More praise for
FIERCE LEADERSHIP

"*Fierce Leadership* has distilled valuable real-life experiences and provides a clear roadmap for leaders, managers, employees, or any group of people working together to make positive change."

—Geri D. Palast, former U.S. Assistant Secretary of Labor, and executive director, Campaign for Fiscal Equity

"Susan Scott nails it again with *Fierce Leadership.* Her powerful imagery and gift for stylish communication lend her message a stickiness and freshness that makes it impossible to forget. As an author, communicator, and leader Susan is peerless. Once again I'm wowed!!!"

—Mark Willis, CEO, Keller Williams

"*Fierce Leadership* is a refreshingly honest and candid book. The author takes a critical look at how our careers and businesses have been held back by so-called best practices, then gives actionable suggestions for revitalizing work and accelerating your success. Read this book for new ideas and to inspire a proactive transition strategy."

—Michael D. Watkins, bestselling author of *The First 90 Days: Critical Success Strategies for New Leaders at All Levels*

"Many of these best practices are anything but. Having applied the principles of *Fierce Conversations* to our organization, I can truly recommend 'Fierce' as a best practice, fundamental to all leadership. *Fierce Leadership* expands these principles by debunking traditional but misguided notions. After reading the chapter on accountability, I am amazed at the amount of time I spend in 'victim' mode. Scott strips bare the self-serving excuses for accepting external influences and the behavior of others as an escape from the pain of not getting the results we desire. For any leader who wants to learn how to move beyond holding people 'accountable' to the rich and rewarding behavior of holding people 'able,' this book is a must read."

—David R. Nielsen, MD, executive vice president and
CEO, American Academy of Otolaryngology

"I loved the book—wrote all over it and used my highlighter and made lots and lots of footnotes. My staff is already hearing all about it."

—Juan Gonzalez, vice president of student affairs,
University of Texas at Austin

"*Fierce Leadership* is not for those who want to become shadows in the crowd; it is for those who are willing to tackle the biggest challenges in their lives, toss out the 'old' corporate way of thinking, and execute at a higher level of integrity, both personally and professionally."

—Faith Green, cofounder of ARC, A Resource Community for Women

"Susan Scott's insightful leadership practices have stimulated my thinking and expanded my context of educational leadership—a must-read for school principals and central-office administrators."

—Debbi Hardy, K–12 curriculum director

"Susan Scott is clearly one of the sages of the ages! This is a book to move the head and the heart. And it can make a huge difference in the success of your business. She fiercely cuts through the slogans and fads that pass for 'best practices' in business today and shows us what it really takes to get where we need to go. This is authentic, original, and powerful—as only Susan can provide!"

—Tom Morris, author of *If Aristotle Ran General Motors* and
If Harry Potter Ran General Electric

"I had to laugh when I read Susan's words . . . 'What you and I are talking about is so fundamental that if I wrote another book, it would have to be titled *The Complete Guide to the Fricking Obvious.*' And yet reading *Fierce Leadership* has instilled in me a new energy! It gives language and support to what has been for me simply 'an instinct' as it relates to leadership, and encourages me to to 'come out from behind myself' and put authenticity and the capacity to connect at the heart of the culture—'the way we do things around here'—in our district . . . well, in ALL my relationships. It gives me the courage to make it an absolute reality and not just an idea vaguely emerging."

—Elaine C. Cash, superintendent, Riverdale Joint Unified School District

"I laughed out loud at Scott's memo to leaders. Humor and the enjoyment of reading for reading's sake in a business book . . . what a concept. I think I'm seeing a new workshop."

—Mardig Sheridan, Beyond Boundaries Learning

Fierce Leadership

Fierce
Leadership

**A Bold Alternative to the
Worst "Best" Practices of Business Today**

Susan Scott

CROWN
BUSINESS
NEW YORK

Published in the United States by Crown Business, an imprint of the Crown Publishing Group, a division of Random House, Inc., New York.
www.crownpublishing.com

CROWN BUSINESS is a trademark and CROWN and the Rising Sun colophon are registered trademarks of Random House, Inc.

Originally published in hardcover in the United States by Broadway Business, an imprint of the Crown Publishing Group, a division of Random House, Inc., New York, in 2009.

Crown Business books are available at special discounts for bulk purchases for sales promotions or corporate use. Special editions, including personalized covers, excerpts of existing books, or books with corporate logos, can be created in large quantities for special needs. For more information, contact Premium Sales at (212) 572-2232 or e-mail specialmarkets@randomhouse.com.

Grateful acknowledgment is made to the following for permission to reprint previously published and unpublished material:

Copper Canyon Press: "The Three Goals" from *Moment to Moment: Poems of a Mountain Recluse* by David Budbill, copyright © 1999 by David Budbill. Reprinted by permission of Copper Canyon Press, www.coppercanyonpress.org.

Graywolf Press: Excerpt from "A Ritual to Read to Each Other" from *The Way It Is: New and Selected Poems* by William Stafford, copyright © 1960, 1998 by the Estate of William Stafford. Reprinted by permission of Graywolf Press, Saint Paul, Minnesota, www.graywolfpress.org.

Tony Hoagland: "The Big Grab" from the forthcoming *I Have News for You* by Tony Hoagland, to be published by Graywolf Press in 2010. Reprinted by permission of the author.

Daniel Ladinsky: "Tired of Speaking Sweetly" and "The Sad Game" from *The Gift: Poems by Hafiz*, translated by Daniel Ladinsky, copyright © 1999 by Daniel Ladinsky (originally published by Arkana Publishing, an imprint of Penguin Group [USA] Inc. in 1999). Reprinted by permission of the author.

David Whyte: "Threads" by David Whyte, copyright © by David Whyte. Reprinted by permission of the author.

Meg Lyman: "Squidlock Holmes" image, copyright © by Meg Lyman. Reprinted by permission of the artist, www.meglyman.com.

Library of Congress Cataloging-in-Publication Data
Scott, Susan, 1944–
    Fierce leadership : a bold alternative to the worst "best" practices of business today / Susan Scott. — 1st ed.
        p. cm.
    Includes bibliographical references and index.
    1. Leadership. I. Title.

    HD57.7.S426 2009
    658.4'092—dc22   2009023316

ISBN 978-0-385-52904-4

PRINTED IN THE UNITED STATES OF AMERICA

Cover design by Jamie Keenan

10 9 8

First Paperback Edition

For Maizy, Clara, Niko, and Uma

CONTENTS

Fierce Leadership

Great things are
not accomplished
by those who yield
to trends and fads
and popular opinion.

—JACK KEROUAC

Introduction

You are always practicing something.
The question is: What are you practicing?
—MARTIAL ARTS SENSEI [1]

What Fresh Hell Is This?

When I was five and woke with my hair glued to my pillow because I'd fallen asleep with chewing gum in my mouth, and when our dog lifted its leg on the neighbors' toddler, who ran to his mother screaming, "Dat doggy peed on me!" and when my brother's forgotten Silly Putty melded forever with the fabric of our new sofa, and when my dad gave my mom a set of pots and pans for Christmas, we anticipated my mother's trademark comment: "What fresh hell is this?" (Fencing foils went over much better the following year.)

I sometimes find myself muttering this same phrase as I sit in meetings with leaders who have apparently gone round the bend, given their latest mandate guaranteed to ensure fresh hell for all involved, taking the company in the opposite direction from where it wants and needs to go. Or when a comment—a throwaway for the person who made it—lands with an audible thud and now, well, now we're into it.

This puzzles me, since the leaders I know are highly intelligent people with invaluable experience on the firing line, a decent amount of humility, a wicked sense of humor, and a strong desire to grow their companies and champion change. They are usually on the right track, and much of what they do works. Yet so many pour considerable time, intelligence, and cash into significant sinkholes—*practices*—with no good outcomes and, in fact, costly implications.

I would excuse the perps as "well meaning," but that term is demeaning, as in: "She means well but is clearly in the late stages of mad cow." It's not that we're trying to deliberately sabotage our careers or our companies; it's just that we don't always recognize the implications of our practices, because most of the time, those on the receiving end of our questionable ideas don't bellow, "Are you nuts?!" Instead, most flinch, then shrug it off as life in a *Dilbert* world, to be expected, what can I do, I'll lay low until this latest hell blows over.

What we need is "squid eye."

Squid Eye

My friend Paul Lindbergh, an advanced aikido practitioner and killer jazz musician, moved to Hawaii as a teenager and soon began diving with native Hawaiians for squid, a highly prized catch that could be sold for a tidy sum or taken home and served for dinner. But after weeks of diving, despite the fact that the local guys always caught plenty, he had caught only one squid, which must have been stupid and unfortunate—the squid, not Paul.

When he expressed his frustration—"How come you guys catch squid and I don't?"—the Hawaiians laughed and said, "You gotta have 'squid eye.'"

"What the hell is squid eye?"

They explained.

"It's the ability to see the squid while he is blending into his natural environment. It's the ability to see him just being himself. It is the ability to see him even when he doesn't want you to see him, to see him even when he is hiding. Be advised he is very skilled. You must understand, he is there."

Knock, knock, Mr. Squid. Are you home? Come to dinner tonight.

The Hawaiians began to tell Paul many things about the squid. For example, one might see a few small stones lying on the bottom of the ocean and understand that the squid put them there. When Paul saw those stones and maybe some shells, they told him to look for a small hole at the base. *Knock, knock, Mr. Squid. Are you home? Come to dinner tonight.*

It was tough to spot the first mound of stones, like looking for morel mushrooms. You can't find any and then suddenly stumble across one. Once you know what you're looking for, you realize you're standing in a patch of them.

As Paul puts it:

> Seeing squid means you see many things that others cannot and do not see. It means having sight in the presence of the blind. It means that you are a selective and efficient information gatherer. This is what "squid eye" really means, and when you apply it to other aspects of your life, you will have, metaphorically, more tuna in your net and fewer guppies and old rubber boots. And if you can see one "tell," you automatically get others. It's almost like beginning to understand the nature of a tell or the nature of signs left behind for our eyes and senses to use.

Once Paul learned the tells—like that mound of stones—he had no difficulty finding squid ever again. And then he learned the tells for lobster, kumu, papio, and other Hawaiian fish and thereafter began to eat extremely well.

Spotting the Tells

For Paul, *tells* signaled the presence of a potential feast, famine, even danger. My fishing reef has been the hallways and conference rooms of global companies. I've watched individuals, teams, whole organizations surf powerful waves all the way to the beach, and I've watched them get their legs stuck in giant clams! At the risk of sounding immodest, over time I developed squid eye *and* squid ear, learning the tells that predict the future more accurately and vividly than how the stock price is trending.

I'm sure you've noticed that even some of the most successful organizations fail to outlast a few generations of management because they are unable to see the threats they face and the imperative to change. And while there are threats we can do little about—a competitor's amazing new gizmo, the price of oil, a housing-market crash, an economic downturn, mother nature, et cetera—there's plenty going on right under our noses that we *can* do something about. But we don't, because we can't see the *tells* signaling that something we're doing is not working, perhaps never did work, is in no danger of working and that, indeed, something is very, very wrong.

For many years, I've coached countless leaders at companies large and small on how to spot the tells in their organization and come up with better ways of doing things. And many of them were so pleased with the results, they asked me to capture my recommendations in a book they could share with colleagues. But over and over I would tell them, "What you and I are talking about is so fundamental that if I wrote another book, it would have to be titled *The Complete Guide to the Fricking Obvious.*" I tried to appease them with the following memo I'd written, inspired by Christopher Moore's novel *A Dirty Job*. Like garlic around our necks, these rules could help protect our souls, keep us human.

Memo to Leaders

Congratulations. You are a leader. It's a heavy load, but someone has to do it. The primary focus of your organization is growth. To help in this regard, it is your duty to lead change, manage, and motivate a multi-generational workforce and execute initiatives that impact the top line and the bottom line simultaneously, while delivering short-term results. You must demonstrate agility, speed, inclusiveness, strategic acumen, and innovation, manage uncertainty and risk, and mitigate the impacts of globalization, off-shoring, a recession, global warming, and the price of oil, et cetera, et cetera, et cetera.

Some time ago, the beloved founders, who kept balance between order and chaos, cashed out, either by dying or by cashing in their chips. Since then, Forces of Darkness have been vying for the top spot. You are all that stands between them and the destruction of the collective organizational soul. If you fail, darkness will cover the earth, the stock value will plummet, and chaos will reign.

Hence, a few suggestions:

1. In order to hold off the Forces of Darkness, you will need to stay awake and locate your body parts.
2. Names and ideas will come to you. The ideas you should write down and act on immediately, or, if you don't have the authority, fight for. The names are of people you need to make available to industry because they are sucking the joy and life out of everyone and everything they touch, or they are the people you should promote and to whom you should give heaping handfuls of freedom and encouragement to break the rules.
3. You will not single-handedly cause or prevent success. Surround yourself with people who model accountability, ferocious integrity, personal authenticity, the capacity to connect with others at a deep level, sheer courage, and a commitment to champion the common good over narrow self-interest.
4. Your central function is to engineer intelligent, spirited conversations that provide the basis for high levels of alignment, collaboration, and partnership at all levels throughout your organization and the healthier outcomes that go with them.
5. People may not wish you well, so pay attention to your emotional wake. You are not invincible. Be kind. Everyone is carrying a heavy load.
6. On the other hand, don't suck up to anyone, ever, or you will turn into a lickspittle and your soul will refuse to accompany you into the building. Just keep describing reality from your perspective without laying blame and you'll be fine.
7. Don't even consider recommending a reorganization. Anyone who requires more than one reorganization over the life of his or her career will forfeit a year's income (including bonuses and stock options) and possibly serve jail time.
8. Do not, under any circumstances, tell a lie—of either commission or omission. Do not stretch the truth, exaggerate, or make shit up to get out of trouble or make yourself look good, not only because that would be bad on many levels, but also because it will come back to bite you in the butt when you're least expecting it, at the worst possible moment, with the biggest price tag attached, and possibly appear on YouTube.

9. Do not attempt to project different images depending on whom you're with. People can spot inauthenticity from fifty paces. Show up as yourself consistently. Unless, of course, you are a jackass.

10. Bear in mind that while no single conversation is guaranteed to change the trajectory of a career, a company, a relationship, or a life, any single conversation can. Take it one conversation at a time. Make them fierce.

A client e-mailed, "Stop stalling and write the damn thing!" I felt myself circling the book that had been circling me. A series of events finally drove me to my laptop. They included:

• Three days observing a sales-effectiveness training for an organization that claimed client centricity was key to its success and whose people wouldn't recognize client centricity if it ran over them. This firm had operationalized dysfunction and arrogance.

• Two days with two hundred executives at a company meeting in which, during a panel on inclusion, a bunch of middle-aged white guys in identical suits rolled their eyes as a young man described how difficult it had been for him to come out as gay to his Catholic boss and an articulate woman described her treatment by her male counterparts as "death by a thousand paper cuts."

• Several conversations with executives who were struggling to retain good people, in part because their leaders and managers were attempting to motivate Gen Xers, Gen Ys, and boomers with the same rewards. Like offering a dog bone to a cat and then scolding the cat for its lack of enthusiasm.

• A conversation with a CEO who labeled employees who questioned his thinking or pointed out problems as "troublemakers" who "just like to throw up obstacles." Meanwhile, there was a fire smoldering in the attic, close to flash point.

• A survey concluding that executives see no competitive edge in graduates from MBA programs. Sure, they can analyze a case study, read a P&L statement, and build a really cool PowerPoint deck, none of which actually predict success. Which begs the question, what *does* predict success? *I have strongly held views on that topic, so keep reading.*

- Debriefs with the team at my company, Fierce Inc., about prospective clients who wanted to hire Fierce but were concerned that their leaders would be uncomfortable with the word *fierce,* and asked if we would mind using a different word, like *powerful* or *honest* or *authentic,* instead. *You know who you are.*

- My general contractor's refusal to divulge the actual estimated costs of completing a tree-house getaway on a nearby island because I might be upset if he told me what the real numbers were. When he finally confessed that he needed four times the figure he had quoted me a month earlier, he became my ex-contractor.

- Newspapers full of stories about high-profile integrity outages, including outright lies, withheld information, scorn for the intelligence of the common man, CEO hubris, and flagrant corporate greed, that tanked the U.S. economy, causing thousands to lose their jobs and in some cases literally put lives at risk.

- A Roz Chast cartoon in the December 15, 2008, issue of *The New Yorker* that pretty much summed up the news. Beneath the heading "The All-Crisis Network," timeslots were allocated to "The World in Crisis," "America in Crisis," "The Crisis in Our Schools," "Cities in Crisis," "Asia in Crisis," "The Economy in Crisis," "The Environment in Crisis," "Religion in Crisis," "Crisis: Housing," "Washington in Crisis," "The Crisis in Europe," and "The Health-Care Crisis."

This is an old list. By the time this book is published, there will be a new list. Watch the news. There is plenty of fresh hell to go around.

During these several months, unlike my usual easygoing, philosophical, quick-to-laugh, quick-to-recover self, I repeatedly found myself shocked, bewildered, sad, frustrated, irritated, and, regarding my contractor, suppressing homicidal impulses. And every time my sense of humor returned, there was another setback.

I found myself ranting! Why are "healthy" companies so sick? Why do we have such a long history of mistaking profitability and stock price as the sole predictors of success? Why have our efforts failed to create real impetus for change? Why are there so many problems within companies that have good people at the helm, none of whom woke up this morning with the thought: *You know what would be really awesome today? To get it completely wrong! What a rush that would be!*

Finally, my use of squid eye resulted in an apostrophe!

I should explain. Years ago, a young relative announced that she had just had an apostrophe—"you know, one of those ideas with shiny lights around it." She meant *epiphany,* of course, but I liked the idea of having apostrophes, and my hope is that this book will provide you with an apostrophe, possibly even an exclamation point, or, at the very least, a semicolon of your own.

My "apostrophe" was the realization that for many people within organizations of all kinds, the major obstacles in making fierce conversations—conversations during which we come out from behind ourselves into our conversations and make them real—a way of life were several of the most prevalent, widely touted, and well-intentioned "best" practices of our times. That so many of these deeply entrenched, long-accepted practices not only fail to resolve the problems they're meant to resolve or achieve the results they're meant to achieve, but actually escalate problems, compromise results, derail effectiveness, weaken execution muscle, limit performance, and drive away talented employees and profitable customers. In other words, "best" practices were the problem!

A tongue-in-cheek website called MBA Jargon Watch (described as "where jargon goes to die") says:

> A widely used term promulgated by the arch-demons of business—management consultants—"best practices" is used to describe the "best" techniques or methods in use in a company, field, or industry. Unfortunately, companies often confuse latest or trendiest with best, and the best practices of one era are soon superseded by the ever-more-ludicrous fads of the next.

At best, these "best" practices are ineffective. At worst, they are costing companies billions of dollars. Yet no one questions them.

The goal of this book is to do just that: To help individuals and organizations everywhere abandon those "best" practices that no longer (and perhaps never did) serve us and replace them with superior practices that get the job done. To show companies and their leaders how to implement these better practices and, as a result, differentiate themselves from everyone else out there, win the promotions, the clients, and the market share they want, attract the most talented employees and ideal customers—and wouldn't it be nice if the stock price went up instead of down?

Here's some really, really good news. You can do this. Whether you own a small business, work for a multinational corporation, or are employed by a school, a nonprofit, or the government, the antidotes to the worst "best" practices are at your fingertips—and they start with *you*. In essence, they require that you simply abandon costly practices and initiatives that aren't working and practice something different. Even a subtle shift in one individual's behavior can set large-scale transformation in progress. I've seen it time and time again.

It may help to imagine a kaleidoscope. When one piece shifts, the entire picture changes instantly, dramatically. Likewise, when we spot a tell or grasp a fundamental new truth (at least, new to us), we see things entirely differently, and we can never go back to the original picture, even if we want to, because we can't unknow what we now know. This book will help you give your kaleidoscope a turn, so that you see more, see differently, and, given what you see at any point in time, are compelled to act.

Before diving into these "best" practices, let's expand the notion of "practice."

What Are You Practicing?

As the Japanese martial arts master known as the sensei suggests, we are always practicing something. The question is: *What* are we practicing? Taking a daily walk is a practice. Watching television is a practice. So is going to church or temple, wearing jeans on Friday, or holding daily staff meetings. At some point, what we've been practicing becomes ha-

I've come to think of "practice" as my way of life, not only what I *do,* behavior visible to those observing me, but also the beliefs that drive my behavior.

bitual. I've come to think of "practice" as my way of life, not only what I *do,* not just the behavior visible to those observing me, but also the beliefs that drive that behavior.

Consider the following definitions from the *American Heritage Dictionary of the English Language*—and examples from me (in italics).

prac · tice (prkts)

Function: verb

1. To do or perform habitually or customarily; make a habit of:
   - practice courtesy in social situations; make a practice of being punctual
   - *practice (makes a habit of) withholding what one really thinks and feels*
2. To do or perform (something) repeatedly in order to acquire or polish a skill:
   - practice a dance step
   - *practice blaming others for our poor results*
3. To give lessons or repeated instructions to; drill:
   - practice the students in handwriting
   - *practice the team in overpromising and underdelivering*
4. To work at, especially as a profession:
   - practice law
   - *practice law (Okay, so I have a bad attitude.)*
5. To carry out in action; observe:
   - practice a religion piously
   - *practice self-promotion relentlessly*
6. Archaic, obsolete: to intrigue, trick, scheme, or plot (something evil):
   - practice witchcraft
   - *practice putting the worst possible interpretation on e-mails from people one doesn't like*

The point is, whether we are practicing nonconformity, one-upmanship, cooperation, truth telling, lying, mentoring, gardening, shamanism, resistance, fluency in three-letter acronyms, fire drills, anonymous feedback, the bagpipe, optimism, cross-dressing, sucking up, giving thanks, giving advice, the tango, meditation, safe sex, recruiting people with pedigrees, complaining, or random acts of kindness, our practices have an impact on those around us.

Sit for a moment and reflect on your practices. Don't restrict yourself to the practices flagged above. Are you practicing being happy, being sad? Telling the truth, telling lies? Being present, being distracted? Being stressed, being grounded? Seeing the best in people, seeing the worst? Doing what's best for yourself, doing what's best for your customer? And what are you practicing at home?

Taking a look at your practices from time to time will help you spot the tells—in other words, recognize your own role in creating or sustaining some of the very problems with which you struggle—and then do something about them.

So write down whatever comes to mind—the good, the bad, the ugly. There's no wrong answer, except a dishonest one.

I am practicing _____.

I am practicing _____.

I am practicing _____.

I am practicing _____.

I am practicing _____.

I am practicing _____.

I am practicing _____.

I am practicing _____.

I am practicing _____.

Any insights?

The Purpose of This Book

The goal of this book is to help you spot the practices that are holding you back, the practices that leave you crazy, cursing, and covered in cat hair, and replace them with practices that will significantly improve both your performance and your pleasure in everything you do and the results you generate.

> Sometimes I feel like a man who practices eating peas with a knife. I'm losing too many. I'm dying of starvation. I can either sit here shoveling peas as fast as I can, trying to stay alive, or use a spoon.
>
> —Paul Lindbergh

During our conversation about squid eye, Paul said, "Sometimes I feel like a man who practices eating peas with a knife. I'm losing too many. I'm dying of starvation. I can either sit here shoveling peas as fast as I can, trying to stay alive, or use a spoon."

Like eating peas with a knife, the worst "best practices" aren't nourishing, don't get us the results we want. But don't worry, by the time you finish this book, you'll have swapped your knife for a huge soupspoon.

You will find in these pages the practices I have defined for myself and for many clients on the path toward great leadership, fierce leadership. Practices to replace those overparsed, acronym-riddled, "best practices" that just don't work. My goal is to help you toss out the Corporate Way and offer for your consideration a New and Unfamiliar Way.

Imagine practices that build execution muscle while enriching relationships with everyone around you. Imagine practices that move you and your team beyond the level playing field and into an entirely new level of competition. Practices that hone your faith in yourself and your company and expand your awareness of the riddle of leadership. Practices that help you map the terrain, the unpredictable landscape in which you retain the right to lead.

Imagine practices that are visible and felt whenever you walk into a room, attend a meeting, or talk with a colleague, boss, direct report, client, or vendor. Practices you'll continue at home, in your community, wherever you are in the world.

The practices you'll learn in these pages, the practices that must now take center stage, are for those who must move organizations from misguided notions of utopia to actually getting the work done. These practices are for people who would choose a fierce conversation (more about *fierce* in a moment), a fierce leader, a fierce colleague, a fierce customer, a fierce relationship, a fierce love, a fierce life over the alternative, any day. These practices are for those who are not interested in living a guarded, careful life and are quickly bored in the company of those who are.

Fierce leadership is a state of mind. A fierce leader doesn't simply *do* the practices in this book like items on a to-do list. Fierce leadership *itself* is a practice, one that becomes woven throughout all that you do, wherever you are, in the same way that an aikido sensei or a Buddhist monk behaves according to core principles of his or her discipline at all times.

A bonus is that you'll not only achieve better results in your career and in your organization, but you'll become a better person, a happier person. It may seem presumptuous of me to suggest that you will become a better person—after all, who am I to judge?—but I'll stick by that statement because that's what people who've adopted the practice of fierce leadership, who've left the "dark arts" and gone toward the light (you gotta have a sense of humor here, people), have said: "I'm a better person." People of all faiths and of no particular faith have told me this. And I believe them.

This book is simply organized. Each chapter will introduce a "best" practice, show you how to spot the tells that signal a need for change, and then explain the alternative fierce practice and how to start practicing it right away.

For those of you who have a death grip on a particular practice simply because you have championed it for years, please look at the phrase *death grip* and notice what word jumps out at you.

You can do better than this. We can all do better than this. And we truly must.

Start anywhere. Pick the chapter that interests you the most. Use what makes sense. Don't loan this book to anybody. Tell them to get their own book. Write in this book. Do the exercises. Begin by writing your name in the front cover.

The Idea of *Fierce*

Everything should be made as simple
as possible, but not simpler.
—EINSTEIN

I would not give a fig for simplicity on this side of complexity, but
I would give my life for simplicity on the other side of complexity.
—OLIVER WENDELL HOLMES

After thirteen years running think tanks for CEOs, I wrote *Fierce Conversations: Achieving Success at Work & in Life, One Conversation at a Time.* The book you're holding in your hands or listening to right now is a sequel to that book, a deeper dive. Far deeper. Ideally, if you haven't read *Fierce Conversations,* read it before you continue. Next best—read it as a companion to *Fierce Leadership* and refer to it as needed.

In case you haven't read *Fierce Conversations,* I offer the following food for thought.

The idea of *fierce* is simple, yet not simplistic.

I am not neutral. I believe that a culture—whether global, national, corporate, or familial—is shaped by our daily practices and that the most powerful practice of all is conversation. Our careers, our companies, our personal relationships, and our very lives succeed or fail, gradually then suddenly—one conversation at a time.

> While meetings pile up, add up, the real work is being done by someone offering a nourishing drink to others— one conversation at a time.

The conversation *is* the relationship, and— while no single conversation is guaranteed to change the trajectory of a career, a company, a relationship, or a life— any single conversation can.

This is true if your company has five employees or fifty or fifty thousand. If you're in retail, banking, graphic arts, or moviemaking. If you work in a restaurant, a bookstore, a hair salon, or a plant nursery. If you're a teacher, a professor, a researcher, or a rabbi. If your expertise is in architecture, manufacturing, clothing design, merchandising, advertising, solar energy, green technology, outsourcing, life coaching, dog training, or software.

No matter what you do, business—small or global, simple or complex—is fundamentally an extended conversation with colleagues, customers, and the unknown future emerging around us. While meetings pile up, add up, the real work is being done by someone offering a nourishing drink to others—one conversation at a time. What gets talked about in a company and how it gets talked about determines what will happen. Or won't happen.

But simply having the conversation isn't enough. It's the *quality* of the conversation that matters. Conversations provide clarity or confusion. They invite cross-boundary collaboration and cooperation or add concertina wire to the walls between well-defended fiefdoms. Conversations inspire us to tackle our toughest challenges or stop us dead in our tracks, wondering why we bothered to get out of bed this morning. A conversation can be deadly boring or a profound experience of humanity, of intimacy.

A leader's job is to engineer the types of conversations that produce epiphanies. Conversations that reveal we are capable of original thought. Intelligent, spirited conversations that provide clarity and impetus for action, for change. Yet too often, we, the results-smitten, speak only of measurable goals, key business indicators, action plans, cash-flow projections, economic indicators, process, and procedure. All are worthy come-ons, yet true success requires conversations that exert a deeper magnetism, a pull as powerful as the tides. Conversations that are intelligent and impassioned. Personal and universal. Meaningful, authentic conversations during which we wouldn't willingly trade places with anyone. Conversations that feel like they could be taking place in a concert hall or a sanctuary. *Fierce* conversations.

Why *Fierce*?

The notion of "fierceness" in any situation wakes me up. At times, in order to break through all the fluff or the defensiveness or the boredom or the complacency or the BS (believability scale), we may need to ask the question that no one will ask, say the thing that no one will say, abandon paint-by-numbers leadership, touch emotion in ourselves and others, and stop trying to keep everything in the discreet neutral zone.

Prior to writing *Fierce Conversations,* I had about twelve thousand hours of conversations with CEOs and key executives, with the goal of helping them increase their effectiveness and enhance their lives.

These conversations often began with the question,

"Given everything on your plate, what is the most *important thing we should be talking about?"*

If someone responded with, "I don't know," I would ask, "What would it be if you *did* know?" And wait. *Silence did the heavy lifting.*

Most of the time, we talked about their companies' knee-buckling goals and challenges—bet-the-farm decisions, costly problems that needed fixing (have you noticed that people burn out not because they've been asked to solve problems but because they've been trying to solve the *same* problem for far too long?), strategies that needed forming, opportunities that needed evaluating (mergers, acquisitions, new hires, technology)—and since no topic was off limits, sometimes we talked about a marriage that was upside down, a kid on drugs, a cancer scare, or a bout of depression.

Our conversations were fierce.

The simplest definition of a fierce conversation is one in which we come out from behind ourselves, into the conversation, and make it real. While most people are uncomfortable with *real,* it is the *unreal* conversations that should scare us to death. Why? Because they are incredibly expensive, for organizations and for individuals. Most organizations want to feel they are having a real conversation with their employees, their customers, and their evolving marketplace. And most individuals want to feel they are having conversations that build their world of meaning.

Real is a change agent's best friend. While no one *has* to change, when the conversation is real, the change often occurs before the conversation has ended. Working with CEOs, my job was to make sure we weren't dealing with the tiny corners of subjects, but the complete picture, the real picture, what Faulkner called "the raw meat on the floor." We didn't waste time, energy, and brain cells waterskiing, skimming the surface of things. We put on scuba tanks and went deep.

> While no one *has* to change, when the conversation is real, the change often occurs before the conversation has ended.

Some of those conversations were uncomfortable, but I ask you, where in our lives did we learn that we should never do or say anything that might make ourselves or others uncomfortable? There's gold in them thar uncomfortable hills.

Don't get me wrong. Fierce conversations can be sweet, sweeter than you can imagine. Not saccharine sweet, but honest sweet. Respectful, kind, generous sweet. Sometimes the fiercest thing we can say to someone is, "I want to tell you exactly what I appreciate about you." And tell them. With no *but* or *however* attached.

And while our conversations were occasionally uncomfortable, the members of my think tanks brought "safety" to our conversations, because when they offered constructive criticism or competing recommendations, it was with deep respect, genuine affection, and the sincere desire to provide helpful perspectives so that the person with the issue on the table would end up making the best possible decision for his or her organization.

Fierce conversations are meaningful interactions. Not just the tough conversations you've been avoiding, but highly productive meetings that have everyone on the edge of their seats, fully engaged. Conversations that provide impetus for action. Conversations during which we connect with our customers and maybe add a digit to our sales figures in the process. Inspiring conversations that include all four generations currently in the workplace; conversations that compel us to hold ourselves accountable, that negotiate through and past those worn-out techniques that result in tepid agreements so riddled with mediocrity and compromise that there's not much to celebrate.

When you think of a fierce conversation, think authenticity, integrity, collaboration. Think execution muscle, innovation, emotional capital. Think collaboration—with your colleagues and customers.

> **When you think of a fierce conversation, think authenticity, integrity, collaboration.**

What Is "Fierce" Leadership?

There's a bold, compelling line between "leadership" and *fierce* leadership. It's okay to cross the line.

Here is the short definition.

fierce lead·er·ship (fi(ə)rs lēdər.ship)
Function: noun, verb
1. A fast-acting antivenom to the business-as-usual mode of high task/low relationship, self-serving agendas, directing and telling, anonymous feedback, holding people accountable, excessive use of jargon, and mandating initiatives that cause people to weep on too many fine days
2. The act of acquiring your most valuable currency—emotional capital
3. The acquisition of squid eye and the demise of truth-telling squeamishness and ethical squishiness

You will begin to cross the line, dropping into a different kind of serious, a different way of being, a different quality of relationship, once you understand and act on the central premise at the heart of everything fierce:

If you want to become a great leader, gain the capacity to connect with your colleagues and customers at a deep level . . . or lower your aim.

Whether your goal is improved workplace relations or improved market share, your most valuable currency is relationship, emotional capital. This is far from a naive, feel-good notion. It's good business sense.

Many of today's business leaders—to use the term loosely—insist that their job is to grow the company and the stock price, by whatever means. And while conventional measures of business success shouldn't be ignored, I propose that human connectivity, as opposed to strategy and tactics, is the next frontier for exponential growth and the only sustainable competitive edge, more visibly useful than ever before.

If Daniel Pink, author of *A Whole New Mind*, is right (and I believe he is), we are moving from the "industrial age" into the "conceptual age." What this means is that today we are making different choices about how we live our lives, who we spend our time with, and how we spend our money.

Pink talks about moving beyond function to engage the senses; adding narrative to products and services (not just listing features and benefits); adding invention and big-picture thinking (not just focusing on details); going beyond logic and engaging emotion and intuition; bringing humor and lightheartedness to business and products; creating meaning and feeling—in other words, true connection—with our employees and customers.

Everywhere, people are hungry to connect, to be seen and known as the unique individuals that they are, and this has an immediate and powerful impact on how we design business strategies and market our products and services and ultimately on whether our businesses succeed or fail.

Yet much business communication is still stuck in the information age. Too often we treat our conversations and our relationships as we do our e-mails—one way, directive, quick, clipped, efficient.

Worse, most corporate training is broken down into theory, processes, charts, graphs, assessments, and models, operating under the assumption that teams can't function until we put a label on the thinking style, learning style, and personality type of every individual who reports to us, as well as those of our composite teams. *Are we red, green, yellow, blue? Thinkers, feelers, judgers, perceivers? Ds, Is, Ss, Cs? What about our derailers? How and when should we adapt our individual styles to meet the needs of others?*

Admit it. We love to learn about ourselves, but most of us are hard wired, so the adapting part is really hard. I have a file drawer full of assessments on myself and confess that I haven't changed significantly in all these years. So while assessments have their place, few people I know—apart from those who sell assessments—would attribute their success or failure or that of their companies to a raft of assessments.

Too often, we confuse inclusiveness with demographics and be-lieve we'll communicate better in a global marketplace if we offer yet another awareness training or perform exhaustive studies on cultural norms. We build walls between ourselves and shut out those who don't match our rank *(you're only level five)*. We identify in advance our "high-stakes" conversations and ignore the potential and power of the conversations that show up at our doors.

In short, we're wedded to ideas about leadership that were intro-duced over forty years ago. Intuitively, this makes no sense—where else do we rely on practices that served us well in another era, when life was at a different pace and change was something you could see coming from a long distance and for which you could take your sweet time preparing?

It's easy to become blind to clues—"tells"—that these practices are no longer working. We yawn and text message our way through a succession of meetings that, were we awake, would reveal evidence of impending trauma, stalled initiatives, malaise. We make excuses and direct blame toward management, the economy, technology, or bud-gets, all the while harboring familiar resentments—barely disguised—toward colleagues, leaders, the whole bleeping plan.

We become anesthetized, accepting this as the way it is, the way it goes, our lot, even our way of thinking, as we continue to beat around the bush, dance around the subject, skirt the issue (insert your favorite metaphor here).

Give us all the luxuries—raises, perks, stock options—and we will manage without the necessities—without deep connection to our work and genuine affection for people other than our own family members.

Now that the notion of "luxuries" has been redefined by those who lost jobs, lost homes, or watched helplessly as their stock options became virtually worthless, we've reprioritized the "perks" that are key to our happiness—food on the table, a roof over our heads, but most of all people whom we love close by—and we realize that we need a renaissance in the skill, art, and definition of leadership. Consider the following implications:

Ye Olde Leadership Model	Fierce Leadership Model
Directing and telling	Really asking, really listening; then directing (in that order)
Feedback-free, development-free zone; little, if any, personal growth	Feedback-rich, development-rich zone; ongoing personal growth
High task/low relationship and the culture of compliance that goes with it	High task/high relationship and the culture of passionate engagement that goes with it
Silos and fiefdoms; competing for resources; not good at partnering	Sharing resources; collaborating; partnering across functions in service to the organization's goals
Information-starved, need-to-know culture	Open, transparent, respectful culture
Impose one's view of reality	Expose one's view of reality and invite those with competing realities to share them
Choking on mokitas—a Papua New Guinea term for that which everyone knows but no one will speak of	A willingness to name and address the issues at the heart of any topic, truthfully and courageously
Profit trumps ethics	Shared values and ethics guide decisions

Resistance to change; sleepwalking through the manual; business as usual	Shared enthusiasm for agility and original thinking; a "new normal," personally and organizationally.

Bonus outcomes: a sustainable competitive edge, increased market share, and deep pleasure in the work.

A fierce leader commits to a way of life, not a business strategy. A way of life that over time becomes about *we,* not me. About one another. About what's best for the greater good. About knocking down the walls that separate us. Not knowing the answers, but *finding* the answers. Not having a business conversation, but a human one.

> A fierce leader commits to a way of life, not a business strategy.

Recently, the head of a business unit in a global pharmaceutical company told me, "I have to believe that I can make a difference in this huge organization. I may be on an ocean liner, but I think of myself as having my own little runabout that I use to stay connected."

Those are the words of a fierce leader.

Where to Begin?

So here we are, you in your runabout, me in mine, with important roles to play in sustaining, developing, and nurturing human connectivity—and reaping all the benefits that come with it.

How might you begin? First, by recognizing that a careful conversation is a failed conversation because it merely postpones the conversation that wants and needs to take place.

Don't linger on the edges. Epiphanies aren't granted to those who play it safe, or pitch a self-serving agenda. Instead, epiphanies seek out those who engage themselves wherever they are and tell the truth as much as they can, who speak directly to the heart of an issue. There is something deep within us that responds to those who level with us, who don't suggest our compromises for us.

Pushing our own limits brings exhilaration. Our edge can be a growing edge. Or it can be an edge from which we topple. The fall won't kill us. Avoiding the topic could.

Consider one of my favorite poems by Hafiz, whose sense of humor and fierce passion for life are apparent in every verse.

Tired of Speaking Sweetly

Love wants to reach out and manhandle us,
Break all our teacup talk of God.

If you had the courage and
Could give the Beloved His choice, some nights,
He would just drag you around the room
By your hair,
Ripping from your grip all those toys in the world
That bring you no joy.

Love sometimes gets tired of speaking sweetly
And wants to rip to shreds
All your erroneous notions of truth

That make you fight within yourself, dear one,
And with others,

Causing the world to weep
On too many fine days.

God wants to manhandle us,
Lock us inside of a tiny room with Himself
And practice His dropkick.

The Beloved sometimes wants
To do us a great favor:

Hold us upside down
And shake all the nonsense out.

But when we hear
He is in such a "playful drunken mood"

Most everyone I know
Quickly packs their bags and hightails it
Out of town.

Don't pack your bags. There's no need to feel overwhelmed. You get time off during which you can be a total slacker, not in the mood for complexity. Or honesty. Or divulgences. Or deep thought. Or connecting with people. Or yard work. Or anything.

> There is something deep within us that responds to those who level with us, who don't suggest our compromises for us.

Spend the occasional weekend unwashed, breath reeking, watching the entire series of *The Office* or *Rome* or *Weeds* or *Deadwood* or *Mad Men* or reality TV or sports or cooking shows or shows about how to lose weight or spiff up your home for five hundred dollars or less, plus stuff you TiVo-ed, while eating Cheez Whiz and Vienna sausages, if you like.

My goal for you is for you to be *you* on your best day most of the time. Which will lead to your career and your company on its best day, your marriage on its best day.

Ask yourself:

What's the most important thing I should be talking about today?
What do I believe is impossible for me to do, that if it *were* possible would change everything?
If nothing changes, what are the implications?
What's the conversation that has my name on it? The one I've been avoiding for days, weeks, months, years? Who is it with and what is the topic? When will I have it?

Note: Please turn to the end of this book and fold down the corner of the page titled "Conversations I Need to Have." Every time you think of someone with whom you need to talk, turn to that page and write down his or her name. Having the conversations that need to take place, without delay, is one of the most important practices of a fierce leader, so you might as well begin.

Fierce Practice #1

From 360-Degree Anonymous Feedback to "365" Face-to-Face Feedback

When I give talks, there's always a sound check to make sure that when I start talking, the audience won't be deafened by an ear-shattering, high-pitched squeal coming out of the microphone. What's that cringe-inducing sound called? Feedback.

Feedback has a bad rap. Think about it. When was the last time you heard somebody say, "Oh, boy, oh, boy, I get my performance review today!" Unless they suspect they will be overheard by the person who gave them their most recent review, most people would probably tell you they'd rather be forced to watch *Jerry Springer* exclusively than receive feedback on any aspect of their professional or personal performance. If you asked them to say more, my money's on a rant.

Several weeks ago, I was sitting with twenty student council members at Miss Hall's School, a college-prep school for girls in the Berkshires that works to develop authenticity, strength, and leadership in its students. The young women had been asked to anonymously write a few sentences on how they felt about their classmates, and now they were going around a large table as each student commented on the anonymous feedback she had just received from her peers. Most of the young faces were tight, anxious. Several girls sat back with arms folded across their bodies. Most looked down, avoiding eye contact. Comments were clipped, careful.

"I guess I don't know who my friends are."

"Pass."

"Pass."

"I really don't know what to say."

This was not a joyful gathering. We were halfway around the table when we came to a girl who was sitting on a windowsill. I had noticed the intensity with which she had listened to each comment. She leaned forward.

"Hey, everybody, I'm really, really glad I have this feedback, so thank you! And I guess what I want to say is: I hope you keep telling me the truth about how you view me, positive or negative. And don't even wait to be asked! Tell me when something happens, right when you're thinking of it. Because if you don't, I probably won't know, and I want to, I really do, because your feedback is the only way I'll understand what I'm doing right and what I'm doing wrong. And that's the only way I can learn about myself and make changes!"

It was clear she meant every word, and in the seconds it took to say what she said, energy returned to the stale room. Eyes lifted and shoulders dropped as the girls gazed at her and located in themselves that place in all of us that recognizes—*someone is here.*

Since this was an opportunity for self-generated insight, the best kind, I sat quietly, trying not to broadcast my thoughts: "Look out, world. We have a leader here." And, of course, there was no need for my input. The comments from the rest of the girls were direct and sincere. This time, no one said, "Pass." They looked at each other and at their colleague on the windowsill with renewed respect, affection, and that loveliest characteristic of all, humility.

A Dangerous Idea

Meanwhile, back in the world of adults, I wondered if others shared my growing conviction that a particular "best practice" associated with performance reviews—anonymous feedback—is failing to achieve its desired results. So one day, while giving a keynote speech to an auditorium filled with executives from a wide variety of organizations, I decided to find out.

I explained that many clients contact my company because they would like to improve their organizations in the areas of honesty, openness, and transparency. Then I paused and asked the audience members to raise their hands if their organization's mission, vision, or values statement mentioned these things. Most hands went up.

I then asked the audience to raise their hands if their organizations provided 360-degree anonymous feedback. Another sea of hands went up, though the audience seemed puzzled. *Where is she going with this?*

"Okay, here's an opportunity to practice squid eye. If an organization declares that it values honesty, openness, and transparency, what's the tell in the words *360-degree anonymous feedback?*"

There was silence, followed by a collective, audible "anonymous!"

"Congratulations. You just spotted your first squid!"

Feedback is invaluable. It's the *anonymous* part that gets us in trouble. We're like Woody Allen, who said, "I'm not afraid of death. I just don't want to be there when it happens." We're not afraid of feedback. We just don't want to be in the room when it's delivered. An Australian colleague told me that when he was taught how to deliver a feedback report to someone, one of the instructions was: "Be sure you are not near a large body of water."

It starts early in our impressionable lives—this attraction to anonymity. This hiding. So it's no wonder that, although most organizations *profess* to value openness, transparency, trust, respect *(yeah, yeah, yeah),* when there are invaluable opportunities for candor, we send in good old underpaid, overworked "anonymous," slip the feedback over the transom, and run like hell.

I discovered an ally regarding my view of this "best practice" in Kevin Kelly, the editor of *Wired* and the author of *Cool Tools.* Each year, a scientific foundation called Edge Foundation asks dozens of scientists one provocative question. Recently, in response to the question "What is your dangerous idea?" Kevin suggested the idea "More anonymity is good." He wrote:

> Fancy algorithms and cool technology make true anonymity in mediated environments more possible today than ever before. . . . However, in every system I have seen where anonymity becomes common, the system fails. Anonymity is like a rare-earth metal . . . a necessary in-

gredient in keeping a cell alive, but the amount needed is a mere hard-to-measure trace. In larger doses these heavy metals are some of the most toxic substances. In vanishingly small doses, it's good for the system by enabling the occasional whistleblower or persecuted fringe. But if anonymity is present in any significant quantity, it will poison the system. . . . Trust requires persistent identity. In the end, the more trust the better. Like all toxins, anonymity should be kept as close to zero as possible.

> Like all toxins, anonymity should be kept as close to zero as possible.
> —Kevin Kelly

Well said! Just look at the definition.

a · non · y · mous (ə nä nə məs)
Function: adjective
1. not identified by name; of unknown name: *an anonymous phone call*
2. having no outstanding, individual, or unusual features; unremarkable or impersonal: *a faceless, anonymous group*
3. used in names of support groups for addicts of a substance or behavior to indicate the confidentiality maintained among members of the group: *Alcoholics Anonymous, Debtors Anonymous*

In what universe would anonymous feedback, anonymous *anything*, be considered a best practice? No one I know wishes to be unremarkable, impersonal, faceless, or unknown—and it would be difficult to argue that anonymity enriches relationships or strengthens connection with others. The fact is that anonymous feedback rarely creates real or lasting impetus for change, which is crazy because the whole idea is to encourage professional growth. There are several problems:

> In what universe would anonymous feedback, anonymous *anything*, be considered a best practice?

1. Anonymous feedback doesn't tell us what we really need to know because it is ANONYMOUS, and most people don't provide specific examples to support their evaluations because more specif-

ics might help the recipient guess who wrote them (and Lord help us if that should happen)! So we avoid specifics and instead use sanitized phrases and a "score" of some sort, all of which tells the recipient very little about how to improve his or her performance. Conversations meant to create impetus for change fail because we don't know how to deliver the message without the load or how to praise people in such a way that they can tell we really mean it.

2. When the feedback is given at regular intervals, usually coming as it does once or twice a year, it rarely immediately follows the behavior that generated the evaluations, so exactly *what* we did right or wrong to merit a certain evaluation often remains a mystery. We are embarrassingly clueless about how our behavior affects others anyway, so unless we get timely, specific feedback, our internal reaction to anonymous comments and ratings is either *"This is totally bogus. I haven't done anything to deserve this!"* or *"This means I need to change something. Unfortunately, I don't have a clue what that change should be."* And even if the feedback is positive, the reaction is *"I must be doing something right. If only I knew what it was, I'd do more of it."*

3. Most so-called 360-degree feedback merely affirms what we already know about who we have been since the day we were born. We're pretty hardwired and unlikely to change. I offer myself as exhibit A. Thirty years after my first assessment, my strengths are still my strengths and my weaknesses are still my weaknesses. I am great at catching people up in the vision and a disaster when it comes to organization. My desk is a hazard area. I'd unplug the technical gizmo that I haven't used in two years but that I got because I'm an early adopter and compulsively adopt myself from one device I don't know how to use to a sexier device I don't know how to use *(I digress),* but I can't identify the plug in the tangle of wires beneath my desk. To find a paper clip, I have to sort through Kiehl's lip balm, the little device used to peel the backing off labels, five or six keys (to what, I have no idea), and a rubber lizard inside a squeeze ball filled with what looks like frog eggs *(I found it on a podium at Microsoft. They said I could have it),* plus other dwelge and lint. All this to say that organizations assess people to death at

great expense, with very little new information or change to show for it. Our reaction is, *"Yep, that's me, all right!"* Creating real impetus for change requires extraordinarily compelling feedback that is clear, insightful, well thought out, specific, and delivered face to face by someone who has observed us in action long enough and thoughtfully enough to tell us something about ourselves that gets our full attention. So 360-degree anonymous feedback fails on all counts.

4. Anonymity is addictive and contagious. We grow accustomed to withholding our real thoughts and feelings. We become anesthetized, barely registering the consistent message our gut has been sending us for years: *Tell the truth.* And we infect others. Ask yourself, where else does anonymity live in the organization and what damage is it doing? At what level in the organization? In what other situations are people withholding what they really think and feel? What are the implications?

So what gives? What is it about this shared addiction that has us in its grasp?

It's our addiction to safety, to being comfortable. Our hardwired tendency to avoid discomfort, even if momentary. And remarkably, it isn't just discussing "weaknesses" and "opportunities for improvement" that makes us nervous; we are also uncomfortable expressing gratitude and giving and receiving praise up close and personal.

What is it we fear?

The consequences of authenticity—intimacy and vulnerability. We fear being real, being ourselves, disclosing our real thoughts and feelings, being seen, being known. It's time to change all that.

Practicing Squid Eye

What might you notice if you were practicing squid eye that would suggest anonymous feedback is causing more problems than it's solving? Check any of the following tells that apply to *your* team or organization. Or to *you.*

Most people hate performance reviews. It's a strong word, *hate*— hardly the response you'd hope for regarding a best practice. Other emotions associated with performance reviews include dread, anxiety, hopelessness, fear, frustration, and a firm conviction that a trip to the bathroom for a surreptitious examination of the boil on your backside would be a far better use of your time. Behaviors associated with performance reviews include anger, defensiveness, withdrawal, and a strong desire to watch movies in which bad guys are impaled, shot, or poisoned, having been revealed as the forces of evil that they are.

Even anonymous feedback isn't honest! This may be the most bizarre, unexpected tell of all. When no one will know it was us, you'd think we would tell it like it is, or at least like we see it. We don't. Jack Welch disclosed in his book, *Straight from the Gut,* that he eliminated anonymous feedback at GE because even *that* wasn't honest, wasn't true. How real are *you* when it comes to anonymous feedback? Do you pull back from letting people know how upset or concerned you are, even anonymously?

Triangulation (otherwise known as talking about people behind their backs) is a popular bonding activity. Friendships are formed over person A and person B's mutual loathing of person C. People don't talk directly to the persons with whom they have difficulty. Instead, they talk *about* them behind their backs. And what fun it is to bring each other up to date on the latest chapter: "You won't believe what so-and-so just did!" Like Mae West, who said, "If you can't say anything nice about people, sit by me!"

> If you can't say anything nice about people, sit by me!
> —Mae West

"Employee engagement" scores are low. Face it, the formal language of feedback is uninspiring and demotivating. Does "satisfactory" capture anything specific that we could feel good about? Would it inspire us to work harder, do better? How about "meets expectations"? Even "exceeds expectations." The colorless language of anonymous feedback, with its numbers, ratings, and boxes to check, is soul killing. There is no life, no joy, no intimacy, no humanity, nothing that enriches relationships. It is a missed opportunity to connect with people. A missed opportunity to be acknowledged as the individuals we are.

People aren't told how much they are appreciated. It's a huge tell if your recognition program occurs every two weeks and is called a paycheck. *More on this later.*

When managers decide to make someone available to industry, they must wait or risk a lawsuit. If people haven't been told that their performance or attitude is not acceptable and that their job is at stake, it is almost impossible to let them go. If you try, the person—even if aware at some level that he or she has been underperforming for quite some time—will likely claim innocence and ignorance: *"I'm shocked! In my last three reviews, my work has been rated as 'satisfactory,' so I thought you were happy with everything I've been doing."* And when we finally reach the end of our rope and ask someone in Human Resources what we have to do to terminate this person, we learn that we'll have to have the conversations we've avoided in the past, give the employee another chance, and document the heck out of everything.

You and others aren't motivated to do your best work. *If Jane keeps getting away with mediocrity, why am I busting my butt?* We get what we tolerate. I don't know about you, but I've not yet witnessed a spontaneous recovery from incompetence. Without timely, candid feedback, people whose behaviors or attitudes are a problem continue unchanged, blissfully unaware, dragging everyone down, including you. Even in a large team, one problem person becomes a rock in everyone's shoes. If it's the boss, the rock is a boulder. It's a tell if, rather than remove the rock, we grow accustomed to limping, while execution is delayed and frustration grows.

Relationships flatline and fail. The conversation *is* the relationship. When the conversation stops because we don't want to risk a negative reaction or if we add yet another topic—our assessments of each other's performance—to the list of things we're unable to talk about, the relationship stops and all of the possibilities for the relationship grow smaller, until one day we realize we're making ourselves smaller in all our conversations.

There is no joy in Mudville. Employees walk around unhappy, unhealthy, on edge. Bored, unengaged. Letter openers and other sharp objects are surreptitiously removed from desk drawers. Your company is not a happy workplace. Just a workplace.

The culture suffers side effects. Most commercials for the latest, greatest drugs include the warning that side effects can include loss of vision, muscle spasms, internal bleeding, uncontrolled barking, and sudden death. *Okay, maybe not barking, but you get the drift.* The warnings for anonymous feedback should read:

> Not to be used within organizations that value honesty, transparency, or openness or by anyone who views authenticity as a desirable character trait. Side effects can include a culture of terminal niceness, avoiding or working around problem employees, tolerating mediocrity, skirting the issues. If you experience rapidly deteriorating relationships or have difficulty maintaining eye contact with others, call your doctor immediately, as these may indicate a serious problem and could become permanent.

The organization's long-term survival is at risk. Profits are down, customers are departing in droves, good employees are leaving. This occurs in part because an organization professing to value honesty and openness while promoting anonymous feedback is out of integrity. Companies in which stated values actually drive behavior and decisions will weather tough times far more successfully than companies whose practices are at odds with their values statements.

Respect for leaders is waning. Everyone is thinking, *How could you, our leader, allow this to continue? Would somebody please bell the cat?!*

You become invisible. No matter what your title or role, if you remain silent in the presence of poor performance or a lousy attitude, you will become increasingly invisible to yourself and to others. Yes, you will be safe. You will also be anonymous, undifferentiated, your identity blurred. With mounting unease, you may realize that *you* are what's missing. It is impossible to sustain forward motion when you know who you are and default on it on a regular basis.

People are failing to grow professionally and personally. It's hard to imagine anyone of substance saying, "I'm so glad I've remained blissfully unaware of how others feel about me, enjoyed few insights into my character, and experienced zero growth as a human being." Those who play it safe, who avoid addressing performance issues and/or talk about people behind their backs can be found on any street corner. And they are unlikely to be viewed by those who identify, develop, and promote "high potentials" as leadership material. Because they aren't.

What Were We Thinking?

If you've spotted one or more of these tells in your organization, you may be asking yourself, "What were we thinking?"

Well, to cut us some slack, we *were* thinking. We've required that feedback be anonymous because our long-standing beliefs, grounded in experience, convince us that this is how we've always done it, this is how it has to be. The problem is that these beliefs, justifiable though they are, squarely block the way forward. In fact, all of the worst "best" practices in this book were born of beliefs that require rethinking. Beliefs like *People won't be honest if their comments aren't anonymous,* or *It's too risky to tell people what I really think.*

Tell us something is true long enough and we will believe it. Call anonymity necessary. Tell us we can't handle the truth spoken directly to us. If we say it enough times, it must be right. Let's all hide.

Complicating matters is that since we like to be right about our beliefs, we will ignore evidence to the contrary. It bounces off our in-

Tell us something is true long enough and we will believe it. Call anonymity necessary. Tell us we can't handle the truth spoken directly to us. Must be right. Let's all hide.

ternal screen entirely, as in the illustration below. On the other hand, evidence, however circumstantial, that supports our beliefs not only gets through, it reinforces those beliefs, even if they bring us pain and complicate our lives. For example, if you believe that someone is basically evil, information to the contrary won't get through your filter, even if he or she saves a drowning puppy in front of your eyes. But if he or she messes up (in your opinion), *that* information registers; it shoots straight through. "See, I told you so!"

WHAT ARE WE WINNING?

Insisting on clinging to beliefs that don't serve us and convincing ourselves and others that we're right can have enormous consequences, and not just in the workplace.

Jim Sorensen, a master facilitator with Fierce, told me a true story. Jim was preparing to leave Seattle to lead a training session for one of our clients and asked his wife, Brenda, to take care of something for him while he was gone. He emphasized that it was critically important, and she assured him she'd get it done.

"Promise?" "Promise!"

When he returned home and asked about it, Brenda gulped, apologized, and admitted she had forgotten. In disbelief, Jim began to rage.

"I can't believe this! You promised you'd handle it!"

"I know. I'm really sorry. I—"

He cut her off, furious. "If you loved me, you could not possibly have forgotten to do something this important to me!"

"Jim, I feel awful. Things just got crazy busy and—"

He cut her off again. "There is NO excuse! Some who loves me would not forget to do something that important after they promised they'd do it!"

"Jim, please, I'm really sorry. I love you, and—"

"I don't want to hear it. I told you this was critical! If you loved me, you would have kept your promise."

Brenda stood very still, then quietly asked, "Jim, what do you win if you win this argument?"

And it hit him. If Jim won this argument, he would have convinced himself and Brenda that she didn't love him. Nothing could have been further from the truth, and he knew it.

Sometimes when we're right, our only prize is a sour taste in our mouth, sadness, a negative view of humanity, anger, stress. What *are* we winning?

If we want to truly change the practices that are holding us back, we need to challenge our beliefs—even when it's hard to do so. Physicist David Bohm wrote, "Normally, our thoughts have us rather than we having them." It is important to occasionally hang our beliefs out in front of us, so we can begin to see our "seeing."

What argument am *I* waging? Are you waging? What are we trying to be right about?

The question is not whether our beliefs are right or wrong. We can tell the stories, point to the evidence, build an impressive case. You're right! Who could possibly argue with the facts? The question is, how are your beliefs working for you? Those with a "positive" context are those that move you toward what you want. Those with a "negative" context move you away from it.

Before considering the fierce alternative, take a look at the list of beliefs on the next page and check those you currently hold. Since at its most basic, "fierce" is about telling the truth, be honest with yourself.

The Fierce Practice: "365" Face-to-Face Feedback

Here are the simple rules of 365 face-to-face feedback:

- Stay current by exchanging feedback 365 days a year.
- Do it face to face whenever possible (and never via e-mail).
- Give it as soon as possible after something occurs.
- Praise is as important as criticism. *Actually, it's more important.* So don't just give feedback when it's negative.
- Always own your comments. Feedback is invaluable. It's anonymity that is the problem.

The goal of the fierce practice is to have open, honest, face-to-face conversations, 365 days a year, with the people central to your success and happiness, whether you report to them, they report to you, or nobody reports to anybody. Give it and receive it. Set aside rank, title. If what someone does or *how* they do it impacts you, your coworkers, or your organization positively or negatively, talk with them directly. If it's negative, no saving up, shoving down, keeping a lid on. No waiting until a formal performance review is scheduled. And be just as timely, generous, and specific with your praise.

When we save up our frustration for a formal performance review months from the actual event, it can feel like an ambush on an innocent person who truly has no idea what we're talking about. I once discovered that someone was still devastated over something I had said years ago, of which I had no memory. If she had confronted me back then, I would have apologized. Hence the 365 days. When we stay current with one another, our *formal* performance reviews will contain

is your context working for you?

(check all that apply to you)

⊖ negative context　　　⊕ positive context

☐ Disclosing my real thoughts and feelings is risky.

☐ Disclosing what I really think and feel frees up energy and expands possibilities.

☐ Most people can't handle the truth, so it's better not to say anything.

☐ Though I have trouble handling the truth sometimes, I'll keep telling it and inviting it from others.

☐ It's important that I convince others that my point of view is correct.

☐ Exploring multiple points of view will lead to better decisions.

☐ I will gain approval and promotions by exchanging my personal identity for my organization's identity.

☐ My personal identity will be expanded as my colleagues and I exchange diverse points of view.

☐ Reality can't be changed. There's no point in fighting it.

☐ Perhaps we can change reality with thoughtful conversations.

☐ As an expert, my job is to dispense advice.

☐ My job is to involve people in the problems and strategies affecting them.

☐ I'll keep my mouth shut; this is a job for the experts.

☐ My point of view is as valid as anyone else's.

☐ I need to ignore what I'm feeling in my gut; just put my head down and do my job.

☐ I know what I know; and what I know, I need to act on.

Shifts in thinking result in changed behavior—the willingness and confidence to engage in the conversations needed to take your organization where it needs to go.

few, if any, surprises, because everyone will already know exactly how they're doing. You will travel light, agenda free. And, of course, this cuts both ways.

Welcome input on your own performance, behavior, and attitude. When someone expresses criticism or frustration, say, "Tell me more." And mean it. Don't defend yourself. Ask questions, listen, and learn. When someone praises you, say, "Thank you." If you're in a playful mood, add, "Would you care to elaborate?"

We drink in acknowledgment for work done well (and don't think for a minute that senior executives don't need praise now and then) and usually correct our course when we learn what isn't working.

So if you'd like to replace anonymous feedback with conversations during which you come out from behind yourself into your conversations and make them real, what do you do?

Simply begin. Beginning is a practice. So is delaying, avoiding, postponing, rescheduling. You'll cross the line between leadership and

Beginning is a practice. So is delaying, avoiding, postponing.

fierce leadership when YOU decide it's time to cross the line. Don't wait for others to bushwhack ahead of you and prove that it's safe. Go first, alone if needed. *Shouldn't leaders set the example, model the behavior?* Yes, ideally, and I'm speaking to the leader in *you*.

Start anytime. Today would be excellent.

Might you be a bit anxious about how things will go? Undoubtedly. Everyone shares this challenge. But as a fierce leader, take the first step even if it scares the heck out of you.

The fourth principle in *Fierce Conversations* is *"Tackle your toughest challenge today."* There's no switch you can flip that will instantly wipe clean the slate on which your long-held beliefs are inscribed, so the fierce approach is to stop talking about it and start doing it! Dip your toes in the water and see how it goes.

The five steps to adopting any fierce practice are:

1. Prepare yourself.
2. Prepare others.
3. Try the practice. DO IT!

4. Debrief.
5. Do it again, only better.

Once you've begun the experiment, you will notice that no one will die, including you. In fact, you will discover that people wake up, that *you* wake up. People will surprise you. *You* will surprise you. The experience will shift your beliefs, not the other way around.

STEP 1. PREPARE YOURSELF.

Prepare to have the conversation in person. Before you give 365 feedback, prepare yourself for the conversation. For starters, come to terms with the fact that you will not have this conversation via e-mail! Master the courage to have the conversation face to face, rather than take the low road (the coward's road, really) and send an e-mail. E-mails are impersonal, inauthentic, and easy to misinterpret. Everyone I know (and I mean EVERYONE) has had the painful experience of sending an innocent e-mail that was interpreted as evil by the recipient.

For example, just the other day, Jim Sorensen told me that since he doesn't like to write long e-mails, his responses are almost always brief and succinct. Recently, someone e-mailed him something to review, and he responded simply, "Good job. Jim." The return e-mail began with, "Well, it's clear from the tone of your e-mail that you're not happy with my work. . . . "

Tone? What tone?

In essence, all conversations are with ourselves, and sometimes they involve other people. We hear one another through our own private filters, interpreting as we go. Even when we speak directly, while I know what I *said* to you, I do not know what you *heard*. E-mail, both wonderful and perilous, triples the risk. I don't know what it is about human beings, but when all we have are words on a screen, we will assign the worst possible interpretation to those words, ascribing meaning and motive that may have never crossed the sender's mind. We will defend our interpretation to the death. And boy, do we often get it wrong. Sometimes we interpret accusation when it wasn't intended. Or we interpret sarcasm when it doesn't exist. (I tend to bond with people over sarcasm but toned it down when I learned that the word *sarcasm* is derived from the Greek word *sarkazein,* which means to tear flesh from the bone in a doglike fashion.)

If we confront via e-mail, well, we're just asking for it!

Clarify (and purify) your intention. Another step in preparing yourself. Ask yourself: Is my intention to . . .

- interrogate reality (mine, as well as theirs);
- provoke learning (mine, as well as theirs);
- resolve a tough challenge; or
- enrich the relationship

If it is, you're good to go.

If your intention is to intimidate, coerce, threaten, put down, or prove someone wrong, don't have the conversation until you've had one with yourself. *If I accomplish this, what will I win?* Momentary satisfaction, perhaps. In the long term . . . not good.

> When men and women come together, they have to abandon their longing for the perfect and each has to enter the nest made by the other imperfect bird.
> —Robert Bly

This is where compassion may enter the picture. Robert Bly wrote, "When men and women come together, they have to abandon their longing for the perfect and each has to enter the nest made by the other imperfect bird." From one imperfect bird to another, let's cut each other some slack and forgive what imperfections we can.

Now prepare your opening statement. *If you read* Fierce Conversations, *this will be familiar to you.* Clarify the behavior or attitude you want to confront and the key points you want to make. Write a rough draft, edit it, say it out loud, and edit it again until it is clear, clean, and compelling and you can say it in sixty seconds without rushing or looking at your notes. *Yes, sixty seconds.* Be selective with the words you speak, so that what you say will go straight to the heart.

Before you begin, review the following pointers.

- **Name the issue.** If you have multiple issues with someone, ask yourself what's at the core, what's the theme, the common thread of all or most of your issues with this individual. Give it a name. The problem named is the problem solved. (Not literally, of course, because there is still work to be done, but if you are not clear about what the core problem is, the conversation may veer off onto unproductive rabbit trails, and you will get nowhere, very slowly, at great emotional expense.) Begin your opening statement with the words "I want to talk with you about the effect *x* is having on *y*." Note the use of *I want,* not *I need.* Note the use of *with,* not *to.* "I *need* to talk *to* you. . . . " has a very different effect from "I *want* to talk *with* you. . . . "

  > "I *need* to talk *to* you. . . . "
  > has a very different effect
  > from "I *want* to talk *with*
  > you. . . . "

- **Select a specific example that illustrates the behavior you want to change.** Say something like, "When you spoke with that customer, you raised your voice, pointed your finger, and leaned forward. I thought you looked aggressive." What not to say: "You were very aggressive with that customer." To which someone might reply, "No, I wasn't," and then you're into it! Behaviors are things that you can record with a camera. Examples bring them into sharp focus.

- **Describe your emotions around the issue.** Creating impetus for change is unlikely to occur if the conversation is purely head based. After all, human beings behave first for emotional reasons, second for rational ones. Emotion gives the lit match something to ignite. Telling people what emotions their behavior evokes in you is intimate and disarming. You are letting them know that you are affected. Note: There's a difference between *naming* an emotion and acting it out. "I am angry," spoken quietly and calmly, will get someone's attention. "I am angry," spoken with ferocity and a red face, will evoke fight or flight.

- **Clarify what is at stake.** Explain *why* you have whatever emotions you have, why this issue is important. What is at stake for the individual whose behavior you are confronting? What is at stake for you, for customers, for the team or organization, for the family? What is at stake for the relationship? Use the words *at stake*. These words have an emotional impact. "I am deeply concerned because I feel there is a great deal at stake here." Be specific and succinct about possible outcomes. If someone's continued behavior could result in termination, tell him or her. Be clear: "If nothing changes, you could lose your job." Even when the message is a tough one, be respectful. Your task is to deliver the message without the "load," so your tone of voice, posture, and facial expression are as important as your words.

- **Identify your contribution to the problem.** Rack your brain to see what, if anything, you may have done to contribute to the problem, and admit to it. If your fingerprints are on this issue somewhere and you don't say anything about it, the other person will, and your credibility will be shot! Say, "I wasn't clear with you about due dates and the implications when they're missed. I want to correct that now," or "I may have overloaded you with too many concurrent projects. If that's the case, I apologize." If you're completely clean, skip this part; just don't be too quick to declare your innocence.

- **Indicate your wish to resolve the issue.** Communicate your intention: "I want to resolve this. . . . " The word *resolve* has a positive connotation. Though there could be a termination—or a demotion or a lost account or a divorce—in the making if nothing changes, at this moment in time, you are expressing your genuine, sincere hope that things will successfully turn around. Then name the problem again, because even though you've been talking for only about fifty-five seconds, the other person may be in shock and have forgotten the topic: "I want to resolve this—the effect your conversations are having on customers." This way you will have come full circle, beginning and ending with absolute clarity about the topic on the table.

- **Invite your partner to respond.** Feedback is not an attack or a one-way conversation. It begins with a clear and succinct statement describing the reality around this particular behavior or issue from one person's point of view—yours—and then you must stop talking and listen. Extend the invitation to your coworker, boss, direct report, customer, spouse, friend, child to join the conversation: "Please tell me what's going on from where you sit. I want to understand your perspective, learn your thoughts," or words to that effect. Where most of us blow this conversation is when we go on and on and on without giving the other person a chance to respond. As soon as someone says something with which we disagree, we jump back in, give more examples, try to build a stronger case. The person on the receiving end of our monologue will tune out and gear up for a perceived fight.

- **Avoid common errors.** Make sure that your opening statement avoids the typical mistakes we've all made in the past.

Error 1: Beginning the conversation with "So, how's it going?"

You already know how it's going, and it's not going well, so beginning the conversation this way is disingenuous. Besides, someone could easily respond with "It's going fine" or "There's been a little creative tension going on, but that's normal. We're on top of it." Where do you go from here? Nowhere, except perhaps "Wrong answer!"

Error 2: The Oreo cookie, or, as Australians call it, "the crap-filled lolly"

This is when we begin by saying something nice, then whack someone with criticism, and finish with a flourish of compliments: "John, I saw the report you're working on, and it's looking good, but I heard that you've been extremely critical of people behind their backs, including me, and this is a serious problem, so we should talk about that, but first, I want you to know that I was really impressed with your proposal for the case study. Nice job there."

This not only makes people crazy but also teaches them that since a compliment often prefaces a roundhouse kick to the solar plexus, they should be on alert, prepared to duck and cover or to defend themselves.

Acknowledging someone for good work is important and should be a separate conversation. *(More about how to praise later.)*

Error 3: Too many pillows

This is the most common error, otherwise known as softening the blow.

We all like to be liked and worry that others will get upset, be hurt by our words; consequently, we put cushions around the real topic of the conversation, and our intended message can get lost. I once heard that a woman who was on the brink of firing someone had a talk with the person and later learned that the employee had left the conversation thinking she was about to be promoted. How fun do you think the follow-up conversation was?

Error 4: Writing the script in advance

Too often, we decide how the conversation is going to go before we have it, playing it in 3-D, Technicolor, surround sound in our minds: "I'm going to say this to so-and-so, and they'll get defensive and say such-and-such. I'm not going to like it, so I'll say this back. . . . You know what, it's not worth it!"

Sometimes we reject ourselves before others can. We decide we won't get the promotion or raise we were considering asking for, so we don't ask. We decide ahead of time that confronting someone about his or her performance won't go well, will make things worse, so we don't do it.

Sometimes we reject ourselves before others can.

Is it possible that we might have gotten the raise we wanted? Is it possible that confronting a problem could result in a happier, more productive relationship? Is it possible your partner won't follow the script you wrote for him or her? I am often pleasantly surprised by people's behavior, including my own.

Error 5: Machine-gun Nelly

Like the Kalahari dung beetle, which collects its feces on its back and flings it at its enemies when frightened (a seriously unattractive image designed to get your attention), we store up anger and frustration, and when an incident triggers all our fears, we hurl the entire load at someone who did not see it coming. And then we wonder why the conversation didn't go so well.

Don't imitate the dung beetle! For about three seconds, you might feel good getting everything off your chest (or back), at which point you will learn how the other person feels, which will not be pleasant. Talk about emotional wake!

An opening statement, broken up into these seven parts, could look like this:

John, I want to talk with you about the effect your tendency to talk about other people behind their backs is having on the team and on the organization.

I recently learned of a dozen exchanges in which you and Audrey expressed contempt for Sarah, yet I'm certain Sarah has no knowledge of your feelings. I also learned that you told Chris that you don't know if you can continue working for a company that has such a flawed strategy, although in our strategy sessions, you've never raised a concern about what we're doing. I learned that even though Martha asked for candid feedback on the article she wrote, you told someone else that you didn't believe she could handle it.

Frankly, I'm stunned and deeply concerned . . .

. . . because there is a great deal at stake for our organization and for you. Talking about people behind their backs violates our company's core values of honesty and transparency and contaminates our culture. And while you may not realize it, people you've talked about eventually learn of your disregard, and consequently, relationships key to your success are faltering, failing. Trust has vanished. In fact, I don't feel I

my 60 second opening statement

Write a rough draft of your 60 second opening statement

1 | Name the issue.

_____

_____

_____

2 | Select a specific example that illustrates the behavior or situation I want to change.

_____

_____

_____

3 | Describe my emotions around this issue.

_____

_____

_____

4 | Clarify why this is important—what is at stake to gain or lose for me, for others, for the team, or for the organization.

_____

_____

_____

5 | Identify my contribution(s) to this problem.

_____

_____

_____

6 | How I will state my wish to resolve this issue.

_____

_____

_____

7 | What I will say to invite my partner to respond.

_____

_____

_____

can count on you to give your honest input on anything. That's toxic to our relationship, and I cannot allow this to continue, so please understand that if nothing changes, your job is on the line.

I am not entirely blameless here. Though I sensed that you sometimes withheld your real thoughts, I disregarded my instincts and did not press you to disclose what you were thinking. For that I apologize. I also didn't take the time with you to emphasize that we take our core values—like honesty—very seriously. They are not just words on a plaque somewhere. We aim to live them.

I want us to resolve this issue—the effect your tendency to talk about people behind their backs and avoid direct conversations is having on the team and the organization.

I'm genuinely interested in learning your perspective on what's going on with you and the team and whether you're willing to behave differently.

Write *your* rough draft, and edit and hone it until it feels clean and clear to you. Practice saying it out loud, covering all seven points in sixty seconds, without looking at your notes.

If you do this well, those sixty seconds will be more useful and compelling than a year's worth of anonymous feedback.

STEP 2. PREPARE OTHERS.

It may seem strange or unfair, but when I give feedback, I prefer not to prepare others too far in advance for the conversation. I don't want them to worry about it, lose sleep, overprepare, or choose the armor or weapons they feel they may need, especially since weapons and armor won't be needed. I often simply choose a time when I'm certain we'll have at least half an hour for the conversation, walk in the door, and begin.

Most of the time, though, it's a good idea to give someone a little advance notice that you would like to have a conversation. At least this allows the person to gather his or her thoughts and anticipate the issue you want to talk about so he or she won't be caught completely off guard. At the very least, it assures that the person will set aside time for the conversation. Simply . . .

- Ask for time to talk: "Jane, I would like thirty minutes or so to talk with you about what happened in the meeting yesterday (or your response to a customer this morning, the missed deadline, whatever the issue is). What's the earliest we can have a conversation?"

- Don't say more, even if asked "What do you mean?" or "What are you talking about?" Just say, "I promise to be clear when we sit down together. When can we do that?"

- Don't begin the conversation then and there unless you have prepared and both of you are able to give the conversation your complete focus for at least half an hour.

STEP 3. DO IT. HAVE THE CONVERSATION.

The bulk of the conversation takes place *after* your opening statement. With your opening statement, you have clarified the issue and extended an invitation for the person to respond, and now you are listening. This is where reality—yours and theirs—will most certainly be interrogated.

If your partner says something with which you take issue or violently disagree, resist the temptation to jump back in and build a stronger case. Simply listen. Ask questions. Don't be satisfied with what's on the surface. Dig for full understanding. The words I often use in this stage are "Say more about that."

Do perception checks by paraphrasing what you think the other person is saying: "May I tell you what I'm hearing? I want to make sure I've understood you." Stay away from hackneyed phrases like "help me understand . . ."

Let silence do the heavy lifting.

We are often severely tested during this phase. It is not easy to stay in listening mode during an interaction with someone whose comments make you want to strangle him or her on the spot. When we struggle to wrap our minds around someone's alternative reality, we need to remember that each of us is interpreting what is said through our own highly individualized filter.

It is not easy to stay in listening mode during an interaction with someone whose comments make you want to strangle him or her on the spot.

Rather than get angry or upset if your partner says something you feel is off base, focus on examining your partner's reality: "You've said . . . What's behind that?"

Remain in question mode for a while: "Given everything we've talked about, what do you feel needs to happen?" "What steps will you take? When will you take them? What could get in your way? How will you get beyond that? Is there anything you need from me or from others? When can I follow up?"

When you confront with clarity, openness, compassion, and skill, most people will join you in a search for a resolution to the problem. And if the invitation to have the conversation is declined, extend the invitation again. And again. If there is someone who consistently refuses to have the conversation that is needed, preface your opening statement by saying something like, "Nobody owns the entire truth about this issue, including me. I would like for the two of us to interrogate reality, side by side. Both of us may gain perspective. If we set aside the issue of who is right or wrong, we may both learn something."

If someone came to you in this manner, you might wonder if he'd taken his meditation practice a tad too far, but it would probably get your attention.

I have used these exact words to prepare the way to address or help others address a highly charged issue. Use different words if you like, but do find the words to invite the open communication necessary to effect real change.

Counter popular defense tactics. Sometimes, when we have this kind of conversation, the other person will immediately go on the defensive and attempt to justify his or her behavior using one or more of the following tactics. Here's how you can counter them:

- **Denial:** "It wasn't me!" or "It never happened."
  If you weren't present when the behavior or interaction under discussion occurred, this is likely what you'll hear, which is one of the reasons I recommend that you require those who *were* present to have the conversation. Otherwise, stop denial in its tracks by saying something like, "I wouldn't be talking with you if it were not clear that there's a problem. You've blown up with customers repeatedly in the last few weeks. Tell me what's going on from your perspective." In other words, bring the conversation back to the problem you named.

- **Defensiveness:** "It wasn't my fault, it was because of . . . "
  An all-time favorite tactic in which people attempt to justify their behavior by going into details about *why* they did what they did: "How long have you known me?! I always take care of our customers, and I'm always professional, but if you had heard what that customer was saying about our company, in fact, what he said about you, well, I think I deserve a medal for my restraint!" Don't get trapped here. You probably wouldn't be having this conversation if there had been only one minor incident or complaint. Bring it back to the issue: "I understand your desire to give me the details about what happened, but I'd prefer to focus on the bigger issue—the effect repeated blowups with customers are having on them and on you."

- **Deflection:** "It's not about this, it's about . . . "
  Some people are skilled at changing the topic: "Okay, so I get a little upset with unreasonable customers, but I'm not the only one who does. Have you listened in on Jack's conversations? He is downright rude. I don't see you talking to him!" or "Do you have any idea how overloaded I am? I've got this project and that project, and everybody wants it now! Give me a break! I'm doing the best I can!" When you gently but firmly insist on keeping the conversation

where it belongs—your serious concern about the effect x is having on y—people usually settle down and stick to the point. People care about how they are perceived, and if you keep the conversation focused, keep asking questions and listening, you will learn what's really going on, including any contributions you may have made to the problem. *I hate that part.*

STEP 4: DEBRIEF.

A debrief is essential at the end of the conversation or in a follow-up conversation, to ensure that the parties leave the conversation with a mutual understanding of the points that have been made.

It's always good to end a conversation by saying something like, "Thank you for hearing what I had to say and for sharing your perspective. Your success is important to me and I applaud your commitment to action. I want to stay current with you, so before we part, I welcome any thoughts you have about this conversation and how I can get better at giving feedback. For example, I noticed that I got a little defensive here and there, and I want to do better going forward."

When we flag our own flaws, it's easier for others to fess up to theirs. In the example above, it's likely the other person will admit to any defensiveness on his or her part as well, which is always helpful.

Then check in with the person later to express your appreciation for the action they took, the change they made, et cetera. And if nothing has changed, have another conversation, making it clear that this issue is not going to go away and that you expect the person to step up to the plate.

STEP 5: DO IT AGAIN, ONLY BETTER.

Remember, the fierce practice is 365 feedback—that means giving feedback any time, any day, 365 days a year. Staying current. Face to face. If you need to confront someone's performance, behavior, or attitude, do it. Don't wait. Don't hide behind e-mail. Fierce leaders don't shy away from these conversations. They have them. And they get better and better over time. If a conversation doesn't go so well, they try again.

Jim Sorensen once told me a story that wonderfully illustrates why feedback should be ongoing. He was standing in his yard with a friend, admiring his neighbor's yard, which was beautiful, luxurious, blooming, fragrant, and weedless. He said, "I sure wish I had her yard." His friend said, "Jim, if you had her yard, in about six months, it would look like your yard." Jim laughed and admitted that his neighbor does things to her yard that he doesn't do to his: "When she sees a weed, she pulls it. When I see a weed, I resent it."

Left to their own devices, weeds thrive, invite other weeds to join them, and eventually crowd out the flowers. Resentment accomplishes nothing. Good gardeners pull the weeds as soon as they spot them, understanding that weed pulling is not a once-a-year job. A garden requires ongoing maintenance. Think of your workplace as a garden and people's negative behavior as weeds. If you notice them starting to crop up again, it's time for more face-to-face feedback. *(Not fertilizer. Don't go there . . .)*

Praising with Courage and Skill

As I've mentioned, feedback is all too often associated with the word *negative*. But in fact, positive feedback—praise, recognition, and acknowledgment—is the most powerful feedback of all. Fierce leaders express appreciation and gratitude up close and personal, in the moment. Their comments are authentic, specific, heartfelt. Consequently, the message is received and people glow. Some even hug people, and no one screams "inappropriate physical contact" or "hostile work environment" because they trust the intent.

Does praising people require courage, compassion, and skill? Yes. As crazy as it sounds, we're just as lousy at praise as we are at confrontation. Maybe worse. Too often, our meager attempts fail to truly reach the people we acknowledge, and that's a shame! What to do?

Besides spontaneous acknowledgments, one of my favorite exercises takes place with a team of up to twelve people. It takes about an hour and a half, and while you may wonder if you can spare that much time, believe me—it's worth the investment. It's called simply **What I Appreciate About You.**

STEP 1: PREPARE YOURSELF.

Think about your team and clarify what it is that you appreciate about each person. Get specific, genuine. Words like "You always do a great job" are lame and unspecific and won't make it through our built-in barriers to accepting praise. Words like "During yesterday's meeting about last quarter's results, I was impressed when you described reality from where you sit without laying blame. You could have pointed fingers all over the place, and I suspect most people in your position would have, but you didn't. It occurred to me that I don't think I've ever heard you criticize others. I admire that in you. You've set the bar high for all of us, including me" . . . will land.

> Specific, public praise is one of the most powerful, most underused leadership "tools" available to you.

What took you seconds to say will be remembered and savored, perhaps for a lifetime. And you will get more of the positive behavior you acknowledge.

You can acknowledge in private or in public. This particular exercise is public. When you praise someone publicly, others will want to demonstrate similar characteristics. In fact, specific, public praise is one of the most powerful, most underused leadership "tools" available to you.

STEP 2: PREPARE OTHERS.

Let your team know you've scheduled a meeting and that they will need to plan on an hour, uninterrupted, no distractions. When they ask what it's about, just say, "I'm not telling you, but you'll enjoy it, so be there!"

Meanwhile, in a room that will afford privacy, arrange chairs in a circle, no table. Ideally, you'll also bring an audio recording device with a good microphone that can pick up voices from a short distance.

STEP 3: HAVE THE CONVERSATION.

As people enter the room and see chairs in a circle, some will joke, and everyone may be a little nervous: "What is this?"

Just smile, get everyone seated, and ask them to put anything they were carrying under their seats and turn off their cell phones and other devices that could beep or vibrate. They'll likely jostle and joke. Wait until everyone is quiet.

Scan the group, making eye contact with each individual, and say *your* version of the following:

> When each of you walks into this building every day, you bring something unique that would be greatly missed if you were absent. Everything you do, including the way in which you do it, is amplified across our organization. Your impact is larger than you know, so I'd like you to hear what I and everyone in this room appreciates about you.

> Here's how this will go. Each of you will take a turn in the warm seat. You'll have sixty seconds to complete the phrase "What I bring to this team is . . ."

> Then each of us will take up to one minute to tell you something specific and genuine that we appreciate about you. We'll each start with "What I appreciate about you is . . ." When we're finished, you've got three choices of what to say: "Thank you," "Thank you; I agree," or "Thank you. Would you say that again?"

> I'll record what people say to you and send you the audio file when we're done, so you can play it for yourself if you're having a bad day or for your spouse and kids if they fail to appreciate your genius.

For the warm seat, I'll pick people randomly, rather than go around the circle. As we give feedback, anyone can speak whenever they're ready. I'd like for us be thoughtful, specific, and genuine in our comments, rather than simply telling someone he or she is doing a good job. I'll say something to each of you as well, when the spirit moves me.

I'll also be our timekeeper. When your minute to tell us what you bring to the team is up, I'll say, "Time." And then whoever wants to be the first to acknowledge you can begin.

Begin recording and call on someone. Allow and encourage silence as people think about what they want to say to their teammates. Don't be surprised if people get choked up while they're giving or receiving this kind of feedback. In fact, hope for it. It's a rare and beautiful thing to be in the room when people hear from their peers how remarkable they are. Even though you need to manage time, be flexible. If someone is saying something particularly meaningful, let him or her speak a bit longer. You're after effect, not protocol.

Set the bar high early in the exercise by your own example. Choose your words and mean every one of them. The key is for your own comments to people during this exercise to be specific and heartfelt, revealing your emotions and your genuine affection.

Note: Don't be surprised if the team insists that you take *your* turn in the warm seat, as well. They almost always do, and you'll have a deeply personal experience of how profoundly moving this level of intimate, sincere recognition can be.

STEP 4: DEBRIEF.

Rather than poll people for their opinions of the appreciation activity, let the debrief occur informally and face to face. It's very likely that people will seek you out to comment about it later that day or week: "That was a really great session" or "Thanks for what you said the other day in the meeting." No need to probe. Just say something like, "You're

Remember, you are
practicing and modeling
what you'd like to see
happen elsewhere.

welcome. I'm glad you liked it." Encourage them to do the exercise with their own teams and with their family members. Remember, you are practicing and modeling what you'd like to see happen elsewhere.

And if you recorded the session, remember to give people copies of the audio file. People will cherish it. I've gotten e-mails and phone calls from family members who told me how excited their spouses or partners were to come home and play it for them.

STEP 5: DO IT AGAIN, ONLY BETTER.

At Fierce Inc., our team does this exercise whenever I sense the time is right. It might be at the completion of a significant, long-term, possibly arduous project. It might be after several new people have joined the team and have worked with us for a while. The point is, you don't have to do this at regularly scheduled intervals. Just do it.

What About One-on-One Praise and Appreciation?

Ken Blanchard got it right years ago with a simple statement in *The One Minute Manager:* "Catch people in the act of doing things right." Praise doesn't have to come in a group exercise; it's wonderful one on one, face to face, in the moment. Or pick up the phone, write a note, send an e-mail. And don't wait for perfection; acknowledge behavior that is heading in a positive direction. Fierce leaders practice this.

Taking It to the Organization

An HR director with whom I recently discussed my view of traditional "performance management systems" counseled me that patience is required, as no organizational culture can move from anonymity to candor overnight. Instead, we should trust that this is an evolutionary process and keep an eye on the goal.

Sadly, patience is not one of my virtues. Given the steep prices we pay every day for anonymity, evolution takes too long! So I don't recommend waiting for the shift from anonymity to 365 face-to-face feedback to happen organically. Make the decision, provide training, and throw the switch.

It starts with you, of course. You, modeling what you'd like from others. And if you have the decision-making power in your company, add a few more steps to your action plan.

1. In most cases, 365 face-to-face feedback does not replace formal reviews. However, it does allow formal reviews to be far more productive and focused. No surprises. A fierce leader considers performance reviews part of an ongoing, extended conversation, a coaching-based alternative to costly, time-consuming assessments and reams of data that based on results, is not serving us. Certainly, while you're at it, build candor and humanity (for lack of a better word) into formal reviews. Let those who conduct performance reviews know that the quality and effectiveness of their performance reviews will be noted by those they review.

2. Announce that since the company values honesty, openness, and transparency, anonymous feedback will no longer be provided. And that, given that you understand people's hesitations about being completely honest with one another, you will provide coaching on how to engage in unabashedly honest conversations that enrich relationships. Let people in the organization know that you believe such conversations are essential in a truly Great Place to Work and that you hold them able to do this.

3. Follow through on this. Provide training. Ideally, begin with senior executives, then branch out. If that's not possible, start anywhere. Start with your own team, your direct reports. Start with a cross-functional team that has been asked to deliver significant goals to the organization.

Personal Action Plan

The practice of 365 face-to-face feedback shouldn't stop at the office. A great marriage, a happy family also require something of us: a change in attitude and behavior, specific actions sustained over time. I encourage you, therefore, to use what you've learned in this chapter to foster open and honest conversations in your personal life, as well. Start by asking a family member or friend for feedback on how you impact your relationship with him or her—for good or bad. Ask if there's anything he or she would like you to start doing or stop doing or continue doing. No matter what he or she says, keep listening, without defense. And thank him or her for telling you.

Once, I was giving a keynote speech in Orlando, and a man who had sat quietly through the session caught up with me outside. He had a kind face and was in his late fifties or early sixties. "Um, I've never actually told anybody this before," he said, "but I'm deeply unhappy in my marriage, have been for years. My wife is . . . well, the only word for it is *cruel,* not just to me, to everyone. I don't think I can take it anymore. I think I need to leave."

I waited.

He continued, "But surely you're not saying I should just come out and tell my wife of thirty years what I'm thinking, like I just said it to you."

Gently, quietly. "I am. Yes."

"Oh, my God." His face lost color.

"Unless you think telling her you'd like sour cream on your baked potato will do the trick."

He looked as if he might be sick there and then on the sidewalk.

"You could begin with 'I love you, but I don't love our life together.' "

He closed his eyes and groaned.

It is hard to look agony in the eye and not flinch, not blink. But in our personal lives, just as at work, a careful conversation is a failed conversation because it merely postpones the conversation that wants and needs to take place. I gave him my card. "Please let me know how it goes," I told him. "I mean that."

About a year later, I got an e-mail from him. He had left his marriage. He had done it with kindness. He was happy in this new phase of his life.

Conclusion

Thankfully, we cut each other a fair amount of slack day to day. This goes for personal relationships, as well. Marriages don't survive unless we are willing to tolerate imperfections in our partners and recognize that we have a few of our own. And when things happen that trouble us, we talk them through until we are whole again, back on track, which is why an honest, skillful confrontation is a gift, a search for truth, a vein of gold worth mining.

Our most valuable, enduring relationships require that we stay current with one another at work and at home—face to face. While most leaders fulfill their basic job descriptions, including conducting performance reviews, filling out surveys, and listening politely (with gritted teeth) to anonymous feedback, fierce leaders do something more interesting, more real. They engage in meaningful conversations that truly connect.

> Our most valuable, enduring relationships require that we stay current with one another at work and at home—face to face.

When our achievements, talents, and positive results are noticed and acknowledged and our missteps are addressed and resolved, we deepen our commitment to bringing the best of ourselves to our work and to our families every day. And this, in turn, translates to stronger relationships and better performance, which translates to success and happiness.

Who deserves your praise? Who deserves an apology? Whose behavior or attitude is causing serious problems? What are you waiting for?

Fierce Practice #2

From Hiring for Smarts to Hiring for Smart+Heart

> We should take care not to make the intellect our god;
> it has, of course, powerful muscles, but no personality.
> It cannot lead; it can only serve.
> —ALBERT EINSTEIN

> Oh, how one wishes sometimes to escape from the meaningless
> dullness of human eloquence, from all those sublime phrases,
> to take refuge in . . . a human understanding rendered speechless
> by emotion!
> —LARA IN *DOCTOR ZHIVAGO*

I am a fan of *Deadwood,* HBO's Shakespeare-goes-to-South-Dakota-during-the-gold-rush hit series. During Keith Carradine's interview of David Milch, the creator of *Deadwood,* Milch said, "Reason is about seventeenth on the list of attributes that define us as a species, and as far as I'm concerned, they can lower it, no problem."

In Nobel Prize–winning author J. M. Coetzee's book, *Elizabeth Costello,* the story unfolds through a series of lectures. Elizabeth argues:

Cogito, ergo sum (I think, therefore I am) . . . is a formula I have always been uncomfortable with. It implies that a living being that does not do what we call thinking is somehow second-class. To thinking, cogitation, I oppose fullness, embodiedness . . . being alive in the world. This fullness contrasts starkly with Descartes' key state, which has an empty feel to it: the feel of a pea rattling around in a shell. . . . The heart is the seat of a faculty, *sympathy,* that allows us to share at times the being of another. . . . There are people who have the capacity to imagine themselves as someone else, there are people who have no such capacity (when the lack is extreme, we call them psychopaths), and there are people who have the capacity but choose not to exercise it. . . . If principles are what you want to take away from this talk, I would have to respond, open your heart and listen to what your heart says.

No great weight rests on whether I agree with Coetzee's formidable character, Elizabeth. I believe, however, that the behavior of those who miss or dismiss her argument accounts for much of the pain humans inflict on one another and for the national and global train wrecks that frequently sweep the headlines.

Far too often, the primary focus of an organization's hiring practices is to hire people with "credentials"—academic pedigrees, high IQs or test scores. What many leaders don't realize is that increasing a company's "smarts" by 25 percent will not translate into revenue growth of 25 percent. Not even close. Consider the following story.

The "Firm"

I was once invited to work with a widely respected, global provider of business consulting services that wanted to improve sales. Because its reputation for excellence was legendary, prospective clients would call with an identified need and the members of the "firm," as they called it (a code word for a company that is enamored with pedigree and probably refers to its executives as "partners"), would craft a proposal for how they might be able to help. The firm would send in its brightest and best, do its due diligence, build an impressive PowerPoint deck, and pitch its solution to the prospective client—who would thank the firm for its proposal and promptly hire the other guys. The firm was losing too many sales, a troublesome and expensive trend, and it wanted to understand why.

After talking with several of the firm's lost customers, the answer was clear. Customers liked the other guys better. Liked their solutions better? No. Liked their pricing better? No. Liked their PowerPoint presentations better? No. They liked the *people* better. They actually looked forward to working with the people on the competition's team. In contrast, they experienced the firm's consultants as a bit arrogant and aloof. They may have been smart, but they lacked warmth, personality.

As John Doerr, legendary venture capitalist, said, "The moment of truth is when you ask, 'Are these the people I want to be in trouble with for the next five, ten, fifteen years of my life?' Because as you build a business, one thing's for sure: You'll get in trouble."

> The moment of truth is when you ask, "Are these the people I want to be in trouble with for the next five, ten, fifteen years of my life?" Because as you build a business, one thing's for sure: You'll get in trouble.
>
> —John Doerr

The firm's ideas and plans were better on paper than their competitors', but the moment-of-truth answer to John Doerr's question was often no. Potential clients simply did not look forward to working with the firm's brightest and best on extensive, long-term projects, no matter how elegant the solutions proposed.

After interviewing staff members, I learned that many of them experienced a similar arrogance from the people at the top. Rank was everything. Partners were God. Everyone else was, well, "administrative staff" (spoken in hushed tones, as if referring to an invalid in the back bedroom with some vaguely diagnosed, potentially fatal malady). Partners were friendly enough, polite, but there was an invisible barrier that was felt, but hard to name, between partners and nonpartners.

It became clear that though the firm was well respected for its skilled and intelligent consultants, the firm's consultants simply did not connect with clients at an emotional level. Nor did they connect with many employees, whose relationship with the firm was merely a business transaction, an exchange of time and talent for a paycheck.

When I finally met with the regional managing director (let's call him Steve, not his real name), he told me that the firm had just lost another significant piece of work—one that would have brought in almost a billion dollars in revenue—after having spent more than 2 million pulling top people together from around the world to design a solution that would have accomplished everything the client wanted and more. The solution was so good, he'd been sure they'd win the work.

He looked miserable. "So what have you got?"

I shared what I had learned from lost clients, particularly the comment I'd heard over and over: *"We like the other guys better."* I began to summarize: "Brilliant solutions are getting you to the table and no further, mostly because the other guys come across as genuinely likable people. They're smart, and they're also relaxed, authentic, natural. They're excited about their solutions, while remaining curious and interested in learning from their clients, rather than arrogant and cocksure. And all of this comes across to prospective clients."

He waited. . . .

I sensed the subtext: *And we fix this how . . . ?*

"So your problem has nothing to do with the quality of the solutions you design or how smart your people are. They're plenty smart. They impress clients intellectually, but they aren't engaging them emotionally."

I thought he flinched slightly at the word *emotionally*.

I continued, "No matter how calm, cool, and collected clients may seem in all those meetings leading up to the proposal, the decision about whom they will ultimately hire, assuming proposals are workable and reasonably priced, will be made first for emotional reasons, second for rational reasons. It's likely they aren't entirely aware of this themselves, but the fact is, their emotions are in the lead position, and this is where you're not on an even playing field. I suspect when you compare credentials to credentials, expertise to expertise, innovation to innovation, fees to fees, this firm can match any competitor. But there is another ingredient. The tiebreaker, the place where you will improve the firm's win ratio and increase revenue, resides in the area of human connectivity."

> The tiebreaker, the place where you will improve the firm's win ratio and increase revenue, resides in the area of human connectivity.

I heard a noise in Steve's throat that sounded like the fracture of ice underfoot. He seemed frozen in his chair. I let silence do the heavy lifting.

He squinted. "So what are you suggesting?"

"I'm suggesting that the task is to improve your partners' ability to connect with clients emotionally as well as intellectually, from the first interaction to winning the work to implementing the solutions. Given the cost of a typical client engagement, the potential can be described as significant. And having talked with your support staff, I would encourage extending this connectivity to them, as well, resulting in happier, more productive associates."

Steve's face began to lose color.

I leaned forward.

"If you doubt that your organization is involved in an emotional enterprise, just ask that client who was considering spending a billion dollars with you. Ask your administrative staff, the people who decide every day how much discretionary effort they will make available to the task at hand.

If you doubt that your organization is involved in an emotional enterprise, just ask that client who was considering spending a billion dollars with you.

"The world is changing. No matter what any of us is shopping for, we can find good products, good services, good solutions. We want to enjoy the experience of *using* those products, those services. This firm doesn't have a lock on brilliance. Your prospective clients can find that elsewhere. They want to enjoy the experience of implementing a brilliant solution in collegial and congenial partnership with the people who brought it to them. And based on their comments, they don't feel assured of an enjoyable experience with the partners of this firm. Meanwhile, some of your employees are restless. Many want more than a paycheck. They would like the experience of working here to leave them whole, proud, feeling good about themselves, happy most of the time, which is not everyone's current reality. As soon as the economy improves, they're outta here. Even partners are bailing.

"High on the list of priorities on the order of 'can't really live without' are deeply rewarding relationships with the people who are central to our success and happiness, at work and at home. And to be joyful much of the time. The lack of human connectivity is robbing many people of joy and is literally costing the firm millions in employee and partner turnover."

I suspected that "joy" was not a concept entertained within the firm's walls. I took a deep breath. "There's a lot at stake for everyone regarding connectivity, Steve. Personally, as well as professionally. It might be worth asking your wife if she is as connected to *you* as she'd like to be."

Steve was still for a long time. A look of pain hovered around his mouth. I was becoming mesmerized by the sound of the ticking clock on his desk.

Finally, he said quietly, "I know in my gut that you are right. That what you are saying is significant. But I also know that I'd never be able to sell this here. It isn't what this firm does."

"You're right, it isn't. And that's the problem," I said.

He shook his head. "Never in a million years. If I brought this to the CEO . . . " He shook his head. "But thank you." His voice trailed off. Then he looked at me and smiled, faintly. "I will ask my wife."

The firm continues to lose ground to its competitors, including emerging companies it hadn't viewed as competitors. It's sad. They are such smart people.

The Business Crisis That Smarts Can't Solve

Let's acknowledge that the übergoal for most organizations is growth—let's amend that to profitable growth—while hoping that the economy doesn't worsen and that Mother Nature doesn't deliver a devastating blow to the general well-being of this planet. To grow profitably, a company needs to

- Provide products and services people want and, if the company is lucky, need;
- Continually win new customers and keep them;
- Recruit and retain top talent;
- Create a work environment in which all employees—male, female, straight, gay, young, aging, fit, disabled, multicultural—can thrive;
- Innovate to stay ahead of the game, ahead of the competition;
- Add new products and services;
- Develop a leadership bench capable of taking the company where it wants and needs to go;

- Execute the strategic plan and change it if it isn't working; and
- Behave ethically!

Clearly this requires smarts. Right? Well, yes, but that's not enough.

In 2003, Howell Raines was fired from his post as managing editor of the *New York Times*. Raines had every managerial advantage and a brilliant strategy, but he "lost the newsroom." He failed to win the hearts and minds of the staff, without which he could not hope to implement his change strategy.

In 2007, Bob Nardelli was dismissed from his position as CEO of Home Depot. He had arrived with impeccable credentials and achieved dazzling financials, but he failed to connect with the shareholders, deal makers, legislators, regulators, and nongovernmental organizations who wanted to have a say in how the company was run and on whom the company's continued success depended.

The problem for Raines and Nardelli and so many other brilliant individuals was that reason did not prevail. Raines and Nardelli alienated people, so their reasoned arguments fell on deaf ears.

Yet despite all the evidence pointing to the fact that it is the deeply feeling, emotionally intelligent people who are best equipped to deliver these results, many leaders continue to focus on hiring and promoting people with pedigrees, graduates of the best business colleges, who, talented though they are, do not view human connectivity as relevant to their success. Why? Because nowhere in their education have they been taught to focus on the human side of their subjects.

Meanwhile, the organization's strategy keeps stalling. Cross-boundary collaboration isn't happening. Leaders play Whac-a-Mole, micromanaging as opposed to leading. Original thinking is happening elsewhere. Employees have little or no emotional connection to the organization and its customers. Loyal customers are hard to come by. Relationships steadily disintegrate, one failed or missing conversation at a time.

At such a crossroads, leaders tend to review measurable goals, economic indicators, cash-flow projections, process, and procedures. Staggering amounts of money are dedicated to reviewing basic business processes, while employees long for one galvanizing conversation. Just one. I know. I've talked with thousands of these employees.

In an article titled "Most Likely to Succeed," Malcolm Gladwell asks, "Who do we hire when we can't tell who's right for the job?" Gladwell points out that in standardized tests that measure the academic performance of students, a good teacher trumps a school, class size, or curriculum design—hands down. The difference a good teacher makes, even in a bad school, can amount to a year and a half's worth of learning in a single year, whereas a bad teacher in a good school may teach half a year's worth of learning in a year and a half!

What makes for a bad teacher? Things like rigid control, broadcasting from the front of the room, and yes/no, right/wrong feedback. What makes for a good teacher? Things like creating a "holding space" for lively interaction, flexibility in how students become engaged in a topic, a regard for student perspective, the ability to personalize the material for each student, responding to questions and answers with sensitivity, and providing high-quality feedback "where there is a back-and-forth exchange to get a deeper understanding."

Sounds like the behavior of a good leader. Certainly, a teacher is the leader of a classroom, with a focus on performance, achievement. So here comes the kicker.

Gladwell writes, "A group of researchers—Thomas J. Kane, an economist at Harvard's school of education; Douglas Staiger, an economist at Dartmouth; and Robert Gordon, a policy analyst at the Center for American Progress—have investigated whether it helps to have a teacher who has earned a teaching certification or a master's degree. Both are expensive, time-consuming credentials that almost every district expects teachers to acquire; neither makes a difference in the classroom."

In *Blink,* Gladwell points to Dr. Wendy Levinson, an international expert in the field of the physician-patient relationship. Dr. Levinson looked at why some doctors who make mistakes that put their patients' lives in jeopardy get sued, and others don't. Dr. Levinson found that patients sued doctors they didn't like and didn't sue doctors they did like, even if the doctor they like made a mistake.

And why do patients like or dislike their doctors? The decision was not rational. Physicians who don't get sued take a little more time—three minutes more than physicians who do get sued. And it was the quality of the physician-patient conversation, *how* the doctors talked with their patients—notice *with*, not *to* their patients—that made the difference. Patients like doctors who really listen, draw their patients out (*tell me more about that*), and answer their questions fully. Those three extra minutes and how they were used were the differentiator. In the blink of three minutes, the patient felt seen, heard, understood, valued, and respected. You don't get that in every doctor's office. Or in every executive's office.

Book smarts don't guarantee good teachers, good doctors, or good leaders, because these aren't cognitive skills. No one's knocking an excellent education from a good school. It's just that this isn't enough. In fact, fewer young people are interested in attaining an MBA, because they recognize that the emerging right-brain economy requires a set of skills and characteristics not taught in most business schools. Many Gen Xers and Yers tell me they see value in forging more meaningful relationships at work, while struggling to get beyond the usual, superficial agenda they can't quite put their fingers on. These are the people—the ones who are both smart and engaged, who value human connection—that we are choosing for leadership roles today, globally. They understand that, while no single conversation is guaranteed to change the trajectory of a career, a company, a relationship, or a life, any single conversation can.

> Fewer young people are interested in attaining an MBA, because they recognize that the emerging right-brain economy requires a set of skills and characteristics not taught in most business schools.

Practicing Squid Eye

What might you notice if you were practicing squid eye that would suggest a focus on hiring smart people is causing more problems in your organization than it's solving? Check any of the following "tells" that apply to your team or company. Or to *you*.

Leaders suffer from excessive certitude. In meetings, people stubbornly cling to their ideas (sometimes at length!) in an attempt to impress others with the brilliance of their thinking. Their goal is to influence. It does not occur to them that an equally valid goal would be to *be* influenced, to have their own learning provoked. Nothing new emerges, because individuals are focused on being right rather than on making the best possible decisions for the organization.

Excessive use of jargon is a badge of honor. Three-letter acronyms (TLAs!) have their use. It takes less time to say ADP than Automatic Data Processing, CBA as opposed to cost-benefit analysis, EAP rather than employee assistance program, FOD rather than field observation demonstration. But when did we determine that as the notable computer scientist Edsger W. Dijkstra said, "no endeavour is respectable these days without a TLA"? My all-time personal favorite four-letter acronym was conjured up within a global organization: FLOG, which stands for feedback log, as in "Have you been flogged lately?" And consider words like *componentize*. Nigh unpronounceable, it apparently means "to turn into a component." For what purpose will remain a mystery. *I digress.* The point is that people who use empty, meaningless jargon are the people who have nothing insightful to say. Internally and with customers, jargon lands like a stone.

The competition is surpassing you. You pull several all-nighters and spend hundreds, thousands, or millions preparing your pitch to a prospective customer. You feel great about the brilliant solution you've come up with and know it will work. You want this job, *need this job.* You go to the client meeting higher than a kite, leave the meeting unsure, a not-so-good feeling in your stomach, and find out a day, week, month later that the customer went with the other guys. You lose sleep for days wondering WHY.

"Loyal" customers are leaving. Joseph Pine wrote that today's economy is an "experience economy," meaning that customers want more than a good product or service; they want to enjoy the *experience* of using a product or service, which begins with their first interaction with a company. So if, in spite of all your customer-service training and "customer-facing" procedures, policies, and scripts, customers aren't feeling the love, you're in trouble. *Love?* Yes.

Your margins are shrinking. Your product or service has become a commodity, and you've been competing primarily on price. Though you believe you offer the best—whatever it is you offer—your customers believe they can find what you offer elsewhere. And they can—for less and/or for a better experience—so they're leaving. Meanwhile, you keep lowering your price, and customers continue to leave. Your top line may be impressive. Your bottom line is troubling.

Implementation—of almost anything—is agonizingly slow, fraught with delays. A costly outcome for companies focused on hiring smart people is a lack of alignment, cooperation, and collaboration throughout the organization. A matrixed organization filled with smart people who fail to connect with one another, have no desire to connect, and, in fact, do not know *how* to connect with their peers in other parts of the organization produces a silo mentality. In its most simplistic form, the thinking is *This solution or decision solves my problem; too bad if it causes new problems for others.* Whether you have fifty employees or fifty thousand, initiatives stall, and you incur financial and cultural penalties as a result.

Competitors can poach your talent. Countless surveys show that human beings desire ongoing, deep connection to their coworkers and to the companies they work for. If your organization's relationship with associates is based primarily on an exchange of time and talent for a paycheck, you're a source for headhunters who will have no trouble luring your "high potentials" to companies with something more appealing going on, where there is more to the human dynamic than "I'm smarter than you are."

What Were We Thinking?

Despite more and more experts writing and talking about the indisputable role of emotions in the workplace, many of us remain reluctant to acknowledge and deal with our own emotions, much less those of others. Sadly, all too often we are decidedly uncomfortable with the thought of actively surfacing and dealing with emotions (notice the negative language—"dealing with") because of long-held beliefs about the role of emotions in the workplace, drummed into us since we took our first business course or began our first job.

Which beliefs do you hold?

I believe that:	I believe that:
Emotions have no place at work.	Emotions are running the show at work, as well as at home, so it's important to surface and acknowledge them.
Any display of emotion, apart from excitement or enthusiasm, is unprofessional and will be judged as such by others.	Emotion is part of what makes us human, what motivates us, for good or bad, so when people express emotion, I need to pay attention.
I don't have time to deal with emotions; I have a to-do list that would fell an ox. People should just do their jobs.	Dealing with emotions can take time; not dealing with emotions will take longer.
If people want love and affection, they should buy a puppy! Not my job!	A central part of my job is to build a culture that includes genuine affection for and an emotional connection with coworkers and customers.

| I will impress colleagues and customers with what I know, persuade them with my intelligence and logic. They should listen to me. If they don't, they're stupid. | If I want people to respect me and commit to the course I recommend, I must respect and commit to them. If I don't, I'm stupid. |

Let's revisit the question, what do you win? What do you win if you win your argument for the beliefs on the left? All of the tells you spotted with squid eye. Since most organizations produce good products and services and offer competitive pricing, the key to disrupting the level playing field must reside elsewhere. It does. It resides in the heart.

If You're Still Not Convinced, Think Nobel Prize

In 2002, the Nobel Prize for economics was awarded to Daniel Kahneman, a psychology professor at Princeton, whose studies proved beyond any doubt that we behave emotionally first, rationally second. This is not a new-age thing. Or a cultural thing. It's the human condition.

The implications are stunning, particularly for companies that have a relationship with their customers based primarily on price and a relationship with their employees based on an exchange of time and talent for a paycheck.

Greatness in individuals and organizations is not a function of intelligence—there is plenty of IQ out there—but of emotional capital, the ability to connect with people on a human level. And each of us accumulates or loses emotional capital—building relationships we enjoy or endure with colleagues, bosses, customers, and other partners—one conversation at a time. Without relationships, we have no voltage. The first company in any industry that significantly improves its human connectivity skills will take the field.

We are emotional beings engaged in emotional enterprises.

We are emotional beings engaged in emotional enterprises. Without an emotional impetus, we withhold our best efforts, drag our feet, delay decisions, or walk away altogether. The competition offers a better price, and "loyal" customers leave. Talented, unengaged employees learn of a work environment in which they sense they'll be happier, and they, too, will be gone, even if they must take lower salaries, pay higher medical deductibles, and endure longer commutes.

This is not hypothetical. The lack of meaningful connections with coworkers and customers is costing companies billions annually.

Consider what the following data means to you and your organization:

- Experienced partners in a multinational consulting firm (obviously not the firm in the story) who scored above the median on the competencies of emotional intelligence delivered $1.2 million more profit from their accounts than did other partners—a 139 percent incremental gain.

- At L'Oréal, sales agents selected on the basis of emotional competencies significantly outsold salespeople selected using the company's old selection procedure. Sales increased by $91,370 for every sales person hired specifically for his or her EQ skills. The cosmetic giant also had a 63 percent lower turnover rate among the salespeople hired for their EQ than among those who weren't.

- Gallup Organization case studies revealed that "regardless of how high a company's customer satisfaction levels may appear to be, satisfying customers without creating an emotional connection with them has no real value. None at all." While an emotional connection with customers is always important, it is a *requirement* during an economic downturn, when customers are hunkered down, giving careful thought to how they spend their money. Trouble is, if you suddenly find you *need* to make that emotional connection, it's usually too late.

- After supervisors in a manufacturing plant received training in how to listen better and help employees resolve problems on their own, lost-time accidents were reduced by 50 percent, formal grievances were reduced from an average of fifteen per year to three per year, and the plant exceeded productivity goals by $250,000.

- The United States Air Force dramatically reduced its annual recruiter turnover rate from 35 percent to 5 percent, which translated into savings of $3 million a year, when it selected candidates who had high emotional intelligence.

- Study after study has shown that teams are more creative and productive when they can achieve high levels of participation, cooperation, and collaboration among members. But interactive behaviors like these aren't easy to legislate.

- A study of 130 executives found that how well people handled their own emotions determined how much people around them preferred to deal with them. *(Ya think?)*

- For 515 senior executives analyzed by the search firm Egon Zehnder International, emotional competencies were better predictors of success than either relevant previous experience or IQ.

- Directors of MBA programs are rethinking their curriculum to include courses that help develop human connectivity skills. *Hooray!*

- An analysis of more than three hundred top-level sales executives from fifteen global companies showed that emotional competencies distinguished the stars from the average.

- A new study of hiring managers across industries reported in the magazine *Chief Learning Officer* revealed that the primary reasons new hires fail are interpersonal, not technical. Twenty-six percent failed because they couldn't accept feedback (you know where I stand on "feedback" of the anonymous variety and why most people have trouble accepting it), and another 23 percent didn't last because they were unable to understand and manage emotions. Thinking back, hiring managers said that there had been clues— tells—but they simply hadn't paid attention to them, and their hiring practices didn't assess a candidate's ability to acquire emotional capital.

Your Most Valuable Currency

The implications for our individual careers are also impressive. Daniel Goleman suggests, "As a leader moves up in an organization, up to 90 percent of their success lies in emotional intelligence." In other words, nine out of ten executives who derail do so because they lack emotional competencies! The three primary derailers are difficulty handling change, not being able to work well in a team, and poor interpersonal relations. *Yep, that would pretty much do it!*

And did you know that in *top* leadership positions, over four-fifths of the difference in performance is due to emotional competence? Four-fifths!

Hafiz wrote, "The idiot's warehouse is full of merchandise." I can picture this "idiot," surrounded by his "stuff"—the beautiful office, framed degrees on the wall, high position on the org chart. And he is lonely and ineffective—emotionally anorexic. His smarts have gotten him this far, but now he's stuck and hasn't a clue why.

> "The idiot's warehouse is full of merchandise."
> —Hafiz

Intelligent people quickly realize that a leader's most valuable currency—*your* most valuable currency—is not money, nor is it IQ, multiple degrees, fluency in three-letter acronyms, the number of technical gizmos attached to your person, the number of reorganizations under your belt, good looks, charisma, self-sufficiency, industry experience, or the ability to analyze a case study, read a profit and loss statement, or build a really cool PowerPoint deck.

Your most valuable currency is relationship, emotional capital, the ability to connect with others. In fact, no matter how much "smarts" we may have, I think we are lonely and empty every moment of our lives until we connect emotionally, as well as intellectually, with at least one other person.

Arjuna Ardagh captured this beautifully in *The Translucent Revolution: How People Just Like You Are Waking Up and Changing the World:*

We constantly resist not only our grief, but also our wild passion and sexuality, our anger, even our exuberance and joy, repressing their free expression. Big feelings overwhelm us. They can easily upset the fragile equilibrium of our lives. We keep a lid on ourselves, till we periodically explode. We don't realize that any deep feeling, pleasurable or painful, can be a wave we surf home into ourselves, into love.

The bold headline, the key message, of this practice, is the main premise of all things fierce:

If you want to become a great leader, gain the capacity to connect with colleagues and customers at a deep level . . .

. . . or lower your aim.

Human connectivity is the überskill that captures the ideal combination of IQ and EQ. You simply cannot connect with colleagues and customers at a deep level unless you are able to bring valuable expertise to the relationship *and* you are able to access and manage your own emotions and the emotions of others.

I have met smart, empty people. *Peas rattling around in a shell.*

Building high-performing, enduring, profitable relationships with employees and customers requires that we explore, embrace, and ultimately rely on emotion in work that is, at the end of the day, deeply human.

I have met smart, empty people. *Peas rattling around in a shell.* You have too. I've also met smart, open-hearted people. Campfires around which we gladly gather. Which would you rather hire? Whom would you like to work alongside?

My personal epiphany has been, *If I'm so smart, I'm halfway there.* Einstein understood this. So does the poet David Whyte, who wrote:

Listen.
In every office
  you hear the threads
  of love and joy and fear and guilt,
  the cries for celebration and reassurance,
  and somehow you know that connecting those threads
  is what you are supposed to do
  and business takes care of itself.

Fierce leaders connect those threads every day.

The great differentiator going forward, the next frontier for exponential growth, the place where individuals and organizations will find a new and sustainable competitive edge, resides in the area of human connectivity.

It is here that significant gains can be made in uncontested market space, employee engagement, leadership effectiveness, and career potential. The benefits are noticeable both within the organization—improved workplace relations—and in the marketplace—improved market share.

This potential is significant.

The Fierce Practice: Hire Smart+Heart People

IQ may get people hired. EQ gets them promoted. Populating an organization with people who have smarts and heart is not an option; it's essential to success. So let's get to it.

STEPS 1 & 2: PREPARE YOURSELF AND PREPARE OTHERS . . . SIMULTANEOUSLY.

Begin by identifying the key emotional attributes of a potential hire. So what does a highly intelligent person who can also connect with people at a deep level look like in person? How would we identify him or her? Like Paul with the squid, you must first figure out what you are looking for. Of course, the necessary skill sets, experience, and attributes will differ depending on the job, but some attributes should always make the list. For example, "integrity" is almost always on everyone's list, but what about "relationship oriented" or "ability to connect with others"?

One of the qualities that Google looks for and measures in potential Googlers is their "Googleyness." Is the candidate able to work effectively in a flat organization and in small teams? Can he or she respond to a fast-paced, rapidly changing environment? Does he or she seem well rounded and bring unique interests and talents to innovate in his or her work? Does he or she possess enthusiasm for the challenge of making the world a better place? This "Googley" factor plays an important role when candidates are evaluated during the hiring process, and note that nowhere in the description did I mention GPA, IQ, number of years of higher education, or any other conventional measure of "intelligence."

Largely as a result of its hiring practices, Google is known to have one of the most engaged and productive workplaces around. While for many organizations the competition for talent is steep, people are eager to work at Google (it typically receives around 1,300 résumés a day), retention of employees is high, attrition is low, and revenues are strong. So what can you do?

Get your team together ("team" being the people the potential hire will work with AND some of the people this person will work for) and build *your* list. If the notion of "smart+heart" is foreign to your team, talk about it or ask team members to read this chapter before the meeting.

To "relationship oriented" and "able to connect" you might add . . .

- Accountable
- Authentic
- Collaborative
- Courageous
- Passionate
- Lifelong learner
- Welcomes feedback
- Biased toward action
- Solution oriented
- Change agent

A word about authenticity. I'm concerned that this word is used so frequently that it has lost meaning and impact, and that's a shame, because authenticity is a big deal when it comes to hiring people with the capacity to connect with their colleagues and customers.

I remember the days when I would have to connect to our Internet server by clicking on "open Internet connect" on my laptop, which then offered options such as "Bluetooth," "airport," and "VPN." I would click "VPN," watch the words "connecting, connecting, connecting, connecting" scroll across my screen and then shift to "authenticating," and I was there. Connected.

One day, while watching this process for the thousandth time, I had the apostrophe (okay, epiphany). Lacking authenticity, there is no connection. It is this connecting and authen-ticating that fierce conversations, fierce lead-ership, and fierce hiring are all about.

> Lacking authenticity, there is no connection.

And, of course, it starts with each of us as individuals. You and I will find it nearly impossible to connect with each other until we have connected with ourselves, our real selves. We can't let others into our real life if there isn't one, if we project images we imagine others desire and those images differ depending on whom we're with. *("Here comes the boss; let me put on my boss face. Okay, the boss has left the room and it's just you and me. That's a different face. Here comes the customer; let me haul that face out of the file. In fact, we call it customer-facing. At home I'll pull out my ideal mommy, daddy, spouse face. And when I'm out in the community, when I see my pastor/priest/rabbi, well, that's a very special face.")*

People can spot inauthenticity from fifty paces. If you hire inauthentic people, your customers and clients will notice—and feelings of distrust will return with disquieting frequency, because they'll wonder what else your company is faking.

At Fierce, we added a few things to our list of required attributes for successful hires:

- Has a sense of humor. (Preferably warped.) *We know who we are.*

- Thrives in a diverse work environment. At Fierce, we are straight, lesbian, married, single, parents, grandparents, "will never have kids!,'" Christian, "spiritual," Jewish, Republican, Democrat, Independent, American, Iranian, East Coast, West Coast, dog lovers, cat lovers, opera lovers, football fanatics, Gen Y, Gen X, boomers, and a partridge in a pear tree. The partridge leads a lot of our meetings.

- Is happy and upbeat, most of the time. Someone who, in general, can focus on the good things that happen, as opposed to those whose lives are a series of freak accidents, messy relationships, and financial emergencies, reinforced by self-loathing.

- Does not harbor an unrealistic sense of entitlement. After all, the world doesn't owe anybody anything. It was here first.

Take a moment to list the attributes important to you in a teammate and, in particular, for the position you're filling.

Attributes essential to success in my company, in this job:

_____

_____

_____

_____

_____

_____

_____

_____

The discussion of ideal attributes will be valuable to everyone in attendance, serving as a reminder of the behaviors and characteristics that are most important, most valued by you and your team members.

Design questions that will reveal whether a candidate possesses the attributes you're looking for. A technique called behavioral interviewing comes in handy here, but I won't belabor it, as there are excellent resources on this topic alone. In general, the principle is that the best predictor of future behavior is past behavior. We learn very little when we ask people to tell us about their strengths, accomplishments, even weaknesses. Clever candidates profess that their weakness is a tendency to work too hard. *Yeah, right.* Instead, ask them to tell you a story about how they actually handled a situation in the past; obviously, this must be a true story, with specific examples and names of other individuals involved.

For example, Helena Ferrari, director of human resources for SDC Technologies, recommends saying, "Tell me about a time when a colleague gave you advice." This question uncovers whether someone is open to feedback, willing to change, collaborative, and respectful of co-workers. Or you could say, "Think back to a time when you were under pressure to get more done than seemed possible, and tell us how you handled that." And just as important, "Tell us about a time when you failed."

Questions that seek examples of previous work situations and how the candidate handled them give us a glimpse of a person's emotional quotient—who someone really is. Such questions are far more revealing than theoretical questions such as "How would you organize a project team?" (a savvy candidate can fabricate a credible response) or leading questions such as "You're a pretty independent worker, aren't you?" Hint: If you say it with a smile, the answer will be "Yes. Give me a job to do, lock me in a room, and let me at it!" If you're frowning, the answer will be "That depends on the project. When collaboration is important, I involve others so that I have all the input and support needed to do a great job."

Candidates are clever devils, indeed.

So write down three behavioral questions that will require a candidate to help you determine if they have the "smart+heart" attributes that are most important to you.

Behavioral questions:

1. _____

_____

2. _____

_____

3. _____

_____

Before you interview, it's also essential that you do the following:

Recognize your hiring traps. A hiring trap is a snare. Sometimes we don't even see it, and other times we recognize the trap, but it's so seductive that we walk right in! Common traps include the following misguided ways of thinking:

- **Personal biases.** "You're like me, and since I am fantastic, I should hire you. Besides, under 'professional and personal affiliations,' it says 'snowboard instructor at Stevens Pass.' I'm a snowboarder, too, so it's clear that you're a cool dude." Or "We both went to Holyoke (or Harvard or Berkeley or Iowa State or . . .)" or "We both started our careers as teachers (or programmers or white-water rafting guides or . . .)" or "We both have certificates in Web development and project management, so I should hire you!"

- **Personal insecurities.** "You are smarter, taller, better educated, more experienced, more attractive, and sexier than I am, which poses a threat to my personal advancement and, more important, my self-esteem. You have more bullets under "qualifications" and "accomplishments" than I could put on my résumé. I can see it now. In meetings, your ideas will be better than mine, so I shouldn't hire you." Or it's the opposite . . .

- **Résumé "puppy love."** You've worked for big companies, you have impressive "qualifications," and you are certified in Seven Habits, Six Sigma, emotional intelligence, Myers-Briggs, e-learning strategies, life coaching, database administration, and log cabin construction, so we should hire you. *I've always dreamed of building a log cabin!*

- **Time pressure.** "It's not just our hair that's on fire. Various body parts are aflame. We need someone now! Your résumé indicates you have skills in the areas we're looking for, and you haven't been convicted of embezzling or stalking, so when can you start?!"

- **Hiring for an ambiguous position.** "We've got to add someone to the team. We'll work out the details about your area of focus later. Meanwhile, it's clear that you're fluent in 'biz dev,' you are presentable, so I should hire you."

- **Ignoring your instinct.** *Very popular.* "During the interview I got a nagging feeling in my gut that says something is off, but I can't figure out what it is, and since I'm tired of interviewing and I have a lot to do and you look good on paper and both of us graduated from Sewanee, which nobody on the West Coast has heard of, and we're both certified time-management trainers, and since we need someone in this position right away, I should hire you."

You've worked for big companies, you have impressive "qualifications," and you are certified in Seven Habits, Six Sigma, emotional intelligence, Myers-Briggs, e-learning strategies, life coaching, database administration, and log cabin construction, so we should hire you. I've always dreamed of building a log cabin!

- **Broadcasting the script.** "I told you what qualities we're looking for, and you profess to have those exact qualities, so I should hire you." If you tell the candidate exactly what qualities you are looking for, you're just inviting a fake, scripted response. For example, if you say, "We are a very collaborative team with a bias toward action. Our focus is on making the best possible decisions, rather than always fighting for our own ideas. Tell us what's important to you," no one is going to respond with "I hate to collaborate. I prefer working in the dark by myself. . . . "

A confession. In the early days of Fierce, we hired a wrong person (wrong for Fierce) because we fell into several of these traps during our selection process. We needed to add a business development person to the team and were charmed by Roger (not his real name), a man who came across as thoughtful, deep, a thinker. He had experience with several high-tech companies, and since we had several technology clients, we felt he would be the perfect person to work with them. We attributed certain qualities and skills to him simply because of his work history. Several of us ignored a gut feeling that he might not be right for us—something about his quietness, his reluctance to smile. We made excuses for what we didn't want to see: "Yes, he was unusually quiet, and there were long silences when we asked him questions, but that probably means that he's a deep thinker." So we hired him.

In actuality, though Roger was "smart," he was a deeply and chronically depressed person whose social skills had never developed. Whereas the rest of us leaned toward relationships, he leaned away. There was no warmth. He resisted taking his first client call, and when we finally insisted on throwing him under the bus, he was hugely relieved when the call was postponed.

Meanwhile, we didn't have a "bench." We were a ten-person company and required everyone to be suited up, on the field, playing for all they were worth. But with Roger, it felt like we were one man down. He wasn't on the bench, wasn't on the field, wasn't even in the locker room.

> He wasn't on the bench, wasn't on the field, wasn't even in the locker room.

We made Roger available to industry after only two months. After he left, someone observed, "Usually, when somebody leaves and takes all their stuff with them, when I look at their work space, I feel the emptiness, but in Roger's case, this space felt empty even when he was here."

And sadly, Roger had little capacity for joy. Suffice it to say that we all breathed a sigh of relief when he left. Then, after having wasted all that time and money, we had to start the selection process all over again!

Take a moment to write down your hiring traps, then share them with the team and ask about their traps.

My hiring traps:

_____

_____

_____

_____

Now that you've built your list of key attributes, identified your hiring traps, and vowed not to be trapped by them, what's next?

Identify three A+ candidates to interview. Not just two that look pretty good and one that looks okay. Three A+ candidates!

Even if you don't have an HR department and you're simply trying to fill a position in a small company, finding three A+ candidates should be your commitment. In fact, in a small company, it's even more important.

Use your personal network, which probably includes online networks too numerous to name (some of which could be extinct by the time this is published). For a recent opening at Fierce, we had great luck with LinkedIn and CareerBuilder. And you can always use Monster, craigslist, Redmatch, HotJobs, Kforce, and other resources that will have emerged by the time this book is published. Ask your friends to keep an eye out for you. Use professional recruiters.

STEP 3: DO IT. INTERVIEW CANDIDATES.

Now that you have waded through the stack of résumés and selected a handful of candidates who interest you, how will you select the three A+ candidates to invite to a face-to-face interview, candidates who not only have the particular brand of smarts your job opening requires, but also have emotional intelligence—and, most important, the capacity to connect with people at a deep level?

Conduct a phone screening interview. This isn't a new idea, though I recommend a few twists to the usual rote phone screening so that you can determine whether someone is an A+ candidate. Part of the challenge is that there are plenty of websites that suggest the "best answers" candidates can give to the questions they will likely be asked.

For example, if a candidate is asked, "What was your biggest accomplishment in your current or last position, and alternatively, what did you fail to accomplish?" one website suggests, "If you didn't fail at anything, say so." I grant you that *failed* is a strong word, but surely we can all admit to falling short here and there. It would be well nigh impossible to connect with someone who has never failed. Besides, they'd make the rest of us imperfect birds look really bad!

And to the interview question, "Why were you fired?" (if you were), one prestigious blog suggests, "Get past the sticky issue of getting fired, so you can move on to your skills and why you're qualified for the job." Now, I ask you, what is honest about "getting past" the sticky issue of getting fired?

So what can *you* do during an initial phone interview to get someone to leave these stock answers at the curb and show up authentically?

- **Show up yourself!** If you ask a bunch of canned questions like an automaton, in a voice expressing no emotion, why would you expect something different in response? Job candidates are probably a bit anxious, hoping to impress you, and most have prepared for the interview and practiced what they will say. Be personable. Go off script. Reveal something about yourself. Not your home phone number. Something you love about your job. Something you don't love is just as important. A whiff of you being "real" will encourage the candidate to be the same. As Maya Angelou wrote, "When someone tells you who he is, believe him." To that I add, "When someone declines to tell you who he is, exit as soon as possible."

  Be personable.
  Go off script.

- **Allow enough time.** Reconcile yourself to the fact that this is not going to be a ten-minute interview. Unless you can tell right away that someone is *not* a candidate, this could take a while. How long depends on how many questions you ask and how important it is to you to get real, thorough answers, which often requires probing. I suggest honing your list of questions to the ones that will tell you what you really need to know.

- **Don't be satisfied with superficial answers.** Dig for candor, full disclosure. If someone gives you a canned answer, a duck-and-dodge answer, a nonanswer, call him or her on it, in the nicest way possible: "That answer sounds a bit like one I read on an interview advice blog. Let me ask the question again, because I'd like to know what really happened, in your own words."

Once you've conducted phone interviews and selected three candidates to interview in person, you're ready for the radical, "fierce" approach to the face-to-face interview that will identify smart+heart candidates. Here goes.

Conduct a team interview. This isn't the most radical part, but it is important. Why the team interview?

- **It sends a powerful message about the importance of collaboration.** Most candidates expect to be interviewed by one person. When a group turns up, it broadcasts the message that this position is important enough to take the precious time of all the people in the room and also signals a collaborative environment in which multiple, possibly competing views are sought on important decisions.

- **It reveals who can really connect in challenging situations.** It's fairly easy to maintain eye contact with one person, but how does a candidate manage three to seven people? Start by having everyone briefly introduce themselves (name and job responsibilities), then notice whether the candidate picks one face and fixates on it no matter who asked the last question or makes eye contact with everyone from time to time. The person who makes eye contact with everyone is the person who'll be able to connect with multiple clients, customers, and/or colleagues simultaneously.

- **It makes authenticity tougher to fake.** At Fierce, we work together as equals. Ideally, a candidate will respond—in tone of voice, personal warmth, facial expression, degree of enthusiasm—in the same way to everyone, regardless of rank, age, gender, or the presence or absence of accents, bling, or tattoos. When people with a wide variety of titles and job responsibilities gather for an interview, candidates who behave differently depending on whom they're with or who's asking the question are not the kind of people you want on your team.

- **Each of us picks up on different things.** I'm often surprised and impressed by the observations and insights of my colleagues following interviews. I might be enthusiastic and learn that someone else is hesitant. Or vice versa. As we talk about it, something emerges that deserves consideration. Something that would have been missed and could have led to a hiring mistake if it had not been brought to our collective attention: "I really liked him." "I liked him too, but I noticed he directed all of his comments to you and rarely even glanced at anybody else, as if we weren't even there. It makes me wonder if he is focused on hierarchy. And how would he conduct himself in client meetings where there are several people present?" Hmmmm.

- **Who should be present?** First and foremost, the person the candidate would report to. Given how busy everyone is, this rarely happens in large organizations, but this is a mistake. The candidate is making a decision, too, and part of the decision has to do with chemistry and personal connection, so if this person is going to report to *you,* take a seat at the table. Ask the questions you want to ask and allow the candidate to ask you questions. Besides, since telephone screening will have identified three A+ candidates, you *can* spare the time. I'd also invite at least two people whom the candidate would work *with,* at least one person who would be an internal "customer" of the candidate, and at least one person who would report directly to the candidate, assuming he or she would have direct reports. At Fierce, there are almost always six people present during an interview. Once we like someone, several of the team members take the candidate to lunch to get to know him or her more personally, but we always start with the larger gathering. It makes quite an impression.

Give the team members the list of the attributes you selected and the questions you designed together. Let them know that you want each of them to ask at least one question during the interview.

Conduct the smart+heart interview. *Here's how it could go:*

Introduce yourselves. Welcome the candidate, and be warm and genuine, not bumps on a log. (I've sat in on meetings during which interviewers came across as stone idols, nary a smile or knitting of brows or anything to indicate that they were living, breathing human beings. What about this would attract an A+ candidate?) Have each person at the table give his or her name and responsibilities, including, "You would report to me," or "I would report to you," or "You and I would work together on . . . "

Begin with a general question. Ahead of time, appoint someone to ask the first question: "Tell us about yourself. What would you like us to know about who you are, where you've been, where you are now, where you're headed?" I suggest that it not be the person the candidate will report to. This signals that you view one another as equals. Following the candidate's response, anyone at the table is free to ask clarifying questions.

Begin Mineral Rights. And look for the tells. Before you ask behavioral questions, spend fifteen to twenty minutes on "Mineral Rights," a deep-dive conversation introduced in *Fierce Conversations*. We call it Mineral Rights because it goes deep on one topic. After all, if you're drilling for water, you're more likely to find it if you drill one hundred-foot well than one hundred one-foot wells.

> After all, if you're drilling for water, you're more likely to find it if you drill one hundred-foot well than one hundred one-foot wells.

In truth, Mineral Rights has many uses. It is used by coaches, mentors, salespeople—it even works wonders with teenagers. I think of Mineral Rights as my Swiss Army knife. It's the conversational model I use most often at work and at home. At Fierce, we use Mineral Rights in meetings to ensure we've identified the real issue that needs addressing. We use it with new customers and during hiring interviews. Leaders use it with direct reports.

There are seven questions, and the rule is questions *only*. Each step in the Mineral Rights conversation breaks through the normal layers of reserve, inauthenticity, or resistance we often encounter in ourselves and others (for more details on the Mineral Rights conversation, refer to your copy of *Fierce Conversations*). You will follow some of the questions with probes inquiring about emotions, in hopes of getting head *and* heart responses.

Don't rescue someone who falls silent or seems uncomfortable. The candidate should be doing 90 percent of the talking.

Question 1: Identify the issue. In coaching and sales conversations, the first Mineral Rights question is "Given everything on your plate, what is the most important thing we should be talking about today?" In an interview, replace this with "Given everything you've shared with us so far, what brought you to our doorstep today?" Give the candidate time to really answer this.

Question 2: Clarify the issue. Draw the candidate out, and don't offer prompts or your own assumptions. The purpose here is to learn what's really going on with this person. If the person is currently employed, why does he or she want to make a change? If the person isn't employed, why not? What is it about your company and this job that appeals to him or her? What's important to him or her going forward? Details are useful. Most important is clarity on why this person is sitting in front of you.

Question 3: Determine current impact. Probe for more information about the candidate's current job or situation to find out what is prompting him or her to leave. Keep the emphasis on *current*: "What results is your current job/situation creating?" "Who else and what else is currently being affected?" and, just as important, "How is this affecting you?" And then ask the question that differentiates Mineral Rights from the usual interview: *"Given this impact, what do you feel?"*

Why ask this? If the candidate isn't in touch with and/or is unwilling to reveal genuine emotion, you don't have a smart+heart person here. But don't be too quick to judge. People aren't expecting to be asked this question.

Question 4: Determine future implications. Ask, "If nothing changes in your current position, what are the implications?" And again, draw the candidate out. It's okay to provide a little help with something like, "If we were talking six months or a year from now and nothing had changed, what might you be telling us?"

Then ask, "When you consider those possible outcomes, what do you feel?"

Question 5: Examine personal contributions to the issue. Ask, "Before we move on, how would you describe your own contribution to the conditions and outcomes at your current position with which you're unhappy? In other words, where is your DNA regarding these results (and whatever emotions the candidate has named)?" This is an opportunity to discover the level of personal accountability the candidate accepts for whatever is not working, not going well at his or her current job. Or to learn that you have an entrenched "victim" on your hands who blames others for failures, disappointments.

If the candidate says, "I don't know" ask, "What would it be if you did know?" Ask this lightly, smiling. This isn't a criminal trial, merely an opportunity for the candidate to fess up to whatever he or she brought to the party. You could prompt with "If you could go back and change something you did, didn't do, said, didn't say, what comes to mind?"

A huge tell is a candidate's inability or unwillingness to recognize and disclose his or her own role in whatever situation displeases him or her. There are a few situations in which a person is truly innocent, but those are extremely rare.

Question 6: Describe the ideal outcome. Say, "Let's imagine you have taken exactly the right job in exactly the right industry and exactly the right environment for you. Tell us about that job and what difference that would make for you."

You'll discover whether candidates really want the position at your company or just any job. Draw them out: "Say more."

Then ask, "When you consider that possible scenario, what do you feel?"

I love when this question sparks excitement, anticipation, light in someone's face. If you don't see it, probe: "Hmm. I don't get the feeling that you're clear about what's important to you going forward." And see what the person says. Or "I don't get the impression that you have a vision for the next phase of your career that is particularly compelling." And listen.

Question 7. Commit to action. Ask, "Given everything you've shared with us, what steps have you taken and what steps do you plan to take to find the right position for yourself, in the right company?" and "What's your time frame?" Note: You haven't yet asked whether the candidate thinks he or she would be happy in your organization, because none of his or her questions about the job or the company have been answered yet. You'll get to that shortly.

Ask behavioral questions. Now it's time to ask the behavioral questions you designed to make sure the candidate has actually displayed the attributes important to you. These might include the following:

> Tell us about a time when a colleague gave you advice.
> Think back to a time when you were under pressure to get more done than seemed possible, and tell us how you handled that.
> Tell us about the toughest conversation you ever had at work. Who initiated it? Topic? Outcome?
> What turns you off? Tell us a story. . . .
> Tell us about a time when you failed.
> Tell us about a relationship with a colleague or a customer that was important to you.

Ask a question they aren't expecting. Once you're clear that a candidate has the chops to do the job you're filling, and once he or she has answered questions that reveal he or she has the attributes you're looking for, ask one or two questions that are out of the blue. Perhaps "What grounds you?" or "What turns you off?" If a candidate asks, "What do you mean?" don't explain the question. Just say, "No wrong answer here. What comes to mind?" A favorite question of mine is

"There's a British sitcom called *The Last of the Summer Wine,* about a group of retired friends living in Yorkshire. One of them confesses that, although he sold linoleum all his life, whenever he had to fill out a form and got to the line that said 'occupation,' he had a hard time writing 'lino salesman.' What he really wanted to write was 'minister of agriculture.' If *you* could write anything above the word *occupation,* what would you write?"

> If *you* could write anything above the word *occupation,* what would you write?

At Fierce, I hope candidates will say "wildlife photographer" or "Duchess of York" or "tree-house builder" or "symphony conductor" or "personal assistant to the Dalai Lama" or "expert on the migratory habits of the brown-headed cowbird." My interest flags if I hear, "Oh, I just want my work to contribute to the organization's mission."

Ask, "What was the last good book you read?" or any other questions you'd like to ask, even if completely unrelated to the job description (assuming the questions are legally and ethically appropriate).

Now it's the candidate's turn. Ask, "What questions do you have of us?" This is where the candidate will ask you to tell him or her more about the job, details, expectations, what you're looking for in a candidate, and more about your company or department or team.

Why not explain all this at the beginning? Because, as I mentioned earlier, you would have broadcast the "right" answers, handed a savvy interviewee the script. Don't talk about the job and what you're looking for until you've gotten all *your* questions answered. If the candidate asks you for information about the job or company earlier (and most will), just say, "We promise to cover that while you're here, and before we do, we'd like to learn about you."

But at this point, don't hold back anything. Tell them the vision, mission, values, expectations, challenges, rewards. Let your own passion, your emotions, show. Remember, the candidate is making a decision, too, and it's just as important for him or her to feel a connection with you as it is for you to make one with him or her.

Have a secret signal. At Fierce, we have a signal when we conduct team interviews. If at any point in the interview, one of us feels strongly that this person is not right for us or for this position, we put our pen on the table. When we notice someone's pen on the table, if we concur, we signal agreement by putting our pen on the table, as well. *(We'll have to come up with a new signal when this book comes out; otherwise, job candidates will freak out if anyone puts a pen on the table!)* We try to be subtle—we don't all slam our pens on the table simultaneously!

If the majority do this (in our case, four out of six people), someone, usually Halley, our President and COO, ends the interview respectfully, warmly, candidly, with no argument, though we will discuss it later. For example, Halley might say, "Thank you for everything you've shared with us to this point. You've been open (if the person has), and given what's important to you, I feel that this isn't the right job (or company) for you." (Give a specific example, but keep it brief; for example, "You prefer to work in the background in a support role, and this job would require that you be front and center, talking with clients regularly" or "Your career goals, which I applaud, are unlikely to be fulfilled at Fierce. So rather than take more of your time, let's stop here. Thank you very much for meeting with us. I sincerely hope you find exactly the right job for yourself.")

Stand up, extend a handshake, and say good-bye. If the person argues (some will try to persuade you that you're wrong, that they should have or could have told you more, et cetera), counter with, "Please don't be disappointed. While Fierce isn't right for you, I have no doubt you'll be the right addition for a great company." And walk to the door.

Why would you do this? One of the principles of *Fierce Conversations* is "obey your instincts." Don't just trust them, obey them! So we do. On the few occasions when we've talked ourselves out of obeying our instincts, we ended up paying the price.

And, of course, if the majority don't put pens on the table, we continue the interview. The pen setter will have a chance to air his or her opinions and concerns after the interview is over. Which brings me to . . .

STEP 4: DEBRIEF.

Allow at least fifteen minutes after an interview to debrief. Yes, I know everyone is pressed for time, but there isn't a more important contribution you can make to the company—well, besides closing a multimillion-dollar deal—than selecting smart+heart people to join your organization, so it's worth those few extra minutes. Plus, if you have several interviews in a row, you will need time between them to refresh yourself. Use this time to debrief two things:

1. What is our impression of the candidate? Right for us? Concerns? How does this person stack up compared to other candidates we've interviewed? Next steps? Make sure you hear from everyone present. Following a recent interview, someone commented, "I can't quite put my finger on his problem, but I'll bet it's hard to pronounce." That is a tell if I ever heard one.
2. How'd we do? Were we happy with our own participation in the interview, with the flow, with the probing? Is there something we want to do differently in the next interview? If so, what is it and how will we manage this? Acknowledge individuals for things they asked or said that were particularly helpful. What did we do well? Vow to do that again!

Clear your heads as best you can in preparation for the next interview.

STEP 5: DO IT AGAIN, ONLY BETTER.

Rinse and repeat, as many times as necessary, until you find the perfect person—with the smarts *and* heart—for the position.

Taking It to the Organization

Share your thoughts about hiring smart+heart people with others in your organization, particularly the data on the importance of the capacity to connect with colleagues and customers at a deep level.

Suggest they read this chapter. Ask for their thoughts. Tell them you'd like to change the practice of hiring smart people to hiring smart+heart people. When it's time to add someone to the team, follow the plan outlined earlier.

If you are a senior executive, participate in the next interview series. If you have the ear of senior executives, ask for time with them and build your case. Make a clear recommendation, a clear request. Help in any way that you can. Offer to coach the interview team and to be a member of it. I cannot tell you how many times one person has advocated passionately for something he or she believed in and ended up shifting tectonic plates.

Provide training to current employees. Luxottica Group is the world leader in the design, manufacture, marketing, and distribution of mid- and premium-priced prescription frames and sunglasses. Following Fierce training, the company enjoyed the best year in its history. While part of Luxottica's success is attributed to acquisitions, there's this, from a senior executive: "The biggest win for this year was how we all came together as one company, the strength of collaboration and connection. The sum total of millions of magical moments."

Personal Action Plan

Like all fierce practices, hiring smart+heart people begins with you. It's tough to hire people who can connect with others if you aren't connecting with others yourself. So now that you know the importance of gauging other people's emotional quotient, how about gauging your own?

Hiring smart+heart people begins with you.

Begin by having a fierce conversation with yourself.

How much emotional capital do I have? To what degree am I connected with the people who are central to my success and happiness? Would others describe me as "smart+heart"?

What words come up for you when you think about your relationships with family members, colleagues, customers?

_____

_____

_____

_____

_____

_____

Write the names of people who would say (and mean it), "I am extremely happy in your company."

_____

_____

_____

_____

_____

_____

_____

_____

_____

Do you desire a deeper connection? If your answer is *yes*, what do you need to do? Make a list of your goals for the next thirty or ninety days. Be specific about the outcomes you want and the actions you'll take. Add names and topics to the "Conversations I Need to Have" list at the end of this book.

Conclusion

Connectivity has revealed itself as my life's theme, my personal challenge, the way through for me, which is sometimes difficult, since I am a card-carrying introvert who thrives on solitude. I came to it early.

As a child, I spent almost every summer weekend at my grandparents' home on Lake Chickamauga in Chattanooga, Tennessee. My grandparents were loving, funny, playful, intelligent businesspeople who built a one-room getaway cabin that evolved over time into the large, comfortable home to which they eventually moved full time.

It was a kid's paradise. My brother, Sam, and my cousins, Gil and Baxter, spent every spare moment there. There was a long pier from which we fished and dived. There were canoes, a tree house, chairs that tolerated wet bathing suits, hammocks to lie in while gazing into loblolly pines, listening to the drone of cicadas and motorboats. There were Indian arrowheads to unearth on nearby islands, forts to build, canasta games to win or lose (the loser served vanilla ice cream with hot fudge sauce), ghost stories to be retold again and again, lightning bugs to catch, screech owls hooting us to sleep.

When I was ten, one warm, humid day, after hours in the woods, I climbed a tree that was home to a muscadine vine. Muscadines are like Concord grapes in that the outer skin slips off, leaving a juicy pearl to savor. After lounging in the branches of the tree, eating my fill of muscadines, I climbed down and sat on the ground, leaning my back against the tree, with my legs stretched out and my palms on the ground. I closed my eyes, dozing in the late afternoon sunlight, not a serious thought or a thought of any kind for miles around. *Ten-year-olds can be marvelously serene.*

Then something strange happened. My palms and legs seemed to sprout tiny tendrils, which began working themselves into the soil beneath my legs. It felt as though my back began to meld with the tree trunk. I was frightened at first, because I literally couldn't move. It was as if my body were fastening itself to the ground and the tree. Then came a growing sensation that I was okay, that in fact, what was happening wasn't strange or dangerous. I began to feel that the tendrils that bound me to the tree bound me to the world. That I was not only connected to the earth and the tree and the breeze and the grapes and the sun and the birds, but also to the people I knew and loved and even to those I didn't know. My ten-year-old self couldn't articulate then what I am writing now, recalling this experience like it was yesterday. The world and everything in it was resident within my own veins. I could taste the world on my tongue, sniff it on my skin. I felt deep love for all of it. What a childhood gift—awareness of my own smallness and insignificance, balanced by the awareness that I was part of something uncomprehendingly vast and beautiful. Connected to it, *literally*.

And then I forgot that experience, got caught up in school, friends, home, boys, the thrills and chills of adolescence. As an adult, the memory returned when I learned that according to quantum physics, an individual's mere presence in a room affects the physical properties of that room and, ultimately, the outcome of scientific experiments. In Steve Toltz's book, *A Fraction of the Whole,* the central character, Jasper, says, "People always say, 'It's good to be a part of something bigger than yourself,' but *you already are.* You're part of a huge thing. *The whole of humanity.* That's enormous. But you couldn't see it, so you pick, what? An organization? A culture? A religion? That's not bigger than you. It's much, much smaller."

Looking back, I recognize that "connection—at a deep level" has been the underlying theme of my work and my life. Every human on our planet, except those with severe disorders, desires to connect with others—whether it's their boss, their colleagues, their friends, their family members. And to do that, they must ask, "Who are you *really?*" Until we know one another, there will be no connecting. So until then, lower your arms. Step away from our hearts. Step away from our companies and our customers.

If you are still resisting the idea that human connectivity is essential to your success and happiness, consider a fortune-cookie aphorism I came across in *Apathy and Other Small Victories,* by Paul Neilan: "The world is your oyster, but you are allergic to shellfish."

The pleasure of connecting with others at a deep level is a total sensory experience, even better than a dozen oysters. But if, after reading this chapter, you think it's only about feeling good, then, well, I haven't done my job. Because the fact is that when we connect at work, we are not only happier, we are more effective, more productive, more profit-

"The world is your oyster, but you are allergic to shellfish."
—Paul Neilan

able. Richer, in every sense of the word. And if you recognize that something within you must shift before you can get there, well, feel free to borrow my mantra for this past year: "Open my heart." Say it in the morning. Think it in the meeting when you feel yourself tuning out or irritated or judging someone. Remember it when you're talking with a customer who is demanding or someone who seems to be wearing a suit of armor encased in concrete.

It's easy to think it's about *them,* about him or her, but it's about *you.* And me. Connecting. Right now, in this conversation. Not that one. *This* one.

Fierce Practice #3

From Holding People Accountable to Modeling Accountability and Holding People Able

I recall hearing the true story of a pilot who landed just short of the runway in San Francisco. Luckily, no one was seriously injured, but the plane ended up partially in the water. When he was hauled to the official inquisition and asked how such a thing could have happened, he faced the battalion of lawyers and industry experts and said, "I f——ed up." End of statement.

Most of us would be stunned (and/or amused) to hear responses like that in business today. After all, when was the last time someone in your organization (maybe it was you) asked, "Who's accountable for this disaster?" and someone rushed forward, arms outstretched, shouting, "It was me! Hold ME accountable! I'm the one!"

Instead, we point the finger. *He, she, they, it did it! It wasn't me.* As Steve Toltz wrote in *A Fraction of the Whole*, "The great thing about blame is that she goes wherever you send her, no questions asked."

The words "I'm holding you accountable" are spoken thousands of times a day around the world during meetings, on the phone, in hallways to individuals, teams, and, yes, teenagers. And my thought is always *Good luck with that.*

Don't get me wrong. Accountability is a big deal, one of the rarest, most precious commodities to be found. Next to human connectivity, accountability is the single most powerful, most desired, yet least understood characteristic of a successful human being and a successful environment. The long-term benefits of personal accountability have enormous implications for the quality of our lives, and there is certainly a direct correlation between a company's health and well-being and the degree of accountability displayed by its employees.

Why, then, in a study by the Table Group, did 80 percent of 132 executive teams score "red," or poor, on accountability? And why are our efforts to improve the level of accountability in organizations so ineffective?

It's because we're so busy trying to find out who is accountable that we forget to check the one place we should be looking: in the mirror.

Common wisdom tells us that powerful partnerships require that we . . .

1. understand needs;
2. clarify expectations;
3. collaborate on solutions; and
4. meet commitments.

Let's acknowledge that few of us are good at all of these steps, particularly the last one, and our efforts are further complicated because we don't understand what accountability really is, how it differs from responsibility, why it shows up, why it disappears, and what it *really* requires.

The purpose of this chapter is to address these issues and to provide a game plan for creating a performance culture that values initiative, problem solving, agility, risk taking, and a bias toward action. A company filled to the brim with individuals who, instead of laying blame, willingly and gladly accept accountability for everything that's got their name on it. Given challenges, they ask themselves, what am I going to do? The answer isn't "duck and cover." They step up to the task and hold others able to do the same.

Before we dive in, to get you thinking, write down your answers to the following questions:

What is an example of an issue confronting you or your team that is made worse by a failure of accountability?

_____

_____

_____

What results is this causing?

_____

_____

_____

What about an example in your personal life?

_____

_____

_____

What results is this causing?

_____

_____

_____

Who's Accountable?

Though you may be clear with others regarding due dates for deliverables, there are inevitably going to be problems, snags, bumps, obstacles, delays. People get busy, waylaid, a colleague doesn't do his or her part, a vendor is late with a shipment, a personal emergency (a sick child, toxic mold in the house, an injury to the family dog) derails a key member of the team.

And, too often, we give people more work than they can handle effectively, hold them accountable for getting it all done, and express frustration when they present us with a list of very good reasons for their failure to deliver. Maybe the package was mistakenly shipped to Ankora, when it was supposed to go to Anchorage. (As we speak, someone in the Niger inner delta region is trying to figure out what to do with six pallets of advanced therapy moisture lotion.)

The point is, when something like this happens, our knee-jerk response is often "I want to know who's accountable for this!" And the automatic reply? "Not me!"

I remember working with a team of high potentials at a global shoe manufacturer. At one point, the founder of the company, a tall, imposing figure, walked into the room and sat in the back. I had just begun to explore the notion of accountability with the team when he stood and thundered, "What I want to know is, if we take a successful store manager and move him into a territory that's struggling, and nothing improves, who's accountable—the manager or the person who moved him?"

In other words, who will receive my wrath? At which point, forty intelligent people—the future leaders of his company—did their best to shrink their subatomic particles and vanish from his radar.

Why? Because most of us associate accountability with blame, culpability, being responsible, being wrong, maybe even being fired. In fact, we'd likely define accountability as "clarity about whose head will roll when things go wrong." Given that *accountability* conjures the image of a firing squad without benefit of blindfold or last meal of Frito-Lays and Milk Duds *(I admit to strange and powerful cravings),* no wonder we don't eagerly raise our hands when we hear the question, "Who is accountable?" Instead, we insist that he, she, it, they did it to us!

And it's no wonder. Deflecting blame seems to be in our DNA!

A marvelous example is Koko, one of the world's most famous gorillas, known for mastering more than one thousand words in American Sign Language and, in doing so, helping to overturn preconceptions about the limits of animal intelligence. One day Koko broke one of her toys (the act was captured on video). The next day one of her trainers came in, picked up the broken toy, and asked, "Koko, what happened to your toy?"

Koko promptly pointed to the assistant trainer. True story!

Non Est Mea Culpa

Humans, including those in high places, often employ a slightly more sophisticated version of pointing. Take a statement from Attorney General Alberto Gonzales's attempt to exonerate himself from any accountability regarding the firing of U.S. attorneys: "I acknowledge that mistakes were made here."

With those words, Attorney General Alberto Gonzales was using a technique often thought to be a politician's best friend: the passive voice. Why is this technique so popular? Because the passive voice takes accountability out of the picture. Think about it. "Mistakes were made." There is no actor in this sentence. Why won't those pesky mistakes quit making themselves!

Passive voice has so cheapened the concept of a mea culpa that various officials in government hearings and press conferences actually seem to be proud of themselves when they acknowledge that "mistakes were made."

Wouldn't it be refreshing to hear an official say, "I blew it"? After fainting from shock, most people would admire that candor and maybe trust that the same mistake would not be made again. Think about how President Obama's candid admissions of error early in his administration bolstered his popularity, rather than harmed it. YouTube features a clip titled "Obama on Daschle: I Made a Mistake," and several other clips in which President Obama models the kind of personal accountability and candor we crave in our leaders today. But let's not hold our breath that everyone will embrace this behavior, wedded as so many are to the passive voice. A duck and dodge if ever there was one.

What we want to know is what mistakes were made and who made them? Please don't give us the generic *they*—as in "They didn't handle this correctly." Which actual human beings had their hands all over this? Give us a name. Was it you? And what exactly is going to be done to correct this and ensure it doesn't happen again?

In one *9 Chickweed Lane* comic strip (rendered by Brooke Mc-Eldowney, my favorite cartoonist) the character Thorax, who sells strange goods and services from roadside stands when he isn't ruminating on his alien origins or dusting off the quantum anomaly in the tractor shed, sits at a roadside stand with a sign reading: REPUDIATIONS R US. He explains to Edda, another character:

> Being as it is election season, I have started up a denial consultancy. While the candidates and the news media uncork their relentless gush of allegations and accusations, I stand ready to provide custom tailored denials for every occasion. I have a new spring line of stout denials, categorical denials, unwavering denials, firm denials, swift denials, flat denials, emphatic denials, steadfast denials, outraged denials and, as summer approaches, a few angry denunciations with matching counter-accusations.

Funny and sad and true.

Of course, failings in accountability happen everywhere, not just in politics. Personally, I'd like someone to explain why Hollywood produces so many lousy movies, why I'm put on hold while a recorded message assures me that my call is important, why hosts of quilting shows sound like they're talking to three-year-olds, why I can only use my hard-earned frequent-flier miles to go to places I don't want to visit at the most inconvenient times imaginable while sitting in the last coach seat next to the toilets, why doctors with whom I have appointments think nothing of making me wait for hours, and why there still isn't a cure for the common cold. A *real* cure. Whom can I hold accountable for all of THAT?

I have a new spring line of stout denials, categorical denials, unwavering denials, firm denials, swift denials, flat denials, emphatic denials, steadfast denials, outraged denials and, as summer approaches, a few angry denunciations with matching counter-accusations.
—Brooke McEldowney, *9 Chickweed Lane*

And while I'm at it, to my knowledge, no individual or group has claimed culpability for the collapse of investment banks, the escalating price of gas, the failure to alert residents of Myanmar of the approaching cyclone that took the lives of one hundred thousand people, or the CIA's destruction of ninety-two interrogation videos. And will someone please tell me why Bernie Madoff did not receive swifter justice, once it was known that he had put thousands of people who trusted him in serious financial straits?

The point is: Are failures of accountability happening in *your* organization, in *your* life—perhaps including how you've handled or mishandled your own financial matters? (Bernie is a rat, in my opinion, but what might you have done differently?)

Before we identify the "tells" and talk about what to do, consider two competing ideas:

The progress of my organization depends on my leaders, colleagues, and customers.

or . . .

In a very real sense, the progress of my organization depends on my progress as an individual now.

To which of these beliefs do you subscribe?

One of the reasons so many of us fail to "succeed," by whatever definition we may choose, is that we believe in the first idea. In other words, we believe someone else is running the show, that our progress depends on our bosses and how they treat us, on our colleagues and how talented and helpful they are or aren't, on corporate politics, on customers and whether they have the capacity to understand why they require our products or services, on our spouses or life partners and the degree to which we do or do not feel appreciated and supported by them. And despite whatever therapy we may have endured, we still lay accountability for our progress, or the lack thereof, on our parents' doorsteps, on the degree to which our parents equipped us with all good things throughout our childhoods or messed us up forever.

This attitude certainly makes for a well-protected ego with built-in excuses for just about every eventuality. It allows us to take

> We're doing the best we can, but really, one can hardly expect us to overcome the pull of the moon.

credit for the good stuff, but when results aren't so good, well, in that case it's not about us; it's about him, her, them, or it. We're merely well-intentioned jellyfish, buffeted by things beyond our control, carried this way and that by the waves, the tides, the politics, the marketplace, the economy, the budget. We're doing the best we can, but really, one can hardly expect us to overcome the pull of the moon.

On the other hand, if someone asked if we considered ourselves a victim, we'd say, "No way! I'm a powerful person, and for your information, my organization recognizes me as a high potential!"

Well, hang in there for a minute or two. Have you ever said any of the following things? Or thought them?

- My department is struggling because the strategy is flawed.

- I'm behind because so-and-so (or such-and-such) is a bottleneck.

- Our industry is suffering because the margins are tight, our unions are threatening to strike, our competition has forced us into a price war, and our customers have unreasonable expectations.

- Our problem? The price of oil! The board of directors, et cetera.

- We can't get this done without the right technology.

- I haven't been able to focus on this project because I have ADD. *(Have you noticed that some people aren't complaining when they tell you they have ADD? They're bragging!)*

I often speak at functions focused on women in leadership, offering my thoughts about what needs to happen for women to step into and remain in senior leadership roles. In 2005, when I read the Catalyst Census of Women Corporate Officers and Top Earners of the *Fortune* 500, I was appalled. Apparently, according to the women surveyed, the three significant barriers they face that men rarely do are

1. gender-based stereotyping;
2. exclusion from informal networks; and
3. lack of role models.

This was not the appalling part. It was the solution offered: Not that women should work to defy gender stereotypes, or make efforts to include themselves in informal networks, or strive to be better role models for their peers and for future generations of women. No, it was that companies should mandate diversity and inclusion, because clearly *companies* are to blame for the barriers facing women. Where's the accountability here?

I'm not suggesting that these barriers don't exist. The glass ceiling is still very real in many industries, and sadly, gender discrimination in the workplace still exists. But what appalled me was how quick the women surveyed were to deny any accountability for the struggles they face. After all, no doubt all three of those conditions existed for Madeleine Albright when she began her stint in the White House as a secretary. Lots of people wondered how "Maddie" went from secretary to secretary of state. Albright's answer: *"By doing whatever I was asked to do, including making a pot of coffee, to the best of my ability. I made the best coffee to be found!"*

Still, many women play the victim, blaming their flatlined careers on the company, society, the world. And then they wonder why things aren't improving. Accountability has to start from within.

For example, I agree with the female director of data management in a financial firm who suggests that where many women fail is in not being specific about their career aspirations with the people who are in a position to point them in the right direction. Not taking the time to reflect or network to understand what's out there for which they might have exactly what is needed. Not actively seeking candid feedback to learn what qualities and capabilities would make them a viable candidate for a new role. And not taking the steps to work on those qualities and demonstrate their considerable talents, abilities, and willingness to learn.

So I confess that I'm not sympathetic when I hear women say things like, "Me, well, the truth is, I don't have a real shot at the top because:

- . . . relationships are formed on the golf course, and I'm not a golfer."
- . . . I have young kids at home and can't put in the eighty-hour workweeks it takes to get ahead around here."
- . . . so-and-so is plotting and scheming for the position I want, and I just won't play those games."

. . . frankly, why would I want a so-called promotion! Those guys in the C suite are miserable. I want to enjoy my weekends."

. . . people don't listen to me because I'm a woman."

I hear this last one from women a lot, and I suspect the reason nobody listens to them is that they say things like that! In my view, the best reasons are really just the worst excuses.

Years ago, a woman who reported to me complained frequently that she hadn't closed any sales because customers weren't returning her calls. I finally said, "Then make yourself the kind of person whose phone calls get returned!" She was shocked, hurt, angry. But starting the next day, her phone calls got returned, and she soon became our top salesperson. In other words, she did something differently. *She* changed, not the customers.

I see victim tells all the time. For example, at some point during every *Fierce Conversations* training, someone will say something like, "I would love to have amazing conversations like this in my company. It would be fantastic. But our leadership and our culture wouldn't support this level of candor."

This statement, this belief is a huge tell. Among other things, it indicates that we don't have a leader here. We may have a *potential* leader and very likely a delightful person, just not a leader. We have a victim. Someone who tells him- or herself and others, *"I can't be myself here,"* when actually, a more honest statement would be *"Right now, I'm choosing not to muster the courage, will, skill, energy, focus . . . whatever . . . needed to do or say what needs doing or saying."*

So if I'm in the room when someone says they can't have fierce conversations because their culture won't support it, I usually say, "Where is this so-called culture with which you're unhappy? Is it out there somewhere? Or is every person in your organization, including you, a walking hologram of the culture? As I look at you right now, I am looking at the culture!"

You are the culture. *I* am the culture.

The point is, the culture is not some nebulous and mysterious force out there somewhere. *You* are the culture. *I* am the culture. And each of us shapes that culture each time we walk into a room, pick up the phone, send an e-mail.

Fierce leaders know that they influence the culture one conversation at a time, responding honestly or guardedly when asked what they think. Since you *are* the culture, you go first! And don't point your finger at leadership—unless you ARE the leadership.

My visual for this:

WHO CAN FIX THE PROBLEMS?
(in the world, in a company, in a family)

X

ATTACH SMALL MIRROR HERE

Revisiting the two competing ideas, remember that in a very real sense, the progress of your organization depends on your progress as an individual now.

So what about the *now* part?

My thought used to be something on the order of *Look, here's the thing. I'm shoehorned into my calendar, got a to-do list that feels impossible! So how 'bout if I focus on some personal development next quarter, next year, when I have a little time?*

That was me not getting it. And then I remembered something a friend said: "Unconsciously, we're always choosing deep growth or slow death. And sometimes sudden death." A bit dramatic, but I got it. *I* was choosing excuses, practicing victim.

So I'm reminding myself and you, the reader, that *now* is where it happens. Great stories, great changes, great results—those fatal moments, events, choices, conversations that put in place something irreversible—turn on *now*.

The Victim Context

Victim is a loaded word, though we all go into victim mode from time to time. It's part of being human. No doubt you know someone who is a bit of a victim. *It could be you.* Be assured that I don't mean to demonize the word *victim*. I personally love the victim mode. Sure wish it worked!

Here's a little quiz.

Do you like to look good? Do you have a tough time admitting to mistakes? When was the last time you apologized to someone? Is your image more important than learning, more important than results? Have you ever said, "Mistakes have been made"? Do you sometimes pretend that you know, rather than admit that you don't? Do you ever blame an outcome on the fact that you weren't coached, or weren't coached well enough, or that you weren't given the tools, resources, support needed to succeed, or that something happened that was simply unfair? Are you somewhat risk averse? When you hear the word *accountability* or when someone suggests that you are accountable for something, what is your internal reaction?

The victim mode shows up everywhere. Some typical examples:

I got a speeding ticket. Everybody else speeds, so why was I the one who got caught?

My work load is too big. I couldn't possibly get it all done.

I didn't get the promotion I deserved. They gave it to the boss's son. I'm better than the idiot they just hired.

My upbringing was flawed.

My partner is a louse.

This kind of thing always happens to me. I must have some big *V* for victim on my back.

They didn't ask for my input.

The world has changed! And without consulting me!

Those younger employees don't have a work ethic. They insist on work/life balance, which is really irritating.

Or have you ever tried to convince someone that you are more of a victim than they are? Victim debates are hilarious.

I have it worse than you do! It's out of my control. They're out to get me.

No, they're really out to get me!

And when we win, we celebrate! *My life is*   **My life is worse than yours!**
worse than yours! Hooray!   **Hooray!**

During the Bush administration, one of our trainers worked in Brazil, and someone there said, "Our president is worse than yours." Taken aback, our trainer replied, "Good for you."

Why is the victim mode so common? It has wonderful benefits! Victimization is easy, a reason to blame. It's not me; it's you, it's them.

How does the victim mode get reinforced? Sometimes it's because everybody agrees that I'm a victim, especially if I'm a good storyteller. We get *oohs* and *aahs*. And lots of sympathy. Some people are victim magnets: *You poor thing, let me help you.* In fact, it's downright irritating when someone interrupts the extremely pleasurable experience of telling our victim story and starts to tell one of his or her own!

The victim mode also gets reinforced because it is frequently rewarded. We have a litigation culture that rewards victims on a regular basis. And the squeaky wheel gets noticed. The people who just work hard—not so much.

Being a victim also gives people a sense of being with the in group, the in crowd. Many people don't go to accountability because they don't want to lose the camaraderie. *Let me tell you how hard this is. This company is evil.* We agree. We are comrades.

Another huge draw of being a victim is that I don't have to look at myself. As we learned in Fierce Practice #1, self-reflection is tough. We have amazing clarity about others, but not about ourselves. I've noticed that BS often sounds true in my head, even if I know it isn't.

Plus, if we're really good at this victim cycle, we don't have to do any work on ourselves or confront our own behavior, because it isn't about us. *I've assessed the problem, and you're it. If you and everybody else would accommodate me, I'd be happier. The quality of my life has nothing to do with me, so I don't have to do anything. I can't. It's out of my hands. If it were in my hands, I'd take action.*

When we shine a light on this, it starts to sound flawed.

The main benefit of being a victim is safety. As long as safety (in the short term) is motivating us, we will pick victim every time. Tempting as it is, the victim cycle is a very addictive and destructive one. After passing the buck, the victim will become depressed and fretful and his or her self-esteem and self-confidence will take a major hit. Relationships will start to suffer; team cohesion will be lost. Then the victim is likely to take these worsening results as further evidence of victimization and further justify the victim mode. At best, nothing will improve, and in most cases, things will get worse.

In order to break out of the victim cycle and improve results, we have to take risks. When you hear me talk about risk, it's a very relative term. For some people, it's a risk to take a long, relaxing day off; for others, it's a risk to work two in a row.

Risking is about leaving the familiar. As human beings, it's amazing what we can get used to.

Are You In or Out of the Cave?

The desire to stay safe has been around a long time. It's hardwired into us. Based on research, brain experts agree that we have what is called the "reptilian mind" or "ancient brain" or "survival mind," which forms the committee of our ancient fears.

Picture two cave people standing in a cave looking out onto the savanna. They notice something moving in the tall grass. What might the participatory learner feel compelled to do? *Go out there and investigate!* And what might happen to that brave soul?

He becomes dinner. So, quite simply, we have more relatives who stayed in the cave.

It's the same for us today. When we contemplate leaving the safety of our comfort zone, we run the decision by a committee of our ancient fears to see if it's a good idea.

What will that committee of fear tell us?

"I wouldn't do that if I were you. My uncle tried that and he died."

What are some of the traits we might exhibit when we choose to stay in the cave?

- Withdraw or attack.
- Be cynical or critical: "That won't work," "Why bother," et cetera.
- Be self critical. And if we are beating ourselves up, we won't be in the mood to leave our cave. Besides, we're busy beating ourselves up.
- Lose self-esteem and confidence.
- Resist change.
- Enjoy and point out the failures of others—because it justifies our having played it safe.
- Play not to lose instead of playing to win.
- Overstructure everything, micromanage.
- Place great importance on distractions—*so that we can stay away from anything where we may fail or make a mistake.*
- Experience no real joy or excitement; life is just okay.
- Have a strong need to be right, have things our way at the expense of . . .

During a training session on fierce accountability, we have a fun, interactive way to identify our cave-dwelling temptations by creating the cave of our dreams. It's called Design-a-Cave. Participants select and affix stickers to a picture of a cave in their journals, decorating their caves with all of the things that would make them comfortable and justify a very long stay.

What might you choose? I'd select a fireplace, a comfy sofa, a glass of red wine, a KEEP OUT! sign, my laptop, my dogs, some good books to read, fresh flowers, my Stevie Award for best entrepreneur of the year, indicating that my work clearly "exceeds expectations," and a framed photograph of someone who took a major risk (one I'm avoiding) and was promptly shown the door as a result.

We love our caves. And while the cave is fine to visit every now and again, it becomes a problem when we live there and never venture out.

While the cave is fine to visit every now and again, it becomes a problem when we live there and never venture out.

When life is primarily about creating safety, we are in no danger of becoming the change agents who bring our highest and best to our own lives much less to those around us. People who stay in the cave are rarely the people who end up as executives and managers of a company. At least, not a company that has any hope of surviving and thriving in the twenty-first century.

Are you in or out of your cave?

Justified "Victim"

Remember, being a victim is not a question of whether we can justify our list of reasons explaining why we are a victim, it's a question of how we use those reasons to justify staying a victim. After all, every one of these justified-victim events may be true. Maybe Maria *did* kick you in the leg, or you *are* working for a boss who is a tyrant. And maybe you *were* raised by demons! If you were victimized, you were victimized.

Being a victim is not the problem. The problem comes in the next stage, where we gather evidence to prove that we are powerless in the situation. Being a justified victim is very seductive, so much so that we start to display our victim evidence, our evidence of powerlessness, on our chests like a badge of pride.

Let's say my manager called me on the carpet. I might say, "Do you know why I'm not successful in my job? *(Whoosh.* I open my jacket and unfurl the stories.) Do you know why my relationships don't work? *(Tada!)* Do you know why I don't feel genuinely good about myself? *(Bullet point, bullet point, bullet point!)* You have the audacity not to buy this list? You come in here and tell me I need to work harder! Can't you read this list? Have you no compassion?"

Why are these well-justified, proven, internalized lists so important to most of us?

Because they become who we are. We identify with our list. If you make my list wrong, you make *me* wrong. And I sense that you identify with your list, so there's no way I want to make you wrong.

The people who buy our list are our friends, truly understanding people, and those who don't buy our list, who don't understand, are a pain in the butt. One of the most common and heartbreaking results of the victim mode is detachment. When we shut out everyone who doesn't buy into our victim list, we run the risk of shutting out the very people we need the most. As Steve Toltz writes in *A Fraction of the Whole,* "When you withdraw from the world, the world withdraws too, in equal measure. It's a two-step, you and the world."

> "When you withdraw from the world, the world withdraws too, in equal measure."
> —Steve Toltz

Interestingly, we like it when people buy our lists: "Oh, you poor thing. Look at what's been done to you. Let me comfort you." Though we get off on that, at the same time, we lose respect for people who buy our list, because it's a list of why we're not able, why we can't, why we're not powerful in a situation.

I love you and hate you for agreeing with me.

If we didn't have these lists, what would we have to do? We'd have to do what we don't want to do, in some cases, what scares us.

Remember, I'm not saying your list isn't true. Every item on your list may be 100 percent true. But it doesn't matter. It's not the event. It's our context, our translation of the event to ward off accountability, and to justify staying in our cave.

Practicing Squid Eye

What might you notice if you were practicing squid eye that would suggest holding people accountable is an unhealthy practice that is causing more problems than it's solving? Check any of the following tells that apply to *your* team or organization. Or to *you.*

People playing not to lose instead of playing to win. Legislating accountability doesn't instill enthusiasm. It usually creates an internal resistance, or at best resentful compliance. "I'm going to be tracking your progress, John. I'm holding you accountable." Accountability is enforced on John. So John does just enough to act accountable only while being watched, like kids when their parents are in the room.

Lack of productivity. Just as in relationships, we create environments we either enjoy or endure. And when no one, including leaders, takes personal responsibility for their results, people simply punch the clock and wait for the day to end. Tick, tock. And if you have people around you who are just enduring the day, my guess is they aren't very productive.

Lack of clarity, lots of confusion. Because people are scared of being blamed for poor results, no one wants to own anything or define their role in the outcome. There is resistance to even partial ownership. It's difficult to solve a problem when it won't sit still and declare itself.

Tunnel vision. People are so fearful of being blamed that they focus on tracking evidence to justify mediocre results, rather than on overcoming the obstacles in their way.

Nasty surprises. Most of us don't like to admit we're struggling, and when "accountability" is added to the mix, the tendency is to delay the discovery of impending doom as long as possible. Consequently, unless a manager has been extraordinarily vigilant, it's often at the last moment—just before the "due date"—that he or she discovers how far short of goal we are.

Generational frustrations. Boomers who try to motivate Gen Xers and Yers by holding them accountable, thinking they'll rise to the challenge if their jobs are on the line, are in for a shock. Baby boomers may rise to that because what's important to them is job security. They will stomach a lot of crap to pay their mortgage. But Gen Xers and Yers will stay long enough to get experience, to get the company's name on their résumés, and then they will leave. The boomers will be retiring soon. Then what?

Unsustainability. In an emergency, legislated accountability can work in the short term. But for the long term, you're looking at a bitter, shut down, passive/resistant work force. What's sad is that when this happens, most command-and-control leaders say, "We need to be tougher on accountability," and what they get is a negative result quicker.

> What's sad is that most command-and-control leaders say, "We need to be tougher on accountability," and what they get is a negative result quicker.

Bitterness toward coworkers. You end up with an adversarial, divisive, tattletale environment in which people are keeping score on who is doing what and are quick to point out one another's faults and missteps.

Difficulty leading. People will stop coming to you and instead go to others behind your back, because they are too afraid to tell you if something is not working. And if you don't follow through on your threats, you lose credibility.

A culture of dependency. People do only and exactly what you tell them to do. Why bother going the extra mile?

Lack of enthusiasm. Some people will anesthetize themselves, numb out.

Stalled strategies and initiatives. "We can't do it because . . . "

Stalled careers. Blaming others for failure is not the behavior of a leader.

What Were We Thinking?

By now, I hope we've established that shifts in our beliefs result in changed behavior, the behavior needed to get the results you want for yourself and for your organization. Which beliefs do you hold?

Negative context:	Positive context:
If other people or the situation were different, I'd have the results I want.	What could I do differently to create the results I want?
Reality can't be changed. There's no point in fighting it.	Perhaps we can change reality with thoughtful conversations.
It's important that I collect evidence to justify my behavior and performance.	I'd rather get the results I want than be right about why I can't get them.
Accountability determines whom to blame if things don't go well.	Accountability identifies who will keep things on track and resolve obstacles encountered along the way.
Delegation requires that I hold people accountable.	Delegation requires that I model accountability, assign responsibilities, and hold people able.
I can't create the results I want because of realities outside my control.	Given my current reality, I need to figure out what to do to create the results, the career, the relationships, and the life I want.
It's not about me. It's about him, her, them, that, the situation.	Part (or all) of this is about me, a behavior, belief, or attitude, which I can do something about once I recognize that I need to make a change.
Other people's excuses are lame. Mine are real!	Everybody's excuses, including mine, are real, including the "lame" ones.
I do the best I can with what I have. It's up to management to solve problems and remove obstacles in my way.	Doing my best includes solving problems on my own, and when that's not possible, I need to suggest solutions and make clear requests to ensure success.

WHAT ARE YOU WINNING?

Unfortunately, lots of people live in the left column, so let's revisit Brenda's question: "What do you win if you win your argument for these beliefs?" You win all of the tells you spotted with squid eye and much more, none of it good.

On the other hand, what happens when the beliefs in the right column are present?

- People bring discretionary effort, creativity, passion, and innovation to the workplace on their own.
- They bring pride and loyalty to the team, to the organization.
- They bring energy. It's energizing to be around people who step up to the plate.
- Challenges are addressed and resolved.
- Things get done. On time.

When I'm around someone who is truly accountable, my first thought is *How amazing!* My second thought is *How wonderful!*

The Fierce Practice: Model Accountability. Hold People Able.

Initially, for most people, the notion of "fierce accountability" sounds frightening, aggressive, full of conflict, smacks of a heavy workload. Yet if you think of *fierce* in the most positive light, like fierce loyalty, fierce resolve, or fierce friendship, you might associate fierce accountability with a bias toward action and passionate commitment to exceptional results, even in the face of obstacles.

> When I'm around someone who is truly accountable, my first thought is *How amazing!* My second thought is *How wonderful!*

Here's the official definition of fierce accountability:

A desire to take responsibility for results; a bias toward solution, action. An attitude; a personal, private, nonnegotiable choice about how to live one's life.

The question is, given my goals, how will I achieve them? Given the barriers to my progress and the current results on my plate, some of which are troubling, what am I going to do?

Complicated times call for simple answers. Simply put, if it's to be, it's up to me.

Complicated times call for simple answers. Simply put, if it's to be, it's up to me.

For example, think back to the question at the beginning of this chapter about an issue made worse by a failure of accountability. If you ask yourself, "What part of this issue, this failure to execute, this disappointing result, has my name on it?" you'd probably recognize your own fingerprints somewhere.

Accountability is not a process or a tool. It's what helps a process or tool become effective. Can you think of a very good structure or process in your company that sings in the hands of some people and weeps in the hands of others? I don't think most processes, procedures, or structures are inherently good or bad. It's who's got their hands on it.

What if, instead of holding others accountable, we held ourselves accountable and others able—able to take charge, take action, and effect change? What if, instead of pointing fingers and laying blame, we modeled accountability and inspired others to do the same?

The fact is that no one can mandate accountability for another person. To say "I'm holding you accountable" is pointless. The only person I can hold accountable is myself. Personal accountability is a way of life—and like all fierce practices, it's an inside job. The accountability conversation is one I have with myself and only with myself. But the good news is, it's contagious. So let's go there ourselves first, and then look at ways to influence others to step up to the plate.

As with each fierce leadership practice, accountability begins (and in this case, *ends*) with you. You being accountable in front of everybody else. Not talking about it, not bragging about it, just modeling it.

Doing what you said you'd do. Taking responsibility for disappointing results. Focusing on taking action. Asking, *given this result, what will I do about it?*

And if things go wrong with others, asking the same question. *Given this result, what are you going to do?* And you must give up blaming. Here's another of my favorite poems by Hafiz.

The Sad Game
Blame
Keeps the sad game going,
It keeps stealing all your wealth—
Giving it to an imbecile with
No financial skills.
Dear one,
Wise
Up.

Take a moment to think about what results you would like to improve or have more of in your job. Some of these things may be tangible, outside of us, easy to measure. We can touch them, see them, feel them, pick them up, or take them to the bank. A bigger paycheck, a promotion, a bigger office, more time, hitting sales goals, maintaining a process, on-time delivery.

Intangible results are inside of us, hard to measure. They include how we feel about our tangible results. Work/life balance, peace and serenity, job satisfaction, less stress, a sense of accomplishment and achievement, camaraderie, a sense of connection, cohesion, pride.

When setting goals, it's important to focus on both tangible and intangible results, because it's possible to achieve your tangible results and not get your desired intangible results. Many of us were raised to believe that if we have the "stuff" that is associated with achieving goals, we'll be happy. And yet I've known many very wealthy, bitter people who had lots of stuff but no fulfilling intangibles. Just because you have one doesn't necessarily mean you will have the other.

While the tangibles tend to be pretty similar for most people (who wouldn't want a raise or a nicer office?), intangibles vary more widely. For example, boomers want job security. Gen Yers and Gen Xers don't believe in security. We might as well be talking about Santa Claus or the tooth fairy. They're looking for personal and professional growth, and if they aren't experiencing that, they look for the next place to go. The point is, we must manage for the intangibles, what people really want from their jobs.

As you consider the results you want for yourself, the first principle of *Fierce Conversations* comes in handy: *Master the courage to interrogate reality.* Not much chance of adopting personal accountability if I'm in denial about the results that have my name on them. Failures, meltdowns, divorces, terminations build up gradually, then land in our laps, on our desks suddenly. If I've chosen accountability as a way of life, I always want to know how I'm doing so I can course correct when needed. Also, *tackle your toughest challenge today.* If you tend to procrastinate, stop it!

Hit the pause button and write your answers to these questions:

For what tangible results should I hold myself accountable?

_____

_____

_____

_____

_____

For what intangible results should I hold myself accountable?

_____

_____

_____

_____

_____

Since it's pretty clear by now that accountability begins with you, let's look at the steps in the "fierce" practice of modeling accountability and holding others able.

The Fierce Accountability Cycle

STEP 1. PREPARE YOURSELF.

If you look at areas of your life in which you are not doing particularly well, my guess is those are areas in which you demonstrate little accountability. To prompt your thinking, take a look at the results cycle on the following page.

Is there a situation in your life with which you're unhappy? An environment that's not working, professionally or personally? Or a relationship with a coworker or family member?

For example, let's imagine that your context is "If my manager were different, I'd be fine." What evidence have you gathered to prove this is right? What are you feeling as a result? What is showing up behaviorally? What results are being created?

Think about a result or an area of your life that you'd like to improve, then fill in the results cycle on the following page.

Taking an accountable stance requires a great deal of courage. We may have to give up being "right." We can be right all the way to disempowerment, failure, total meltdown, a lost job, lost customers, bankruptcy, divorce.

As I said earlier, as long as being right or playing it safe is most important to us, we will always pick "victim" and stay in the cave. The rub is that it is very difficult to improve results while we are in the cave. So the challenge is to leave the cave and the comfort and safety of "victim" and move into accountability.

> We can be right all the way to disempowerment, failure, total meltdown, a lost job, lost customers, bankruptcy, divorce.

When fear is whispering in our ear to go back into the cave, we need something or someone more important to us than fear to motivate us out to the delta in search of better meat. Sometimes it's pain, or

results
What results are being created?

↑

behavior
What is showing up behaviorally?

↑

emotions
What am I feeling as a result?

↑

evidence
What evidence have I gathered?

↑

CONTEXT
What is a victim context I hold today?

hitting rock bottom. Sometimes it's the knowledge that the status quo isn't working, that someone needs to take the risk or everyone starves.

I'm sure you have an example of constructive context that has gotten you the results you wanted, and if you look at the areas of your life that are working the best, my guess is that those are areas in which you demonstrated accountability.

For example, you may be in a relationship that is extremely positive and rewarding. What was or is the context that allowed you to create this amazing relationship? What risks have you taken? How often have you found yourself far from your cave, exploring entirely new territory, with no guaranteed outcome? Or perhaps you are surrounded by colleagues who are committed to you at a deep level. Or you completed a complex project within your deadline and came in way under budget, in spite of serious challenges along the way.

You made choices every day that produced these great results.

Take a moment to capture an example of your results cycle in an area of your life that is successful (see the following page).

But what if you inherited a problem? A dysfunctional work team? A key project with inadequate resources? You are being treated unfairly. You don't like it. You want it to be different.

Let's look at an extreme example.

Let's say I wake up in a stainless-steel room. Stainless-steel ceiling, stainless steel floor, stainless-steel walls.

I notice a sign on the wall with a little light above it. The sign says, "When the light blinks, the walls will begin to move together and touch." Like in the spy movies. Yowza!

The light blinks. The walls begin to close.

I notice there are two holes cut into the floor. Both are large enough for me to fit into, are lined with stainless steel, and have labels that say "8 FEET DEEP," and "4 FEET DEEP." They are both filled with sewage.

Now, do I have a choice? I could do nothing and become very thin, or I could pick a hole. So I pick the four-foot hole and jump in as the walls close in.

Did I make the best choice I could, given what I knew? Probably, and now I am sealed in a stainless-steel cylinder in four feet of sewage!

Do I have a choice now? Yes. The ultimate choice, my context. I can say, "Ick, ick, ick. This is the worst thing that has ever happened to me. It's not fair. Why do things like this always have to happen to me?" or I can say, "Thank goodness it's only up to here."

I'm not suggesting that when things are really bad, your context should be "Oh, boy, sewage! Gotta love it!" But in this case, compared to the alternative, I'd take it. I suspect that one source of much of our unhappiness is that we compare our reality with a fantasy of what we think should have been. We compare our real mate with mate charm-

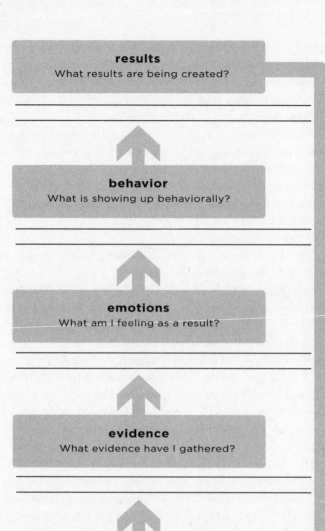

ing, our real job with job charming, our real company, clients, et cetera, with the charming versions of them.

How 'bout I embrace reality, explore my options, clarify the results I want to produce, and take a step in that direction?

Don't ask me how I'd get out of the sewage-filled cylinder. I haven't a clue. But after reviewing how I got there in the first place, I'd try to figure something out.

Why do we pick the context of "Oh, why me?" Why don't we want to acknowledge that we always have choice, especially in the difficult areas of our lives? Because then we would have to leave the cave, venture into the tall grass, and get to work. It's easier to complain, resent, and blame than to embrace the reality of sewage and do something about it.

Years ago, a Native American gave a talk at a conference. He said it always felt like two dogs were living inside him. One was a mean, adversarial dog, and one was a nice, compassionate dog. They fought constantly. Someone in the audience asked, "Which one wins?" He answered, "The one I feed the most."

Accountability is a choice. We can choose to feed the victim dog or the accountability dog. Victim mode is about short-term safety, at the expense of long-term growth. What I want is for you to have a tool that works for the long term, regardless of the environment, not in reaction to it.

Victim mode is about short-term safety, at the expense of long-term growth.

You are powerful. The question is, In what direction is your power pointed? You can be powerful in resistance—*I've been downsized, lost my job. Whom can I blame?!*—or you can point your power in a positive direction: *This is an opportunity to change my life for the better, so I will gather evidence about how I can be successful at this.*

Think of something you want to accomplish, even though your current reality might feel like four feet of sewage. Think of something big, something that's really important to you, something you yearn for. Even though you might think it's impossible, write it down below.

"Why I can _____." Now, what do you know about yourself that serves as evidence that you *can* create the result you want, even in your challenging situation? Write these things down. They might be experiences, traits, strengths, anything you can think of that reminds you that you are able.

I will tell you that for most people, this list is harder to fill out than their victim list.

My List (Why I Can _____)

_____
_____
_____
_____
_____
_____
_____
_____

Given this assessment, how are you feeling? Hopeful? Encouraged? And given these emotions, what shifts in behavior might you make? What decisions might you make? What actions will you take? What results do you think you might create?

Instead of gathering evidence for why you can't, gather evidence to ensure your success. That includes finding others who will support your success rather than bond over mutual scars and wounds.

Might you fail? Yes, and in failure you will learn. None of us can avoid failure now and then. What we can do is change the context in which we place failure.

In general, who takes better care of their homes, those who rent their homes or those who own them? I want you to own this situation, not rent it.

Fierce accountability is about ownership. You own the problem. This is essential. Think of this analogy: In general, who takes better care of their homes, those who rent their homes or those who own them? I want you to own this situation, not rent it.

From ownership, move into decision. It's amazing how our decisions change when we own them. And then we go into action—we do something about it. At this point, we are nowhere near our caves—we're miles away. And each time we take a risk, we build our confidence.

I will summarize the benefits of accountability by quoting people who have made the choice of fierce accountability and who have been truly practicing it for a while.

I've learned not only what doesn't work, but also what *does* work.
I've grown. I've gotten stronger.
More people want to hang out with me.
I've increased the possibilities for myself.
My perception is expanded.
My brain and spirit are awake. I live more in the moment, present, rather than moping about the past.
I spend much more time outside of my cave having adventures.
I've gained admiration and respect.
I've produced some amazing results.
I am emotionally enriched. I feel good about myself. I am happy.

STEP 2. PREPARE OTHERS.

If you have done the exercises so far, you've had a fierce conversation with yourself, which is where accountability begins. Now what about "others" in your life—colleagues, friends, family members— whose results and the results of everyone around them would be greatly improved if they chose personal accountability as a way of life?

Here's a true story, one you can emulate.

In order to build internal confidence, stimulate cross-boundary collaboration, and achieve five knee-buckling, high-stakes goals, Peter Neill, who was an executive director with AT&T Wireless, hired me to engage engineering directors spread around the country in a series of strategic dialogues focused on accomplishing their goals and developing the leadership characteristics that Neill believed would define the success of his team.

When Peter took the reins of Transport Engineering, he found an organization that was divided into five regions, with little or no communication among them. Peter explained, "We were a collection of independent engineering teams accountable for common results, all with different road maps of achievement and varying degrees of successful implementation."

And when it came to accountability, Transport Engineering had a reputation for missing deadlines, failing to deliver, and offering detailed excuses and reasons that put the blame on individuals and situations outside of Transport Engineering. Like Koko the gorilla, group members pointed the finger at others, never at themselves. One popular comment was "I/we knew this would be impossible. There was no way we could get all this done in the time frame we were given."

Meanwhile, the organization had defined four key themes—measured results, speed, financial performance, and innovation—that described technical and financial success for the overall business. And achieving these, Neill saw, would require new and fresh dialogues across the business divisions.

During a kickoff session, I began by grounding the team in the principles and practices of *Fierce Conversations,* including an issue-preparation form that ensured all future discussions would hit the ground running. Then we identified specific high-level, measurable goals for the year, like financial accountability, system capacity and performance, national initiatives, tool development, and evolving network planning and engineering.

I asked the directors if they believed the goals were doable in the time frame they had been given, with the resources available. There was some gulping, but they agreed that yes, though the goals were a stretch, they believed they were possible. A sixty-day action plan was fleshed out, including a chart that clarified exactly *who* was going to do exactly *what* by exactly *when.*

Then we talked about accountability. What is it? How does it differ from responsibility? Who assigns it? What happens when it's present? What happens when it's absent? Why does it disappear? What is an issue of accountability confronting this team right now that is made worse by a failure of accountability? *You know the drill.*

We talked about their reputation as victims, hardly something to be proud of, and discussed the definition of *fierce accountability,* and then

I forbade them (as much as anyone can forbid grown men) to point the finger at anyone other than themselves, going forward. Then I said:

You've got fifteen minutes to stand up, walk around the room, and examine everything we've taped to the wall. Focus on the Who, What, When chart and in particular any item that has your name on it. When we reconvene, this will be your opportunity to tell us if you don't believe it's possible for you to do what's on this chart by the time indicated. And if that's the case, tell us what you would need to pull it off, so we can figure out how to give it to you, or else give us a different delivery date, a more realistic one given the real world in which you operate. Once you sign off on this chart and we leave this meeting, we hold you able to deliver what you've said you'll deliver when you've said you'll deliver it. We'll meet again every other month, and we'll begin each meeting by checking off the action items that were due. Then we'll discuss anything that has changed since last we met, tackle the next set of issues on which you'd like input, and continue building out the plan.

> Unless the world comes to an end or every bone in your body is broken in an accident, we are all counting on you to deliver what you've said you'll deliver when you've said you'll deliver it.

Almost everyone changed at least one "by when" date, identified missing resources, and figured out how to get them. Then we took a solemn oath involving a dead chicken and some stump water. *Okay, not really, but we did take an oath.*

The team met for five additional sessions over the next twelve months. Team members explored and practiced leadership characteristics specific to the success of AT&T Wireless. Using the conversational models they had learned earlier, they interrogated reality, tackled their toughest challenges, designed strategies and road maps for key projects, developed a growing appreciation for the talents of individual team members, and outlined further collaboration needed to ensure that no member of the team would fail.

Neill was happy. "As a result of my team's skill at engaging colleagues in 'strategic conversations,' " he said, "the level of personal accountability across the organization drove our results." The benefits, Neill proudly pointed out, were visible. "First and foremost, we . . .

- Exceeded four of our five annual goals. And met the fifth.

- Became more efficient, leading to greater than 25% same year improvement in our financial performance.

- Acquired the foundation required to support year-over-year improvements critical to our business success within the wireless industry.

- Gained cross-boundary collaboration, which allowed Transport Engineering to deliver connectivity in support of our next generation network six months ahead of schedule.

- Gained the skills we needed to play our particular business game at the next level.

- Learned ideas and techniques to use in our own teams, applying principles to staff conversations and conference calls.

- Know each other better. We listen to one another. We have a higher level of empathy and understanding.

- Share common goals. The program opened us up to new ideas. The coaching helped individuals and the entire team focus."

Neill summarized, "My team can match any team. Now our goal is to drive what we've learned and how we're operating together down into the organization. In an industry as growth oriented and competitive as ours, we can't afford not to have conversations like this every day."

Back to you and your world. It's hard to work with someone who is invested in persuading you to buy their victim list. But there are certain things you shouldn't do to break people out of this cycle. Don't tell them to get a grip. Don't avoid them. Don't complain about them to others. Don't get angry. Don't tell them what they need to do and how to fix things. Don't tell them that they're delusional.

Remember, the victim cycle is fear based. A lot of the things we do to try to break others out of the victim cycle actually increase their fear, because we are essentially putting fire in the cave to force them out.

If you avoid people, the same thing occurs. Inclusion is a strong human need. Exclusion stimulates fear. Yet if we placate a victim, make allowances for him or her, others see that victims get treated better, so they may go into victim mode, too.

Whether we avoid or placate victims, the issues don't go away. In fact, they will get worse. And for those of you who are parents, the worst thing you can do—assuming you want your children to live accountable lives—is to buy their victim list and build a cave for them that's so attractive, so safe, that they'll never want to leave.

Fierce leaders model accountability, and people follow their example. If you want your children to risk and challenge, you have to risk and challenge. You must model accountability right in front of them and hold them able.

A powerful and effective way to hold anyone able—child or adult—is to engage him or her in a Mineral Rights conversation, which accomplishes the four goals of all fierce conversations:

1. Interrogate reality
2. Provoke learning
3. Tackle tough challenges
4. Enrich relationships

In "Fierce Practice #2," we used a version of Mineral Rights in an interview. Now we'll modify it slightly and use it to break someone out of victim mode. The conversation allows us to mine for "gold" in the form of greater clarity, improved understanding, and impetus for action—and for change, when needed.

Let's look at a classic Mineral Rights conversation and consider how it holds individuals able and points them toward personal accountability.

STEP 3. DO IT!

1. Identify the issue. If you notice that someone is in victim mode, ask him or her about it. Say something like, "You seem angry (sad, frustrated, withdrawn, et cetera). Please tell me what's going on." Your own context is very important here. Find the place within yourself that genuinely wants to hear.

2. Clarify the issue. Get very curious. The details aren't always important. Listen for the real issue, because the problem named is the problem solved. It is important, therefore, to spend time in the problem-naming part of the conversation.

Though clarity will increase throughout the conversation, ask questions that will help your partner further clarify the issue for himself or herself. Take time to get the whole story. This venting can help to empty the person emotionally and make him or her more receptive to change.

The challenge here is to remain empathetic. This person is describing his or her list, and to him or her, it is very real. When people sense that you are empathetic, they are usually more open to possibilities.

Please note that there is a difference between empathy and sympathy. If you are sympathetic and placating, people often feel somewhat patronized. They might get defensive and/or lose respect for you if you readily buy their list. Remember, we love and hate people who buy our list. So convey empathy without buying the list.

Say things like, "I bet that's hard. Sounds like a tough situation." Validate the person's reality, not his or her defense of it.

3. Determine current impact. The focus here is on *current* impact. You might ask, "How is this currently affecting you?" If your partner veers off track, bring him or her back: "Let's stay focused on the current impact for a moment. I am also interested in who else and what else is currently being affected."

This question is useful in breaking someone out of the victim cycle because the answers catalogue the prices that are currently being paid, reinforcing the importance of stepping up to resolve the issue. Ask, "What else?" until the list of prices is complete and robust.

There is now a second question that is very important: "When you consider all of the results you just catalogued, what do you feel?" Listen intently.

Hearing someone's words is only the beginning. If we don't also inquire about his or her emotions, it's as if we are leaving our companion sitting in a car that is going nowhere because it has an empty gas tank. Emotions give the lit match something to ignite, propelling us into action.

During a Mineral Rights conversation, if your partner is not in touch with his or her emotions, he or she is in no immediate danger of doing anything differently . . . and tomorrow will be a lot like today.

Draw out your partner. You might say, "You say you're frustrated (or angry or worried . . .). Say more about that, please." Ask, "What else do you feel?"

4. Determine future implications. The focus now is on what's likely to happen if this issue is not resolved. You could ask, *"If you and I were talking six months or a year from today and nothing had changed regarding this issue, what might you be telling me?"* Draw the person out: "What else could have happened?"

Then ask about emotions again: "When you consider that possible scenario, what do you feel?" This question requires someone to look at the long-term repercussions and heightens their resolve to take action.

5. Examine personal contribution to the issue. This is a critical part of this conversation because it points the person in the direction of accountability. Just a little opening will help. Simply ask, "Can you see any ways in which you have contributed to this situation?"

Many people are surprised, even offended, by this question. After all, they have just invested a fair amount of energy unfolding their impressive victim list for you—the long list of reasons why this bad thing has happened to them. They've pointed the finger at what or who is to blame, even named names. "He/she/it/they did it to me." Plus, you've asked them what they feel, which suggests you are a compassionate person and now you've thrown a bucket of cold water on the conversation by asking a completely insensitive question that suggests they may have had something to do with this stinker of a story. Sometimes I detect a look of panic, as if the person is thinking, *"Dang! I was so close to freedom, so close to getting out of this conversation with a new recruit to the blame game."*

Hang in there. Sit quietly and wait for a response, even if the wait is a very long one. If they say they don't know what you mean, simply repeat the question.

If they say, "I don't know," persist by asking, "What would it be if you did know?" Obviously, tone of voice is important here. You aren't being sarcastic or superior or threatening. You're genuinely curious.

Let silence do the heavy lifting.

6. Describe the ideal outcome. This is the step I must resist rushing toward because of its powerful impact. This step really connects emotionally. I often say, "Let's imagine this is no longer an issue. It's resolved, completely, elegantly. What difference would that make?"

A negative view of the future creates fear. When the voices of fear are whispering in one ear, we need something whispering louder in the other. A strong vision of a positive future will do this. Once again, ask about the person's emotions. Use the same question you asked in step 4: "When you imagine this possible scenario, what do you feel?"

7. Commit to action. This step seeks action, brings closure. Once someone considers constructive action, he or she has moved into the accountability cycle.

Ask, "Given the situation you're in, as onerous and unfair as it seems, what is an action step you can take to turn things around?" Probe and push for clarity here, for a commitment. Have the person create a deadline for the action, the sooner the better. If you don't think the solution he or she came up with will work, get curious. Say something like, "I don't see how that will work. Will you tell me more about that?"

Ask how the person is going to create support: "Who can help you and how?" Remember, new behavior without support becomes extinct.

Ask, "When can I follow up with you?" Take your partner's phone number or e-mail address and commit to following up with him or her once he or she has taken this step.

Thank your partner for his or her good work.

Keep your commitment and follow up with him or her!

I forgot to give you the secret rule regarding this conversation: NO declarative statements. NO advice. Questions only! And no fair using leading questions like "Have you considered trying . . . ?"

This rule is incredibly difficult for most people to follow, because oh, how we love to give advice! But when you take someone through a Mineral Rights conversation, it's essential not to give any advice until you are on the other side of step 7! Otherwise, you create dependency. If you tell someone what to do and how to do it, he or she will become dependent on you. The point of accountability is to empower *the other person,* not for you to become the new source of his or her power.

Besides, what *you* come up with may work for you, but may not work for the other person, and the more he or she comes up with the answers, the more he or she will own them. If you do have a suggestion or two, offer it at this time. Because you have listened, your partner will see you as wise, intelligent, and compassionate.

This conversation is so powerful, it has literally changed the course of people's careers, marriages, lives. I highly recommend that you ask someone to take *you* through a Mineral Rights conversation on an issue that is troubling you at work or at home.

> This conversation is so powerful, it has literally changed the course of people's careers, marriages, lives.

Trust yourself to answer the questions you'll be asked. The answers to your issue are in the room. You have them. Allow someone to assist you in unfolding them.

Don't write anything down. Just show up authentically for this conversation.

Avoiding the traps Most of us are sorely tempted by common traps that are guaranteed to derail a Mineral Rights conversation. So don't:

- discount your partner's list *("That doesn't sound so bad")*;
- get caught up in his or her story, sympathize, or placate: "Oh, you poor thing!";
- give advice (this is especially important for a victim, because victims are accustomed to the power being outside themselves);
- skip some steps and jump right to "What are you going to do about it?";
- become judgmental *("What the heck were you thinking!")*;
- top your partner's victim story with one of your own: *"Wow, that reminds me of something that happened to me!"* Now it's about *you*, not him or her.

Some other important reminders:

- Mineral Rights is not a race. When competitive people see a list of steps, they tend to figure, *First to the end wins.* Wrong. This conversation is about depth, not speed. Slow the conversation down so you can help your partner gain real insight.

- Make sure your motivation is to help, not further a hidden agenda.

- Dig deep—"What else?"

- Find the neutral place from which you can remain empathetic without judgment.

- Let silence do the heavy lifting.

- Listen, for what is *not* being said, as well as what *is* being said.

- Your partner should be doing most of the talking, overhearing him- or herself thinking out loud, saying things he or she didn't know he or she knew.

- No matter what the reporting structure may be, consider this a conversation between equals.

- Bring nothing but yourself and the purity of your attention to this conversation.

STEP 4. DEBRIEF.

Even if you're convinced the conversation went well, check in with the other person to see how he or she felt it went. The conversation wasn't merely a task on your to-do list. There's a lot riding on the outcome.

I suggest waiting a day to check in with someone. While he or she will, hopefully, have had some insights during the conversation, once he or she has had a chance to sleep on it, the penny may truly drop.

A quick phone call or e-mail could say, "Just wanted you to know that I appreciated your candor and hard work during our conversation yesterday. Now that you've had a chance to sleep on it, please let me know how you felt it went and if you had any additional insights. You can count on me to follow up with you on your action step. Again, thank you for talking with me. I hold you able to take it from here. I'll be cheering from the sidelines."

STEP 5. DO IT AGAIN, ONLY BETTER.

At this point, you might be wondering if the Mineral Rights conversation is too formulaic, if it would seem awkward, unnatural. For example, might your partner dig in his or her heels and refuse to answer some of your probing questions or feel that you are playing shrink or being inappropriate?

You are not playing shrink. I'm not a shrink and wouldn't presume to tread on that territory. And while a few of my colleagues, friends, or family members have felt a bit uncomfortable from time to time, I don't believe anyone has ever felt I was being inappropriate. Bold? Yes. Fierce? Of course. Inappropriate? No.

Still, it may seem awkward the first few times you practice Mineral Rights, so practice it at home with your partner or a friend. Ask, "How was your day?" If your partner's day was lousy, out will come the story, and you're launched. Step one. Many people have reported that when they practiced Mineral Rights at home, they had the best conversation they'd had with their partner in a decade. Once you've done Mineral Rights three times, it will feel natural, and, more important, you'll frequently be blown away by the results.

I believe this model will work 95 percent of the time, with patience and practice. But no one is perfect; even though I'm pretty good at it, I still allow the conversation to derail a bit from time to time. So I go back to the person, acknowledge what I noticed about my role in lessening the effectiveness of the conversation, and let him or her know I'll try to do better next time.

This is me modeling accountability. I would receive low marks in accountability if I told myself or anyone else, "The conversation was a bust. That person was impossible to talk to!"

Taking It to the Organization

If you want to build the practice of fierce accountability into the fabric of your organization, I suggest you:

1. Schedule and conduct Mineral Rights conversations with each of your direct reports. Let them know that you'll ask them what's the most important thing the two of you should be talking about. Remember to ask about their contributions to the issue they put on the table, and don't give advice.
2. Schedule a brief team meeting each morning or each week to ensure shared clarity about priorities and time lines. Telling someone "This is a priority" leaves a lot up to interpretation. A better communication would be "I'd like you to complete this by the

end of day Thursday. We'll review it Friday morning." People can't hold themselves accountable to deadlines if clear deadlines haven't been set.

3. Be clear with everyone about WHY the things on their to-do list are a priority. An associate could easily think and possibly say, "I haven't done much about this because I don't understand why I should. What's at stake? What's the bottom line? What business issue does this solve? What impact will this have?" *Answers to those questions raise people's level of accountability.*

4. At the team meeting, ask each team member to give a succinct report on what he or she has accomplished and what's on his or her to-do list for the coming week.

5. Stop "victim" conversations ("If this or that were different, our lives would be easier") by saying something like, "I assume you are all aware that we are acting like victims around this topic." That will shift the conversation from what they can't do to what they can do. Encourage people to have the internal conversations they need to change and create better outcomes for themselves. *"Think about what you can do to change or improve things."*

6. Express ample, public appreciation for getting stuff done despite obstacles!

7. If someone is lagging, ask at the team meeting, in front of everyone else (yes, in front of everyone!), "What's your plan to catch up?" Instead of pointing a finger, have a private come-to-Buddha meeting with those who regularly fail to execute.

Personal Action Plan

The movie *The Departed* opens with Jack Nicholson saying, in his listen-up-you-piece-of-shit-because-I'm-only-going-to-say-this-once voice, "I don't want to be a product of my environment. I want my environment to be a product of me."

"I don't want to be a product of my environment. I want my environment to be a product of me."
—Jack Nicholson in
The Departed

Yes, his tone is menacing and his hands are drenched in blood for most of the movie, but he had the right idea. The environment is all about you; in fact, it already *is* a product of you.

Personal progress isn't a cakewalk. Which is why my goal for you, as presumptive as that may seem, is for you to positively and indelibly shape the environment of any company, team, room—whether boardroom, conference room, or living room—into which you walk. I'd like others to sense that "someone is here!" I want people to feel that way about you and to be happy in your company.

To sum it up, I want you to spend most of your time being you on your best day. Not a version of someone else, but YOU, awake, accountable, in motion! And like all practices, accountability is an inside job.

Write down your top personal and professional goals for the next thirty to ninety days, which you formed as a result of reading this chapter. For starters, how 'bout getting *your* stuff done when you said you would! Remember, you can't hope that others will choose accountability if you're not modeling it yourself. So if things aren't getting done, ask yourself, "What part of this failure to execute has my name on it?" If you haven't completed a project assigned to you and the due date has come and gone, your cavalier statement to the team that you're "still working on that" doesn't cut it. Want others to deliver on time? Lead by example.

Here's what a good action plan might look like:

1. Begin by having a fierce conversation with yourself: "To what degree do I model accountability for my colleagues and family members? What's on my victim list? When things haven't gone well, what reasons and excuses do I often point to? What is this teaching those around me? What am I winning?" Be specific about your goals and the actions you'll take.

2. Tell the truth. **Tell the truth. Tell the truth.** Since there is no connection without authenticity, be extremely attentive to your level of honesty in all your conversations.

3. Find someone to support you in modeling accountability. Without support, most people find it difficult to move out of victim mode,

into accountability, and stay there. Ask someone to let you know if he or she sees you being "right" in a destructive way.

4. If you have been passive about your career progression, stop it! It's up to you to further your career. Get specific about your career aspirations. What's out there in your organization that you might be good at? Take advantage of your transferable skills. Where could you add value? Declare where you want to go, and ask for honest feedback. Ask your boss to advocate for you.

5. If your boss isn't willing to advocate for you, ask what you need to do differently to get a wholehearted yes from him or her. And then get to work on yourself.

6. Add names and topics to your "Conversations I Need to Have" list at the back of this book. And have them.

Conclusion

The progress of the world actually does depend on our progress as individuals, now. It's true for me, it's true for *you*. It's true for prime ministers and presidents, for the young woman (girl, really) who took my order at Chimayo Mexican Restaurant on Orcas Island, for the Maasai herding goats near Kilimanjaro, for the craftsmen who built my tree house, for the FedEx guy, for the woman at the help desk with CenturyTel. It's true for the priest, the cop, the robber, the saint in training, the new parent, the insurance salesman, the snake expert at the pet store, the guys throwing fish at Pike Place Market.

On a metaphysical plane, each of us is, indeed, the center of the universe, and all that we think, feel, and do impacts everyone else. Gets a little tricky, but you've been exposed to this idea if you have paid any attention to quantum mechanics, watched *What the Bleep Do We Know!?*, have any leanings toward Buddhism, or have simply been noticing what's going on around you.

Here's a footnote from *Rats: Observations on the History & Habitat of the City's Most Unwanted Inhabitants,* by Robert Sullivan: "Once, in Rome, I went to a church, San Clemente, also known as Saint Clement's

Basilica. When you enter the church, you enter a medieval church with eighteenth-century additions—a Baroque basilica. When you go down a level, you see that the upper basilica was built on an early Christian church, with frescoes dating to the ninth century. *That* church was, in turn, built on the site of a mithraeum, a third-century temple for the cult of the god Mithras, which revolved around the life-giving slaying of a bull. (A major feast day of the popular cult of Mithras was December 25, and the cult competed with Christianity for popularity.) You take an ancient set of steps down into the mithraeum, and when you get there—it's a dark, dank, stone-walled, basement-like place—you see in the floor a stream running beneath a metal grate. When you do, you realize that the mithraeum was built on a Republican estate, which was most likely built where it was built because it was alongside a stream, a stream that was probably beautiful at the time, not that I personally have anything against streams piped through basements. My point is this: religions built on religions, cultures on cultures, cities on cities, just the way one rat moves into the previous rat's old rat hole—or hole of any kind, really."

In other words, what we do can leave lasting impacts greater than we can ever know. Sure, the world changes—layers are built upon layers upon layers, until the original structure is barely recognizable—but without the foundation, progress can never occur.

Let's conclude with a wonderful poem by Hafiz that gets to the heart of the notion of personal accountability. In summary, you're it!

YOU'RE IT
God
Disguised
As a myriad things and
Playing a game
Of tag

Has kissed you and said,
"You're it—

I mean, you're Really IT!"

Now
It does not matter
What you believe or feel

For something wonderful,

Major-league Wonderful

Is someday going
To

Happen.

Fierce Practice #4

From Employee Engagement Programs to Actually Engaging Employees

Connections are made slowly, and sometimes they grow underground. You cannot tell always by looking at what is happening. More than half a tree is spread out in the soil under your feet.

—MARGE PIERCY, "THE SEVEN OF PENTACLES"

I know you consider me your equal. That's what bothers me.

—AN OVERHEARD CONVERSATION

A company is like a huge power-generating station. Press your ear to the door and you will hear individuals talking, and underneath, you will make out the hum of the organization. Or the sputter and cough.

My own poll got off to an awkward start when I asked a woman in line in an employee cafeteria, "On a scale of zero to five, five being completely engaged, how engaged are you?"

"You can put me down as a definite zero!"

"Zero, wow . . . "

"Oh yeah. It's gonna take a helluva man to beat no man at all!"

Clearly I needed to refine my question.

"How engaged would you say you are in your work, with your team, your boss, what it is your company hopes to accomplish?" *(No one has ever accused me of being scientific in my sleuthing, but answers such as the following don't require a great deal of translating.)*

"I'm here, aren't I?" said with exhaustion.

"You must be with HR. You guys got another waste-of-time poll going on?"

"I guess I'm as engaged as a person of color can be in a place like this."

"Oh, I absolutely love my job and my boss and I'm just thrilled to be here!" *Further probing revealed that this woman loves everyone and everything on this planet, has never had a bad thing happen to her, and has never entertained a negative thought. She is probably on major drugs. Or should be.*

Are there highly engaged employees? Of course, but they are the minority in most organizations. Most people are just trying to get by. So what's the big deal?

The State of Engagement

The big deal is that if employees aren't engaged, your company will suffer. Good people quit, defect, disappear, or worse, show up every day—in body—but their souls are occupied elsewhere. They become disgruntled, disenchanted, disillusioned. And this affects your bottom line.

Yet despite all that companies are doing to promote employee inclusion and engagement, which go hand in hand, many still see this as merely something that makes people feel good—or at least better—about their jobs. Of course inclusion and engagement make people feel good. They also increase productivity, reduce turnover, and build revenue.

I think of it this way:

inclusion + engagement = execution muscle

. . . and without execution muscle, you might as well hang it up. Let's define terms.

Employee inclusion suggests that people of every stripe—gender, age, sexual orientation, ethnicity, religion, aspiration, disability, position or title, and whatever other differences are possible in the human population—feel that they have a place at the table, that they are seen, heard, and valued and that given stellar performance, they have an opportunity to advance. That they do not feel marginalized, "less than," left out, overlooked, invisible, made wrong, taken advantage of, disrespected, ignored, or mistreated.

At its heart, inclusion is about membership, belonging to a community, whether a family, a school, a company, a country, or the human race. I'm grateful that my granddaughters, Maizy and Clara, are in inclusive classrooms that resemble the diverse environments in which they will eventually work. They are in daily conversation and collaboration with Nishi, Santiago, Bora, Kaichen, Ayush, Alejandro, Garima, Enikö, and Lavente. And loving it. Children who learn together learn to live together, a requirement if we are ever to achieve that elusive concept known as world peace.

> Children who learn together learn to live together, a requirement if we are ever to achieve that elusive concept known as world peace.

Employee engagement is generally viewed as the degree to which employees view the goals of the company as in line with their own lives so that when they have choices, they will act in a way that furthers their organization's interests and vice versa. In *Getting Engaged: The New Workplace Loyalty,* author Tim Rutledge explains that truly engaged employees are attracted and committed to, inspired and fascinated by, the work that they do.

It's no surprise that "employee engagement" is a key initiative within many companies. After all, engaged workers are more productive, make more money for the company, and create loyal customers. They contribute to good working environments where people are happy, ethical, and accountable. They stay with an organization longer and are more committed to quality and growth—in fact, engaged employees outperform their unengaged counterparts by 20–28 percentage points.

Yet according to the *Gallup Management Journal*'s semiannual Employee Engagement Index . . .

- 20 percent of employees are actively engaged in their jobs;
- 54 percent are not engaged; and
- 17 percent are actively disengaged.

To break it down further, BlessingWhite issued a report titled "The State of Employee Engagement 2008." The study, based on a survey of more than 7,500 employees and interviews with forty human-resource and line managers on four continents, revealed that only 29 percent of North American workers (fewer than one in three) are fully engaged. Moreover,

- 27 percent are "almost engaged";
- 12 percent are "honeymooners" or "hamsters" (new to the organization or to their role and not yet fully productive, focused on the wrong things, and contributing little to the success of the organization);
- 13 percent are "crash and burners" (disillusioned, potentially exhausted, sometimes bitterly vocal top producers who are not satisfying their personal definition of success and satisfaction and, if left alone, may slip into disengagement and bring down those around them); and
- 19 percent are disengaged (not getting what they need from work and, if left alone, likely to collect a paycheck and enjoy favorable job conditions but contribute minimally).

If companies are so committed to including and engaging their employees, why these dismal scores? Because inclusion and engagement can't be feigned, trained, or forced. They can't be mandated or taught in some dry management seminar. Because like the other fierce practices you've read about so far, inclusion and engagement start with you.

What Matters Anywhere, Matters Everywhere

A few years ago, former secretary of state Madeleine Albright and I spoke in Washington, D.C., to an audience of women who were in positions of power within the government. Following our talks, someone asked, "Ms. Albright, if you could give only one piece of advice to those who are in positions of political power globally, what would you advise them?"

She answered unhesitatingly, "I'd advise them that what matters anywhere, matters everywhere."

I've shared that comment with thousands of people because I feel it's brilliant and applicable to the planet, to communities, to families, to organizations, and to every workplace. I've shared it because until we grasp this concept, we're in no danger of enjoying the benefits of true collaboration—across borders, across teams, across functions, or across ideological lines drawn in the sand.

You will experience "inclusion and engagement" to the degree that you and others in your organization appreciate and act on Madeleine Albright's advice.

Picture your organization. Does it look something like the graphic on the following page, a highly matrixed organization where everyone works within a "silo"?

Imagine that the CEO of this company asks everyone to answer the question "Where should we focus our resources over the next twelve months?" Chances are, the head of Finance & Accounting in North America would answer that quite differently from someone in Product Development in South America or Information Technology in India or HR in Europe.

What does *your* organization look like? To make this relevant and real for you, take a moment to fill in names, divisions or responsibilities, and locations—even if the location is simply a different corner of a small office—on the graphic on page 156.

As you look at your organization, consider how each area affects the others. Consider whom you talk with, who talks to you, who else they talk to. Who is left out? Whose voices and perspectives are missing? Who is not on this chart? What individuals and groups should be included and engaged, depending on the topic?

I came across something several years ago and wish I could remember where I found it, so I could attribute this properly. The suggestion was that in every organization, large or small, there are three basic units: in no particular order, the company, divisions of the company (large and small, geographical and functional), and the employees (the individual contributors, who come in every shape, size, and color). Each unit (company, divisions, employees) has its own identity—unique in all the world, deserving of recognition, celebration, guidance, support—with its own goals, its own pack to carry, its destination clear or un-

where do *you* live?

where do *you* live?

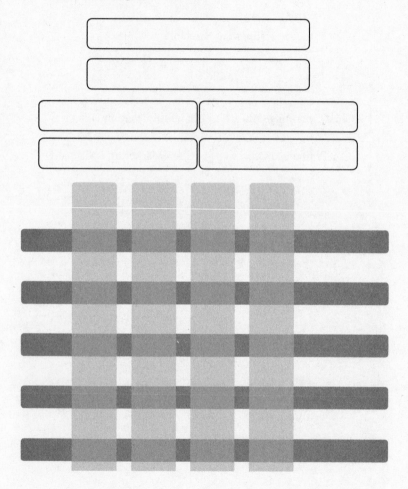

folding. And all are connected, dependent on one another, affecting one another with every drawn breath, every missed deadline, every bit of work won, every new initiative.

What matters anywhere in your organization matters everywhere in your organization.

Or should.

The challenge is to impart this understanding across the organization, and to do that, we must expand the idea of "inclusion" beyond the usual suspects and expand the idea of "engagement" beyond that tired old phrase, "inspirational leadership," as if reciting the mission statement or giving an inspiring pep talk will do the trick!

In *Field Notes on the Compassionate Life,* Marc Ian Barasch writes, "Einstein himself once referred to our sense of separateness as 'a kind of optical delusion of consciousness'—a delusion that limits our caring because it 'restricts us to our personal desires and to affection for a few persons nearest to us.' "

Physicist Henri Bortoft wrote: "Everything is in everything. The part is a place for the presencing of the whole." Fail to engage one of us and you lose all of us.

The point is, we're all connected. Whether we work in the mailroom or the showroom or the corporate suite, whether a company has offices in Minneapolis, San Diego, or Dubai, any sense of separation is an illusion. You affect me, and I affect you—even if we never meet and have no idea of each other's existence. Our thoughts, the makeup of our cells, our emotions, our beliefs affect others in ways more powerful and profound than we could ever realize.

Fail to engage one of us and you lose all of us.

I've mentioned that in scientific experiments, the mere presence of someone affects the outcome. And if *you* were that person, the outcome would be different than if I were that person or Yoshiko or Delaram or Fred or Sam or Catherine were that person. So something about *you*— something unseen by the naked eye—is keenly felt by everyone and everything with which you come into contact. And vice versa.

Here's a favorite poem by David Budbill:

The Three Goals

The first goal is to see the thing itself
in and for itself, to see it simply and clearly
for what it is.
    No symbolism, please.

The second goal is to see each individual thing
as unified, as one, with all the other
ten thousand things.
    In this regard, a little wine helps a lot.

The third goal is to grasp the first and the second goals,
to see the universal and the particular,
simultaneously.
    Regarding this one, call me when you get it.

Let's call him, shall we?

What matters anywhere literally DOES matter everywhere. But for now, let's point the telescope at your company.

Organizations are webs of relationships, and relationships are forged one conversation, one meeting, at a time. Each conversation, each meeting, creates a chain reaction, like Rube Goldberg's "simplified pencil-sharpener":

Open window (A) and fly kite (B). String (C) lifts small door (D) allowing moths (E) to escape and eat red flannel shirt (F). As weight of shirt becomes less, shoe (G) steps on switch (H) which heats electric iron (I) and burns hole in pants (J). Smoke (K) enters hole in tree (L), smoking out opossum (M) which jumps into basket (N), pulling rope (O) and lifting cage (P), allowing woodpecker (Q) to chew wood from pencil (R), exposing lead. Emergency knife (S) is always handy in case opossum or the woodpecker gets sick and can't work.

Likewise, your conversation with me (A) prompts my conversation with Rob (B), which shapes the tone of Rob's message to the team in the meeting this afternoon (C), which is passed on to other associates (D–J) and customers (K–N) and shared that evening with every spouse (O–X) who dares to ask, "How was your day, sweetheart?"

You, all by your lonesome, are having an impressive impact on your world.

Your conversations with your assistant affect his sense of esteem and well-being and also his impression of what matters to you, which he conveys in every conversation he has with all of the people in your world.

Your conversations with peers affect their willingness to collaborate and cooperate with you when they really don't have to. They pass on their opinions and experience of you to others in the company.

Your conversations with your boss move your career trajectory forward or backward or stall it indefinitely.

Your conversations with customers ultimately win or lose the day. More about those in Fierce Practice #5.

Depending on what you're consistently putting out (thoughts, beliefs, behaviors, et cetera), you're affecting everyone around you, who then affect everyone around them. So harkening back to "Fierce Practice #3," who is the great mover and shaker in your world? That would be YOU. Your universe does, indeed, revolve around you. And you influence that universe one conversation, one meeting, one e-mail at a time.

To give you an example, below is my web of relationships at Fierce Inc. My conversations with Halley, our president and COO, influence her conversations with Aimee, our director of training, which influence Aimee's conversations with everyone who is leading Fierce-related trainings around the world. And because I believe that a training course is only as good as the person who leads it, this is a big deal to me!

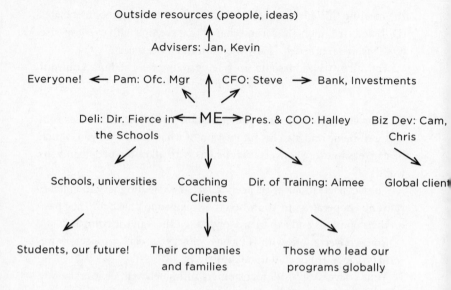

In your web of relationships, with whom do you talk? Play with the graphic on page 161, add arrows and lines, or just grab a piece of paper and begin doodling. The point of this exercise is not to capture an org chart, but to capture the web of people—your boss, your assistant, colleagues—that you directly influence and who then, given your influence, influence others.

As you look at this chart, whom have you been forgetting to include? Whom do you fail to engage? Whose input could be valuable, even though he or she is not in a formal leadership role?

While there have been many studies on employee engagement, the overriding theme, according to the Conference Board, which reviewed all of the studies, is "a heightened emotional connection that an employee feels to his or her organization, that influences him or her to exert greater discretionary effort." And *all* studies, *all* locations, and *all* ages agreed that the direct relationship with one's manager is the strongest driver of employee engagement.

It's true that most employees want to do stimulating work that impacts the success of a company they're proud to work for. They want opportunities to develop professionally and advance their careers. They want to make friends at work. Ideally, a best friend. But what matters most is their relationship with their leader. With YOU.

I don't like to say "I told you so." But I told you so. Employee engagement and inclusion isn't a cognitive issue. It's an emotional issue. As I've said earlier and will repeat, possibly risking your wrath, if you want to become a great leader, you must gain the capacity to connect with colleagues and customers—at a deep level—or lower your aim.

It's understandable that most of us try not to think of, much less speak of, the prices we've paid because of professional relationships gone sad, gone bad, gone missing. So

> Employee engagement and inclusion isn't a cognitive issue. It's an emotional issue.

wouldn't it be great if we could simply mandate employee engagement, deep pleasure in the work, the quality of our relationships, with the turn of a dial!

"John, your level of engagement seems to be hovering around 40 percent. I realize that 100 percent might be asking too much, so I'd like you to dial your engagement up to 75 percent during the next three weeks and hold it there. Okay?"

"Karen, I'd put your ability to generate innovative solutions at about a four on a scale of one to ten, ten being high. Would you please notch it up to a nine by the end of the day today? Our clients are expecting some original solutions. Thanks."

"Candy, whenever you see me coming, you slam your door and jab pins into that voodoo doll you crafted from crumpled memos and rubber bands. I get the impression you don't like me very much. So I'd like you to recognize that I am the finest boss you've ever worked for. That's a directive."

"Norm, every time I give you the benefit of my advice—and God knows I advise you all the time—you slip into a slack-jawed stupor. Yesterday you actually drooled, indicating a lack of appreciation for the brilliance of my thinking. I'd like you to increase your respect for me from its current level of zero to a five by the end of the month, with an additional increase to eight by year-end."

"Team, I'm tired of you guys showing up late for meetings, leaving early, text messaging under the table, and offering no ideas or suggestions when I ask you what you think. So from this point on, you will show up on time, fully engaged, eager to tackle tough challenges. Ready, set, go!!"

I believe you'll find this approach in the dictionary under "fat chance."

Practicing Squid Eye

What might you notice if you were practicing squid eye that would suggest your organization's initiatives around employee engagement and inclusiveness are ineffective? Check any of the following "tells" that apply to *your* team or organization. Or to *you.*

Employee-satisfaction survey scores haven't improved significantly over last year's troubling results. You see it in faces, body language, absenteeism, and performance, dramatized by exits. Gradually, then suddenly, employees absent their spirits from their work, followed by their bodies.

The definition of *diversity* is narrow and limiting. "Diversity" is too often thought of as male/female, straight/gay, Christian/Buddhist, black/white, et cetera, and rarely moves beyond such distinctions. This is too bad, since within each group to which any of us "belong," there are equally diverse views, opinions, beliefs, priorities, motivations, intentions, goals, and modes of operating in this world. No one speaks for *all* women, *all* gays, *all* blacks, *all* Christians. Diversity in all its forms deserves our attention and respect.

Having said that, there is little diversity around the table. No matter what the topic is, the same people attend meetings and make decisions affecting everyone—decisions that often fall short of brilliance and consequently meet with resistance. Diverse perspectives from those who will be affected and who will implement strategies are not actively solicited in the early stages and in some cases are not solicited at any point in the process.

Necessary conversations aren't happening, because people are fearful of giving offense, of being considered disrespectful, insensitive, or politically incorrect. Let's face it, there are always a few people in every "diverse" category who are loaded for bear, looking for a reason to be offended, and if you say something they don't want to hear, you could be the recipient of their wrath, accused of insensitivity, discrimination, or prejudice! So you tiptoe around them. In the name of "respect," you withhold your real thoughts. Guess who's running the show!

You are a global company behaving like a local one. When making decisions that will affect colleagues and customers around the world, you fail to solicit input from your international counterparts. Consequently, you get major push back regarding policies, protocols, and initiatives deemed by international colleagues to be culturally unworkable—because they *are*.

The language of your organization is in no danger of engaging anyone. Your objectives include intensifying customer focus, valuing growth, ensuring ongoing productivity improvements, accelerating succession cycles, strengthening risk management, maximizing international leverage, emphasizing distinctive capabilities . . . *Oops, sorry, I dozed off.*

Leaders attempt to "engage" everyone in the same way. For example, many leaders work effectively with people in their own age group but fail to get through to younger or older employees whose goals and priorities are *significantly* different.

Your employee-satisfaction surveys are anonymous. Any form of anonymity is a huge tell that you've got an employee-engagement issue. If you doubt this, please revisit "Fierce Practice #1!"

Employee feedback hasn't been translated into meaningful action. If there is consistent feedback regarding an area of dissatisfaction, and yet nothing is done to improve things, it would have been better not to have asked in the first place. To think that employees don't notice the lack of an action plan focused on driving behavior change is foolish. Lack of action usually leads to even greater disengagement and apathy.

There is little employee enthusiasm for feedback. Why should employees spend time and energy filling in feedback forms when historically, feedback hasn't produced significant change or improvement? Like a line from a Bob Dylan song, "I'm not saying you treated me unkind. You just wasted my precious time."

There are very few women and minorities in positions of leadership. Look at the org chart. It's a huge tell if everyone in the C suite looks the same.

Employee inclusion and engagement are not tied to executive compensation. In spite of embarrassing survey results, frontline managers aren't motivated to change, because they are still rewarded for metrics tied solely to the top and bottom line. What's interesting is that the top and bottom lines *are* affected by inclusion and engagement, but few leaders make the connection.

Headhunters view your organization as a source for job candidates, not a destination. Some of your best people have been recruited out from under you. Their exit interviews (assuming there *were* exit interviews) were telling, and yet little has been done to remedy the problems they revealed. Meanwhile, recruitment and replacement costs are excessive, and the loss of knowledge and experience suggests you can kiss growth and innovation good-bye.

What Were We Thinking?

An HR executive in a global company once told me, "The big lie we tell ourselves is that if we continue offering awareness training about inclusiveness, things will change. We launch programs focused on women and minorities. We broaden this to include LGBT—lesbian, gays, bisexual, and transgender people. And still, nothing changes, so what do we do? Offer more classes."

Prior to joining Fierce Inc., Chris Douglas, who was an HR executive at Alaska Airlines for twenty-five years, told me, "We had mandatory diversity programs at Alaska Airlines that addressed 'leading diverse teams' and 'performing successfully in a diverse workforce,' and they were good—full of statistics, good information, good intent. And we did a good job of trying to address context, filters, et cetera.

"The unintended impact was that people felt the company was implying that attendees were biased or prejudiced, and since most people don't believe they are biased or prejudiced, even if they are, the word *diversity* developed a negative context. In fact, companies all over the world are moving away from that term but haven't changed tactics, so now the new terms are being painted with the same negative brush."

Conversations such as these and many others led me to suspect that (a) most awareness classes don't get through to people; (b) awareness doesn't automatically translate into action; (c) we abandoned the term *diversity* and switched to *inclusion,* and it still turns people off; and (d) we make inclusion so complicated, it's laughable.

Dr. Linda Twiname, with the Department of Strategy and Human Resource Management at Waikato Management School in New Zealand, researched the question "What might be the outcome of genuine employee voice and participation in organisational decision-making upon workplace well-being?" (The spelling is hers.) The question she asks is a good one. The problem is, her answer begins:

> The co-option of employee empowerment discourses used by organisations seeking to maximise performance has been documented as contributing to the intensification of control rather than enhancing real employee participation in employment decisions. Through a participatory action research (PAR) programme in a medium sized internationally owned manufacturing firm located in New Zealand, employees sought to transform aspects of their workplace lives that they believed would enhance their well-being. Together we generated PAR processes designed to reflect a Habermasian notion of communicative action by striving towards "ideal speech acts."

Did you catch all that? Me neither. You know you're in trouble when something begins with "The co-option of employee empowerment discourses . . ."

I will not be enrolling in a course taught by Dr. Twiname. I'm certain she's a lovely person, and I might enjoy her company if we were talking about exciting places we have been or our favorite recipes involving wild mushrooms. But the "Habermasian notion of communicative action"? Give me a break! And what, pray tell, is a "speech act"? Is this unintelligible jargon supposed to move us toward inclusion and engagement?

I want to yell at Dr. Twiname. I want to stand in front of her and scream, "What is the matter with you? No, really, WHAT IS THE MATTER WITH YOU?" *In case you read this, Dr. Twiname, I'd apologize for taking a shot at you, but with stuff like this, you had it coming.*

On the other hand, Jamie Dimon, CEO of JPMorgan Chase, describes an inclusive culture as "the way you feel when you enter a building. It's the people who take time to say hello and are interested in answering your questions. It's about respecting the people you work with; about knowing they're there when you need their support and that they're willing to listen to your opinions." This I can understand.

So what's the real problem in most organizations? The problem isn't out there. It's in here. We want employees to be engaged and feel included, while we ourselves are detached, distracted, disengaged, focused on our to-do lists. We want others to bring that elusive, coveted "discretionary effort" in the door with them every day, but we don't have time to engage in the conversations that would enrich our relationships with them. We are busy, not to be found. And even when we are willing to spend more time with people, we don't want to get too close to them. After all, there's a professional distance to maintain. Conversations and meetings that create actual intimacy make us nervous and uncomfortable. Besides, intimacy requires too much upkeep on an emotional level, and conversations and meetings that really engage and include take too much time. We're kinda busy.

The fact is, *not* having those conversations will cost more in the long term. When you disengage from the world, fail to include it, the world disengages, too, in equal measure. It's a two-step, you and the world, you and your organization. Your colleagues, associates, employees lose interest in you because you've lost interest in them. Calling them *associates* isn't enough. If you want to engage and include the people who surround you at work, then gain the capacity to connect with them at a deep level—or lower your aim. *I know, I know. I'm repeating myself.*

WHAT ARE YOU WINNING?

Our efforts at inclusion and engagement won't be sustainable unless we shift beliefs that have kept us stuck. The beliefs on the left below are commonly held. Opposite each one is a contrasting belief that creates an entirely different set of outcomes.

Which beliefs do you hold?

I believe that:	I believe that:
My plate is full, and my focus is on my department. If what we do causes problems for other departments, that's their problem to solve.	What matters anywhere in this organization matters everywhere in this organization, so I should include and engage other parts of the company before I make decisions.
People who don't look like me or who don't share my religious and ideological beliefs do not merit my respect and inclusion.	There is more than one right way to live a life.
Only people in management roles should be invited to meetings about strategy, problem solving, and decision making.	I should invite to meetings people whose perspectives I need to understand and should involve them in the problems and strategies affecting them, regardless of title, role, or "rank."

People who haven't been here as long as I have should keep their mouths shut. This is a job for experts.	A new or young employee's point of view is as valid as anyone else's and critical to designing strategies that will be effective in the future.
It's important that I convince others that my point of view is correct.	Exploring multiple points of view will lead to better decisions.
I don't appreciate it when people question my view of reality and my suggestions about what we should do.	Since my goal is to get it right, rather than to *be* right, I want others to express differing, even competing, realities.
There are some topics no one should mention because they are extremely sensitive and might make some people uncomfortable.	It's important to surface and address significant issues that are causing problems, no matter who might be implicated or upset.
As the leader, I need to share information and assign tasks. I don't have time to listen to the opinions of people who just don't get it.	I encourage candid dialogue during meetings, especially when others don't see things my way, since we all might learn something and execute more effectively.
To be effective, I must maintain a professional distance from those who report to me.	I have genuine affection for and an emotional connection with the people who report to me.
My pedigree, title, income, experience, and achievements mark me as superior to and more valuable than others.	My education and experience allow me to bring value to my company, and at my core, I believe that we are all equals.

No organization wants low employee-engagement scores, high turnover, and the accompanying defection of customers to the competition, and none of us, apart from a few troubled individuals here and there, wants anyone to feel devalued or disrespected. Yet if you hold the beliefs on the left, your efforts at inclusion and engagement will falter. Remember, it's not about whether your beliefs are right or wrong. It's about whether they're working for you. So how can you shift a belief that isn't getting you what you want?

Try this. Choose a belief on the right that you find hard to embrace. Write it down:

_____

_____

_____

Let this be your private mantra, so to speak, for the next twenty-four hours. Say it to yourself. Wear it, walk around in it. Repeat it. Think about it when you interact in person, on the phone, or via e-mail with others. Behave as if you believe it.

When twenty-four hours are up, debrief yourself. How'd it go? What did I do differently? What happened as a result? Were those results positive or negative? How did I feel about myself? Did I like myself more? Less? Did I feel happier, more effective, more peaceful? How did others respond?

If you like what happened and how it felt to you and others, then keep the belief as a mantra until you really *do* believe it. When you're ready, try on a second one, then a third.

As your beliefs shift to the right side of the chart, and you are ready and eager to include and engage, chances are, your question is HOW!

The Fierce Practice: Include! Engage!

As with every fierce practice, the first step is simply to begin! Stop *talking* about inclusion and engagement and start *including and engaging* in every conversation, every meeting. And yes, there is a bit of serious business that will influence the outcome before you walk into a room or open your mouth. That bit would be your intention, your motivation. What do you want and *why* do you want it? We often forget to consider the "why" part, and it's the more important of the two questions. For example, we can set a goal to include people, to engage them, but apart from the usual language on this topic, why would we want to? Really, why? Get this wrong and no amount of personal charisma or process and procedure will save us. Our answers will determine if our story ends with "happily ever after" or "was last seen wandering in the forest."

For me, the poet William Stafford has a wonderful answer to the *why* part—why inclusion and engagement are so very important. Consider the first stanza of this poem.

A Ritual to Read to Each Other

> If you don't know the kind of person I am
> and I don't know the kind of person you are
> a pattern that others made may prevail in the world
> and following the wrong god home we may miss our star.

That pretty much nails it for me. Based on results, many of us have been following the wrong god home, especially the "what's in it for me" god. We're in a new, challenging time, and I don't want us to miss our star. Given all the suffering so many have endured; all the prices paid; and all the personal, national, and global consequences of our flawed intentions, motivations, and behaviors, one would hope that most people would be eager to abandon old patterns, yet the gravitational pull of business as usual is strong. To break the pattern, we must show up in our conversations and meetings with the intention of getting it right for all of us, for the greater good. And to think of these conversations not as top down or bottom up, but side by side. Listening to each other, not to correct and instruct, but to truly understand. A genuine intention to understand cannot be faked. If people pick up even a hint of hidden agenda, condescension, or patronizing attitudes in any way, you're toast.

And the final stanza:

For it is important that awake people be awake,
or a breaking line may discourage them back to sleep;
the signals we give—yes or no, or maybe—should
be clear: the darkness around us is deep.

"A breaking line" refers to an earlier stanza about what happens if an elephant in a circus lets go of the tail of the elephant in front of it. The line breaks and the circus won't find the park. If you or I wander off on our own, making decisions with no thought of how others may be affected, tuned only to our own self-interest, well, there are consequences. Sometimes, the darkness around us is not only deep, it is sad, ineffective, and unworthy of the organizations for which we work, the lives we want to live.

Given the darkness we've experienced, my hope is that we have grown tired of isolation, that we perceive old patterns and the prices we've paid, and that we will begin to seek connection and, through connection, the best way forward.

As Rūmī wrote:

Out beyond right doing and wrong doing,
there is a field.
I'll meet you there.

Inclusion and engagement take place in Rūmī's field, not just when we're exploring easy topics—safe topics with easy answers—but when we identify and tackle our toughest, most pressing issues. Leadership that is not practiced under fire is without value. Only by applying inclusion and engagement in trying situations do we have a genuine experience of them. So don't hold meetings on a tiny, tyrannical lawn. Throw the doors wide open and invite many people to the conversation, so that you and others can act *in unison* to further what wants and needs to happen. Our power as individuals is multiplied when we gather together as families, teams, and communities with common goals. It will be your collective intelligence and strength that make positive change possible within your circle of influence.

In the book *Harry Potter and the Chamber of Secrets,* the character Mr. Weasley gives Harry Potter a piece of advice: "Harry, don't ever trust something that thinks for itself unless you can see where it keeps its brain." Unless we can see where every one of us keeps his or her brain, we tend not to trust one another. Remember, trust requires persistent identity. When the right people—those who have line of sight to key priorities, who possess the ability to make decisions and allocate resources, and who will be impacted by those decisions and allocations—meet in order to interrogate everyone's reality regarding an impending decision, surfacing built-in conflicts, and clarifying directions and priorities . . . well, we all end up seeing where each person keeps his or her brain.

At Fierce, we are often in conversation, and twice a year we come together formally to make sure we're clear about where each member of the team keeps his or her brain. Each December, each of us comes to the meeting with a PowerPoint presentation answering the following questions (which ensures everyone has given considerable thought to the questions BEFORE the meeting). We ask that they not discuss their answers with other team members prior to the meeting. We are more interested in learning one another's "first thoughts," personal and honest thoughts, than in groupthink. *Note: I will explain "my stripe on the beach ball" later.*

When I look at Fierce from my stripe on the beach ball

- Within the next three months, it is essential that Fierce . . . (name three things, in order of priority)
- Within the next twelve months, it is essential that Fierce . . . (name three things, in order of priority)

When I look at my goals and what I am responsible for

- Within the next three months, it is essential that I . . . (name three things, in order of priority)
- Within the next twelve months, it is essential that I . . . (name three things, in order of priority)

My greatest achievement this year was . . .
My greatest achievement next year would be . . .
Our revenue goal for next year should be . . .

In addition to clarifying priorities and goals, we share our answers
to questions such as

- What is the current chapter title in the book about Fierce Inc.?
- In the coming year, what would Fierce do if we had no fear?
- Imagine images of us working together throughout the new year.
  What are our most common behaviors, values, virtues, and accom-
  plishments?
- What values will define us in moments of truth during conversa-
  tions with each other and with clients?
- Five years from now, I want Fierce to be described as . . .

We always have a brilliant two days and begin implementing the
resulting action plan, which we revisit formally in June, sharing what
has changed, what we've learned, and whether or not the plan is still
sound. If it isn't, we change the plan.

So to include and engage, invite people to a meeting, tell them you're
going to show them where you keep your brain around an important
topic, and ask them to reveal where they're keeping theirs. Invite the
vetoes early; let the built-in conflicts surface. Tell people you want to
be influenced by them. And mean it. In the process, you will not only
make better decisions, but you will also enrich relationships with all
those present.

The powerful tool you'll use is the Beach Ball meeting, which is essential when you have . . .

- decisions to make;
- strategies to design;
- opportunities to evaluate; or
- problems to solve

. . . which for most of us, is every day! And you want to get it right
for the organization and for the ultimate "call" to be implemented im-
peccably, willingly.

STEP 1. PREPARE YOURSELF.

Earlier, I asked you to picture your organization as a web of relationships that are shaped one conversation, one meeting at a time. Now picture your organization as a huge beach ball.

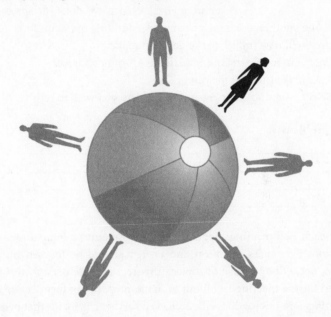

Each person in your company operates from a different colored stripe and experiences reality from that perspective. People in marketing, human resources, manufacturing, accounting, out on the loading dock—and let's not forget your customers—obviously have significantly different, perhaps competing perspectives. Blue, red, green, gold . . .

A Beach Ball meeting is an opportunity to uncover the perspectives that people share and don't share—to connect to the real, personal voices and minds of others whose input is essential in order to make the best possible decisions for an organization. During Beach Ball meetings, what matters is not whose perspective is correct. What matters is that everyone in the room puts his or her brain on the table

"Harry, don't ever trust
something that thinks for
itself unless you can see
where it keeps its brain."
—*Harry Potter and the
Chamber of Secrets*

for all to see (assuming that attendees brought their brains with them).

Rūmī's field is where Beach Ball meetings take place. When we get this right, we leave a meeting with ideas no one person had coming in. Differing agendas are revealed, and consequently, even if we don't all agree, we trust one another and gain a clear understanding of the multiple realities that will now influence the decision maker.

We begin to understand Madeleine Albright's advice.

Let's make this real for you.

Select a significant or recurring problem you wish to resolve.

The problem is:

_____

_____

_____

_____

Beach Ball meetings begin with clarity about the issue under discussion. Everyone's attention and energy should be focused on *the* topic, not a hodgepodge of topics. This requires the person who has asked for the meeting to fill out an issue-preparation form *before* the meeting, an exercise that will force even further clarity for that person and will ensure that the meeting hits the ground running.

Please stop reading and fill in the form now. Remember, the problem named is the problem solved. What is the topic or problem you want to address? Don't linger on the edges.

Now that you've clarified the issue, whose perspectives will be important for you and others to understand? Get creative here. Forget about titles. Who sits at the juncture where things happen? Who is impacted by the problem or will be impacted by the solution? Whose cooperation will be needed to implement the solution? Who is likely to resist the solution? Who often disagrees with your perspective? Who is the "customer"? Who has nothing to do with the topic but, though he

Beach Ball
Preparation Form

the issue is

Be concise. In 1 or 2 sentences, get to the heart of the issue. Is it a concern, challenge, opportunity, or recurring problem that is becoming more troublesome?

it's significant because

What's at stake? For example: how does this affect profitability, people, products, services, customers, timing, the future, or other relevant factors? What is the future impact if the issue is not resolved?

my ideal outcome is

What specific results do I want?

relevant background information

Summarize with bullet points: What, why, where, when, how, who, etc.; which forces are at work; what is the current status?

what I have done up to this point

What have I done so far?

options I am considering

What options am I considering? What am I leaning toward doing?

the help I want from the group is

What do I want from the group? For example: alternative solutions, confidence regarding the right decision, identification of consequences, where to find more information, critique of current plan, etc.

or she would be very surprised to be invited, might bring something unique to the table?

Write down these people's names.

I will invite to this meeting:

_____

_____

_____

_____

_____

_____

Prior to this meeting, send out any material others will need to review. If you start the meeting by passing out a bunch of statistics for people to review, you will kill the energy in the room. If you want to hit the ground running, ask that everyone review whatever information you've provided *before* the meeting and come prepared to share their perspectives.

Materials I will send out ahead of time:

_____

_____

_____

STEP 2. PREPARE OTHERS.

In your invitation, let everyone know

1. The topic to be discussed;
2. Its significance;
3. Your desire to understand their perspectives about how to solve it; and
4. Your expectation that they will come to the meeting prepared to focus their energy and attention on the topic.

STEP 3. DO IT!

Hold the meeting. Here is how it should go:

1. Begin by thanking everyone for coming, and urge them to unplug. That means turning off their cell phones and any high-tech distractions that are likely to ring, hum, or vibrate. If anyone has a laptop open, ask them to close it and go laptopless. Tell them that you want eye contact in this meeting, deep listening, and, in fact, that you would prefer that no one take notes, so everyone should set aside paper and pens. *This includes you!*
2. Give everyone a copy of the issue-preparation form, and talk through it quickly to focus attention and resources on the topic.
3. Tell your team members that you want to hear the perspective from each stripe of the beach ball, especially if it differs from what you see or the direction in which you are leaning. You could even put a beach ball on the table or draw one on a flip chart or whiteboard. Say something like:

   We're here to solve the problem of . . . (or operate as a think tank on the topic of . . .). I will tell you what I think needs to happen and why. My view is based on my position on the beach ball. I'm standing on the blue stripe, so that's what I see. It's hard to see other colors from where I stand, so I need you to tell me what it looks like from your stripe on the beach ball. That requires that you push back on anything I say that doesn't match your view of reality. Tell me what I'm missing. That's how you'll add value to this meeting. My hope is to be influenced by you. I want to be different when this meeting is over.

   And mean it!

4. Ask for clarifying questions about the issue preparation form and answer them.
5. Make sure that you hear each team member's thoughts, concerns, ideas. I usually tee this up with humor: "While you have the right to remain silent, I've noticed that some of you don't have the ability, so

be reminded that I want to hear from everyone." (This usually gets a laugh and sends a clear signal to those who talk too much.) Your goal is not to persuade them to your way of thinking, not to defend your position, but to understand theirs. If you disagree with a comment or don't understand, please don't say, "Yes, but . . . " That's a surefire way to indicate that you're not really asking. Replace *but* with *and*. "Yes, and . . . " will keep all the doors and windows open. If someone says, "I don't know," ask, "What would it be if you did know?" If someone says, "I have nothing to add," ask, "What would you add if you did have something to add?" Don't let anyone off the hook. Everyone must show up in this conversation, and if you get this part right, no one will show up unprepared at the next one.

6. When you have heard from everyone and the conversation is losing steam or people are starting to repeat themselves, ask each team member to write down a concise answer to this question: "Having heard from everyone here, what is your strongest recommendation?" (or "What would you do if you were in my shoes?" or whatever question fits best).

7. Have each person read his or her advice aloud. Do not respond, except to say, "Thank you."

8. After everyone has read his or her advice, tell the group what you've heard and ask, "Did I miss anything essential?"

9. Thank everyone for his or her contribution and tell the group what action you are prepared to take and when you will take it. If you don't know yet, tell them you need time to think and that you'll let them know your decision.

10. Ask them to sign their recommendations and give them to you so that you can follow up with them if you'd like more information.

Conclude by saying something like, "Thank you for your time and intelligence. Well done!"

START AND END YOUR MEETINGS ON TIME. I'll say it again. Start and end your meetings on time. I confess that I am seriously turned off when the person who called the meeting is late himself or says, "Let's wait a few more minutes so more people can get here." And then there's the frequent comment, "It's always like this. We never start meetings on time," *said as if describing a mildly irritating but endearing trait in a child.*

Starting meetings late has consequences beyond just inefficiency and inconvenience. A poll of 360 workers, including senior management, conducted by the Workplace Intelligence Unit, found that turning up late for meetings was considered by many workers the height of disrespect, with four out of ten feeling that colleagues who did so or canceled at the last minute were simply showing that they did not value the respondents' time.

People feel disrespected when they show up and others don't. The message received is that those who arrive late value their own time more than that of their colleagues—an attitude that doesn't exactly foster inclusion and engagement. Don't waste anyone's time, either at the beginning of a meeting or at the end. If you start on time and stay focused, you'll be done when you said you'd be done. The meeting *will* end on time.

Early in my coaching relationship with Will (not his real name), a wonderful, seriously evolved chairman of an organization in Los Angeles, I asked his assistant what advice he would like to give his boss. This is what he said:

> "I'd like him to clean up his behavior around meetings. He's created a monster by scheduling meetings and keeping people waiting. For example, if a meeting is supposed to start at 10 A.M., I can guarantee you that no one will be in the meeting room at 10 A.M. Except me. So I start calling people who are supposed to be there, and they ask, "Is Will in the room yet?" And of course, he isn't, so the waiting continues. Until he's in the room, they won't leave their offices. Part of it's a power dance—who's more important?—but mostly these are busy people who can't afford to sit in a conference room waiting for who knows how long for Will to show up. And sometimes, he's not there even when he's there. He's distracted."

"It's always like this. We never start meetings on time," *said as if describing a mildly irritating but endearing trait in a child.*

Will cares very much about every one of his executives, and yet his meeting behavior sends the opposite message. Sadly, maddeningly, this is a dynamic that exists in many organizations, a huge time waster.

Here's another example.

I traveled with Chris Douglas, who handles business development for Fierce, to spend a day with a dozen decision makers in a global pharmaceutical company. The purpose was to walk them through a Fierce training course for their sales managers and then collaborate with them to customize the course. We were to meet from 8:30 A.M. to 5 P.M.

Chris and I weren't bothered by the 6 A.M. call requesting that we arrive an hour earlier. The trouble began when we were met by an outside consultant who had been working with the organization for a year. Let's call him Jim (not his name). Actually, let's call him *Dr.* Jim, as that's how he prefers to be addressed since he has a PhD. And let's call the person spearheading the sales training initiative Steve.

Dr. Jim: I need to prepare you for the day.

Chris: Terrific. What do we need to know?

Dr. Jim: It's about the culture, what it's like around here. I need to warn you so you won't take it personally.

Me: Sounds ominous.

Dr. Jim: It's just the way things are. Let's start with . . . you don't have a full day.

Me: Has something happened?

Dr. Jim: Nothing that doesn't happen every day. People have to attend other meetings. They're double booked. Very common here.

Chris: Lay it out for us, please.

Dr. Jim: Well, Steve won't be here until noon. *(Chris and I barely stifle a dual gasp.)* And he'll need to leave around 3 P.M. A couple of people, including the head of sales training, will be here for the first hour, then out for an hour or two. Four people have to catch planes, so they've got to leave at 2 P.M. Others, I don't remember who, told me they'll need to step out from time to time to take phone calls.

(Chris and I look at each other, our eyes starting to glaze.)
Dr. Jim: It's nothing against you or Fierce. It's the culture here. You just have to work with it.

What I didn't say is *"And exactly how long have you been consulting with this company? And what part of 'totally messed up' haven't you noticed? Did they hire you to build a case for dysfunction?"* I was thinking it, but I kept my mouth shut because I have matured a bit (just a bit) over the years and recognize my tendency toward expressive compulsive disorder!

We stayed and did the best we could, given that people were constantly in and out of the room, but looking back, we should have made an immediate, courteous exit and offered to return when they could guarantee the presence of those we had agreed on.

Do you know this culture, live in one like it? Everyone always checking their BlackBerrys and cell phones to see if "something" has happened while they were in the meeting, in the subway, in the bathroom, on the plane, uneasy at the thought of being out of touch, thinking someone may need to tell them something, may need them for something?

What is this "something" we anticipate? And do we really imagine that, if we, personally, are unable to show up and intervene or provide input immediately, all will be lost? If so, this signals someone who does not hold others able. How'd you like to work for her, for him?

If you are enabling this culture, modeling this kind of behavior yourself, STOP IT! Thank you.

I understand you're busy. Who isn't? So shape your schedule to suit you, rather than the other way around. What depth of involvement do you want, and what is appropriate, in what areas?

Pull your assistant into this conversation. He or she can help you organize your days better, so that you are not letting your schedule or other people dictate too much, but instead are focused where you need to be, so that everything isn't a crisis, a priority, and so that you can make better use of your time and not keep people waiting. The fierce conversation needed is one in which you clarify the *best* use of your time and stop accepting that things are this way because things are this way.

STEP 4. DEBRIEF.

You can do this at the conclusion of the meeting or informally later on. Ask,

> "What insights did you gain from this meeting?"
> "What could we do to improve the next meeting?"
> "What did we do well?"
> "Looking back, who else should have been invited to the meeting?"
> "What valuable perspectives did we miss?"

Get back to people once you have made a decision or taken action based on their suggestions, and let them know the results and/or next steps.

STEP 5. DO IT AGAIN, ONLY BETTER.

Get increasingly creative about who is invited to meetings. Support staff. People from other parts of the company. Customers. Vendors.

Recognize and correct any missteps on your part. Did you talk too much? Did you catch yourself being argumentative? Did you use the word *but*?

If someone was disruptive during the meeting—made others feel diminished or wrong, took too much airtime, withheld his or her view—bring it to that person's attention privately and say that you hold him or her able to do better next time.

To sum up, Beach Ball meetings should be well thought out. The right people should be brought together to share diverse perspectives on a clearly defined topic of importance and operate like an ad hoc think tank. Each person's thoughts should be solicited and listened to. Reality should be interrogated, learning should be provoked, tough topics should be tackled, and relationships should be enriched. The meeting should be focused and fairly fast paced and should start and end on time.

When this is the case, you are facilitating connection. Respect is deepened with understanding. Most of us are happy to let leaders lead, yet we'd still like to feel that each of us has a place at the table, that when we are asked for our perspective about bet-the-farm decisions, we're really being listened to. This should be a regular occurrence, part of daily life as we know it, rather than a rare event. In fact, failing to show respect for other people's views is a major problem within many workplaces.

Respect is deepened with understanding.

Because Beach Ball meetings are far more productive, provocative, and engaging than the kinds of meetings most of us are used to, the idea tends to catch on. Those who attend your beach ball meetings will behave far better in other meetings and will encourage others to do so, as well.

Taking It to the Organization

In addition to Beach Ball meetings, there are several highly inclusive, engaging team exercises I strongly recommend that you take to your organization. The first is called Lifeline. It allows people to see one another as more than their jobs, their roles. To see one another as human beings with lives that include work and extend beyond work.

Here's how it works.

LIFELINE

Gather your team together and give each person a sheet of flip chart paper and a marker. Tell them you'll give them fifteen minutes to draw their lifeline, starting from as early in their lives as they can remember. They should start by drawing a flat line across the center of the page. This line is neutral, neither good nor bad. Then ask them to mark the major highs and lows in their lives—personal as well as professional—with Xs above and below the neutral line. Each X should be labeled with the event, the year, and the primary emotion they felt at the time. Then they'll connect the Xs, so that their lifeline looks like a sales or stock price history.

When they're finished drawing their lifelines, ask for a volunteer to

lifeline

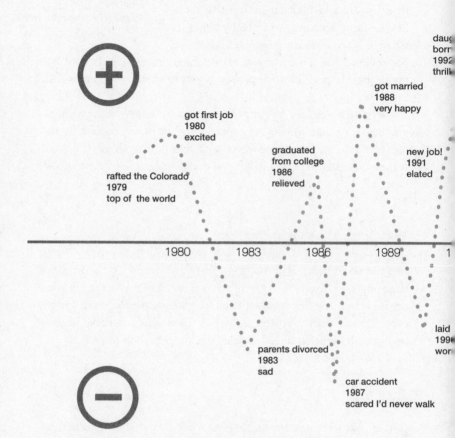

rafted the Colorado
1979
top of the world

got first job
1980
excited

graduated
from college
1986
relieved

got married
1988
very happy

daug
born
1992
thrill

new job!
1991
elated

parents divorced
1983
sad

car accident
1987
scared I'd never walk

laid
199
wor

1980   1983   1986   1989

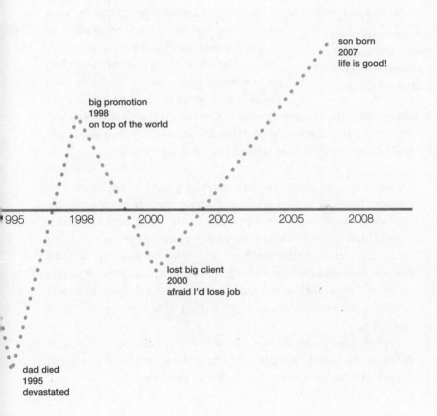

big promotion
1998
on top of the world

son born
2007
life is good!

995   1998   2000   2002   2005   2008

lost big client
2000
afraid I'd lose job

dad died
1995
devastated

go first. Have him or her stand in front of the room, put up the lifeline chart, and talk the team through the key events of his or her life. Encourage the team to ask clarifying questions along the way.

When the person is finished, ask, "How have these events shaped who you are?" When he or she has answered this question, ask, "How have these events shaped how you lead?"

How have these events shaped who you are? . . . How have these events shaped how you lead?

You'll need about twenty minutes per person, so this may be a long exercise, depending on how many people are on the team, but I assure you it's worth it. Participants will learn things about their teammates that they didn't know before and will better understand not only *what* they do, but *why* they do it. And there will be considerable self-generated insight along the way.

Be aware that there may be a surprising level of disclosure. I remember listening to a team member whose presentation was punctuated every sixty seconds by the sound of the pump on his portable chemotherapy drip. Another team member had been present when his father accidentally fatally shot his mother on a hunting trip. Another had lost his entire net worth after Eliot Spitzer knocked on his former employer's door. We also learned of great successes, magical moments, wonderful accomplishments. And wouldn't Eliot Spitzer's lifeline be interesting . . .

When this exercise is given its due, whoever is in the room will be far more connected, included, and engaged with everyone else in the room than they were when they walked in the door.

"SIGNIFICANT EVENTS"

Every Monday morning, the Fierce team meets at 9 A.M. for "Ducks" (short for Ducks in a Row) to touch base about what's on everyone's plates, the status of projects and work with clients, any help needed, et cetera. But before we dive in, we take time for "Significant Events," an exercise in which each person tells us—briefly—about his or her most significant personal and professional event since last we met.

Since we meet on Mondays, on the personal side, people often talk about what they did over the weekend. Sometimes it's news of relatives or a child's recent accomplishment, or the latest chapter in a house hunt, or a paragliding thrill. Then they add any late-breaking work-related news. Significant Events usually takes about sixty seconds per person, and that's all that's needed, really. Still, that's valuable time, so why do this when we're all so busy? Because it allows us to get a sense of how and where each person is, emotionally as well as intellectually. It gives us a chance to congratulate and commiserate. It helps us get to know each other better when we're all present. To see the person, not just the job.

Significant Events was standard procedure with the think tanks that I ran. It brought the CEOs closer together, reminded them that each CEO had a family, outside interests, a personal life, and it reminds me of a question I've heard in England: "Who is he when he's at home?"

I am not suggesting that you begin every meeting with Significant Events, but it's a good thing to do periodically with a team that works together regularly and a good way to engage and include those who may be new to the team or only visiting before kicking off almost any kind of meeting. It levels the field—*we are all people with accomplishments within these walls and vivid lives outside these walls*—and it allows us to "see" each other as more than our jobs or titles. It facilitates connection.

If your team is too large for this (more than twelve to fifteen people) and/or you're truly pressed for time, there are other variations you could use. Just do a quick version, including only personal significant events: "In fifteen seconds or less, please tell us your most significant personal event in the last thirty days." Or have people share their significant events in groups of three.

Or just start your meetings with something to make people smile, something to break the ice. When Cam Tripp led teams at SPU (Seattle Pacific University), he says, "We always started out with something fun—even if it was a silly border on the agenda. Sometimes we laughed so hard that people down the hall wondered if we got any work done. Indeed we did. We performed at very high levels; in fact, because of our work, out of 250 other universities, ours was number one for student leader satisfaction, likely because it was a connection-rich culture."

In another example, Peter Lynch of AIMCO starts meetings with "ZenMo"—a Zen Moment—usually some funny YouTube video or cartoon that gets people laughing and produces high connectivity levels and high performance. People NEVER show up late, because they don't want to miss their ZenMo.

LEARN A NEW LANGUAGE (OR AT LEAST A FEW WORDS IN A NEW LANGUAGE)

This isn't a team exercise. This is just for you. I once witnessed a wonderful opening welcome at a conference. One of the senior executives stepped to the microphone and said, *"Welcome. Benvenuto. Huan ying. Salaam. Buenos días. Guten Tag. Bienvenue. Goddag. Irashaimasu. Karibu. Hola. Jambo. Tervetuloa . . . ,"* continuing his extended welcome in all of the languages spoken by the organization's employees. No notes, no teleprompter. He looked directly at people's faces as he welcomed them in their native tongues.

His greeting showed that he valued the diversity of the audience, and it signaled his respect for them. This was warmth, human connection at its best. The applause was enthusiastic, and everyone was smiling broadly.

He grinned and confessed that the hardest and most important thing he'd had to do in the last twenty-four hours was learning and memorizing all the greetings.

If you have employees from other countries and cultures, I hope you will follow his lead.

UNDERSTAND AND EMBRACE GENERATIONAL DIFFERENCES

It would be a grave mistake to put each "generation" into a box labeled "This is who you are." Most people are delighted and relieved to discover that people of all ages share many core values and priorities. In fact, we are more alike than different. At the same time, there are differences among generations that you should take into account if you want to create a truly engaged workplace.

In *The Way We'll Be: The Zogby Report on the Transformation of the American Dream,* John Zogby says that Gen Yers, also known as First Globals (born between 1979 and 1990), consider the notion of generous pensions and lifetime job security laughable ("While you're at it, tell me about Santa Claus"), which it is these days. First Globals are ready to go anywhere, experience everything, and work and live in exotic places, and for them, family life takes priority over work life and a flexible, diverse, collaborative, fun learning environment is key. So if you run a company or lead a team or have a customer base that includes members of this generation, you'll do well to create an environment that offers these things.

Boomers, whom Zogby calls Woodstockers (1946–64), also value work/life balance and hope to achieve it after they retire! Zogby suggests that to engage members of this generation, you'd do well to offer jobs or positions that allow them to have a second act—"something with more social utility than an endless obsession with self."

Gen Xers, or Nikes (1965–78) made "Just Do It" their mantra, but as they age, they are going to spearhead the search for what they believe to be the real American dream—greater spiritual, rather than material, fulfillment. So they are less likely to be engaged and motivated by loftier job titles and high salaries than by work they find fulfilling.

And we should not write off the Veterans or the "Private Generation" (1922–1945). They've got decades of healthy living ahead of them, and they're going to fill those golden years with volunteering, mentoring, and lifelong learning opportunities.

When working with people of a different generation from yours, until you appreciate the similarities and the differences, you may find that your best efforts are not appreciated, are not striking a chord. At Fierce Inc., all generations are present and play well together. Our differences are hugely valuable. We provoke one another's learning, and our similarities are deeply reassuring.

Many organizations offer training (like our Fierce Generations workshop) on this topic. A quick search will turn up multiple resources, which, as a leader committed to engaging employees, I encourage you to consider. But simply attending a training course or running a workshop is not enough. If you want to expand and implement a practice of inclusion and engagement throughout your organization, you can follow my personal action plan.

Personal Action Plan

1. Stop *talking* about leveraging the diversity of ethnicity and talent within your organization and start *doing* it. Build a diverse team and focus that team on something tough, important. One of the quickest, most powerful ways to bond people for life is to bring a group of people together and ask them to accomplish something significant and difficult in a short period of time.

2. Bring together the best thought leaders within your organization. Make sure that all the different departments, teams, and perspectives are represented—from the mail room on up. Get them to think out loud about a problem that needs solving, a decision that needs making, a strategy that needs designing, an opportunity that needs evaluating.

3. Don't fire and forget. When a person leaves, do exit interviews to find out where you went wrong. And act on what you learn. *And* make it easier to fire people who aren't right for your company or the job or who think that just coming to work each day is enough. Don't let them get away with anything less than their "A" game.

4. Select a generations workshop that doesn't simply point out generational differences, but also reveals their similarities. I have found that each of us is a surprise for everyone else. The "card game" that kicks off the Fierce Generations workshop results in the wonderful surprise that we are more similar than different. This realization helps to connect us.

5. Work with HR to make it easier for people to say what they really want to say about why they want to hire or fire someone, rather than what is judged politically correct. HR should be helpful, not a hurdle.

6. Focus on creating consistent, enduring connections everywhere you go—connections that highlight and focus the unique capabilities of individuals on your business model and on employee and client relationships.

7. Have a Beach Ball meeting focused on resolving a problem or designing a strategy. Invite to the meeting two people who have absolutely nothing to do with your team or the topic—people whom no one would expect to see sitting at your table—and include them as equals. It could be someone who works in an entirely different area of the company. A maintenance person. An intern who works in the building across the street. The EVP of another division. Your favorite barista or sales clerk. A customer. A prospective customer. If you're a small company, invite someone from another small company in the same building. Or someone from a large company that you admire. Ask for their thoughts and listen hard.

8. If you have a relatively new team, do the Lifeline exercise with them.

9. Start a meeting with Significant Events.

10. When you ask people how they are, don't be satisfied with "fine." *Fine* is a four-letter word. Help employees and customers articulate the true answer. Keep your tone encouraging, not fear inducing.

11. Ask people where they want to go careerwise and why they want to go there. Tell them the truth about how they're doing relative to their goals. *Did you get the "Tell the truth!" part?* Advocate for your top performers moving up in your organization even if a move might have a short-term negative impact on *your* progress. Too many leaders will only support someone's advancement if it's both good for that person and in the best interests of the leader. This is shortsighted and will win you zero points. If you see a natural move for someone and would like him or her to stay with you to complete a particular project or initiative, then make that clear. Part of a leader's job is to build a stellar bench.

12. Add names to your "Conversations I Need to Have" list, and have those conversations. Who deserves your praise? Who deserves an apology? Who deserves your support? Who deserves the truth? Who might have a thing or two to teach you?

13. Have these conversations in person. Technology is marvelous, but inclusion and engagement require that you get up out of your chair and spend time with people, face to face. Don't send an e-mail when you could talk with someone. When all a person has are words on a screen, he or she will likely attach a tone and meaning that are a far cry from what you intended.

14. Delegate more, and don't usurp responsibility. Support as opposed to command. Coach as opposed to convince. This is not about your "winning," looking good. It's about developing others. Come from a place of goodwill.

15. Tell a family member how much he or she means to you. When I asked a friend why she chose the man she married, she said, "Because he knows how he feels about me." Who needs to know how you feel about them?

Conclusion

In *The Elegance of the Hedgehog,* by Muriel Barbery, a supersmart twelve-year-old, Paloma, describes her response to the annual performance of her school choir in Paris:

> Every time, it's a miracle. Here are all these people, full of heartache
> or hatred or desire, and we all have our troubles and the school year
> is filled with vulgarity and triviality and consequence, and there are
> all these teachers and kids of every shape and size, and there's this
> life we're struggling through full of shouting and tears and laughter
> and fights and break-ups and dashed hopes and unexpected luck—it
> all disappears, just like that, when the choir begins to sing. Everyday
> life vanishes into song, you are suddenly overcome with a feeling of
> brotherhood, of deep solidarity, even love, and it diffuses the ugliness
> of everyday life into a spirit of perfect communion. Even the singers'
> faces are transformed: it's no longer Achille Grand-Fernet that I'm
> looking at (he is a very fine tenor), or Deborah Lemeur or Segolene
> Rachet or Charles Saint-Sauveur. I see human beings, surrendering
> to music.

Every time, it's the same thing. I feel like crying, my throat goes all tight and I do the best I can to control myself but sometimes it gets close: I can hardly keep myself from sobbing. So when they sing a canon I look down at the ground because it's just too much emotion at once: it's too beautiful, and everyone singing together, this marvelous sharing. I'm no longer myself, I am just one part of a sublime whole, to which the others also belong, and I always wonder at such moments why this cannot be the rule of everyday life, instead of being an exceptional moment, during a choir.

When the music stops, everyone applauds, their faces all lit up, the choir radiant. It is so beautiful.

In the end, I wonder if the true movement of the world might not be a voice raised in song.

I understand what Paloma feels and imagine you do too, when music takes you someplace you'd like to stay and you want to gather everyone you love around you, gather everyone you don't love, too, so that maybe we could see beyond ourselves and truly meet one another. When these emotions strike me, wash over me, I vow not to allow the sense of connection and goodness and joy and love and longing that was mine for a moment to slip away. And then the music is over, the phone rings, the dogs bark, the news headlines announce another preposterous event or horrifying outcome, a deadline looms. Poof, there it went, all that connection. To get it back, I often return to music.

I wrote much of *Fierce Conversations* while listening to the music of Kelly Joe Phelps. As I explained, "I am in love with his sound, a cross between Springsteen, Dock Boggs, and someone from somewhere on the banks of the Mississippi. The lyrics are lovely but secondary. It's simply what this music evokes in me. Unbidden. Dropping me into a funky, smooth, and groovy place where I want to pour a glass of red wine, light a fire, and reminisce. I remember evenings with friends, playing our guitars and singing by the Missouri River my freshman year of college. I can see Kelly Joe Phelps's music with my eyes. He's tapped into an artery somehow. You can't get that just anywhere."

Many pages of *Fierce Leadership* were written while listening to

Trio Mediaeval, three gorgeous voices who sing traditional ballads, hymns, and lullabies from Norway. Days and days were also spent writing to the sounds of Pete's Pond at the Mashatu Game Reserve in Botswana, Africa, via the National Geographic WildCam. The cameras are focused on Pete's Pond. As I wrote, a bird with impossibly long tail feathers sang a gorgeous aria in the dead of night. Hyenas patrolled, hoping a small animal would find itself without protection. Moths the size of dinner plates floated across the camera lens at night.

Hamish, my cairn terrier, spent a few minutes in my lap each morning, watching the goings-on. It was part of our morning ritual. The frogs in Pete's Pond sound like the frogs in my pond, only more exotic. All these sounds—birds, animals, insects, water, wind—have an effect on me. They transport me to a state of mind in which there is the possibility of a deeper intellectual, emotional, or spiritual dive.

Why am I telling you this? Because I believe that part of being engaged is amassing a diverse collection of thoughts, ideas, emotions, and worldviews through the words, songs, and actions of others.

Part of being engaged is amassing a diverse collection of thoughts, ideas, emotions, and worldviews through the words, songs, and actions of others.

It isn't easy—this connecting, this looking beyond hardwired assumptions and beliefs, this seeking out people and seeing beyond. Some people have given up trying to meet others, completely missing those who are not from their world. But these people will never grow, because they just meet themselves over and over, because they are only looking in the mirror, entranced with their own form, their own face and ideology.

Seeking out people with different views, different perspectives, different ideas is often challenging, because it requires us to set aside judgment and open our minds. But we have to remind ourselves that to get beyond where we are, where I believe most of us are, we would all be well served to choose our music carefully, to stop talking and listen to one another.

Employee engagement, inclusion. A worthy goal that will remain just that—a goal—unless and until, here and now, we create deep connection in this moment, *this* one, with *this* person, the person across the table in the meeting, the one holding forth or sitting quietly, the one cooking dinner, the one with whom we disagree, the one we haven't valued, haven't really *seen*. Until now.

Fierce Practice #5

From Customer Centricity to Customer Connectivity

Your call is important to us. Please listen carefully to the following options.

If you would like directions to the store nearest you, press "1."

If you would like to know the status of your account, press "2."

If you would like to make a payment, press "3."

If you feel there has been an error in billing, press "4," then enter your account number followed by the pound sign, at which point you will be prompted to enter your social security number and the complete text of the Serenity Prayer, then "star."

If you are experiencing technical difficulty placing your order, please use our online help desk, which you won't be able to access since you're having technical difficulty.

If you have forgotten your password, you may select a new password, provided you can decipher a set of garbled letters and numbers impossible to read.

If you would like to speak to an actual human being, say "human being." You will then be put on hold indefinitely where you can listen to cheesy hold music and annoying ads while our staff attends a meeting on improving client centricity.

If you press "0" in the hopes of getting to an actual person, you will be returned to the beginning of the menu.

Should you get to an actual person by some loophole we have not yet plugged, you will be asked to repeat all of the information you have already entered, since none of it will have been captured by our new and improved system, at which point you will be disconnected. If you have forgotten why you called and are losing the will to live, press "5." Nothing will happen, but it gives you something to do.

If you would like to hear these options again, press "3825star-sign63."

We fall back on the language of "client centricity" in the unoriginal, secondhand language that is currently the best we can manage. Look at the words—*client centricity*. How do they strike you? To me, they sound formal, hygienic, cold, mechanical. I've never heard a customer say she left because someone wasn't centric with her. Would you use such language at home? *Come on baby, let's get centric tonight!*

Come on baby, let's get centric tonight!

"Client centricity" is one of the most common terms in business today and a key initiative for many companies. In service to this "best practice"—which refers simply to a focus on customers—companies invest millions in "CRM" (customer relationship management) initiatives aimed at training "customer-facing" employees. There's no question that acquiring and retaining customers is vital to every company, but it's the way companies are going about it that's dead wrong.

Consider the fact that 55 percent to 75 percent of all CRM and customer centricity initiatives fail to meet objectives. Charles Green, coauthor of *The Trusted Advisor,* points out that many companies have the client focus of a vulture—they pay close attention to what the clients are up to, but only in order to figure out the right time to pounce and tear at their flesh. Green suggests that most CRM systems are not really plans to build a relationship at all—they are just a list of features and benefits advertising the wonderful things the company could do for customers.

I agree. My excitement soared when I read the heading for an advertisement for Kaiser Permanente. "Unleashing the Power of Connectivity in Health Care." Two bold headings said: "A health-care crisis of communication." And "Connectivity. The overdue next step." *Bravo!* I thought. Let's see what they're doing to fix this. Well, what they're doing, what they've done, is replace a paper-based information sharing system with "a continuous loop of information around the patient that will give clinicians secure access to all data, on all relevant patients, all of the time."

This is a good thing in health care, an excellent use of technology. But what struck me is that for lots of people, the term *connectivity* is automatically associated with technology. And *only* technology. The ad goes on to say that Kaiser Permanente spent 4 billion dollars building this system and that "secure, computerized data sharing can reduce errors, redundancies, lost information, and costs."

Data. Costs. Both are important, no question, and while I suspect that Kaiser Permanente's considerable investment in technology was one of the right things for them to do, I wonder what else they're doing on the "connectivity" front.

Sales plans, computerized data sharing, and advertising strategies are not relationship-building vehicles. While an automated phone system may improve an organization's operational efficiencies, it rarely improves the customer experience. In fact, most have the opposite effect. Recall your latest experience with automated customer service, trying to get to the right place and the right person. Want to get a heated conversation going? Pick an industry and pile on. Try "airlines" and stand back. I used to love Gershwin's "Rhapsody in Blue." Now the first bar of "Rhapsody" brings me right back to all those wasted hours in airports due to delayed or canceled flights, with no information, much less empathy, from United employees, and causes a new conditioned response, a flash of frustration—a far cry from what United would hope for.

The Trouble with Customers

Here we are, all set, having plastered on our customer-facing faces, and a client or customer walks in, or calls or e-mails us with a question, problem, or goal that our script doesn't address. How annoying! The problem is, we advertise for customers and *human beings* show up. And they never remember their passwords! So we return to the script we've memorized, while our customer grows increasingly disgruntled. Go "off script"? We don't dare.

The point is, though we can learn the language of our industry, sit up straight, dress appropriately, and speak knowledgeably about product, when the conversation doesn't feel natural, doesn't respond precisely to the customer's questions, doesn't engage the customer in an authentic way, there will ultimately be no sale. And no matter how many times we hear the same feedback *(You didn't listen to me. You focused on features and benefits before you found out what I was trying to accomplish. You didn't even look at me)*, we struggle to behave differently because we don't know *how* to get beyond our customer-facing "script." Besides, we aren't particularly interested in, much less skilled at "seeing" and responding to, each customer as a one-of-a-kind human being, which is a shame, since way back in 1982, in *Megatrends,* John Naisbitt posed "the triumph of the individual" as a new direction that would transform our lives. And it has.

Today, more than ever, consumers are seeking to be acknowledged as unique individuals with lives, needs, tastes, and desires that differ widely from those around them. One size doesn't fit all. Consider the myriad options to customize our computer desktops and cell-phone ring tones. Mine is a barking dog. What's yours?

CRM programs are designed to manage a relationship with a typical customer. The problem is, there isn't a typical customer. Yes, I know your data says there is, but there isn't, not really. And even if there were, what customer wants to be *managed?* Worse, most companies don't strive to create an actual *relationship* with customers—they view exchanges with customers as merely transactional, to be completed as quickly as possible.

A client in the manufacturing business told me recently about a vendor who lost out on hundreds of thousands of dollars of her company's business. When the vendor questioned why he lost the business, the client replied, "It wasn't because you couldn't accommodate our needs. You have the capacity to fill the order. It was because you were attempting to push a particular product that we didn't need or want. You were on a mission to close the deal. If you had taken more up-front time to talk with us, to listen to us, you would have discovered what we were actually looking for."

In other words, what the customer was really hearing was:

"Kelly, you're an important client and we value your feedback, which unfortunately has been that we are self-serving, frustrate you regularly, and only consider you a cash cow. You'll be happy to know that we have now put the words client centricity *on our website and named it as a key initiative. Since that should put your concerns to rest, we'd like you to make another purchase."*

Don't hold your breath. Use a phrase like *client centricity* and you'll not only fail to win back the business, you'll put savvy customers on edge. Your customers don't want to hear about your client-centricity initiatives. They want to hear that you will work very hard to understand their unique needs and then do everything possible to meet those needs, assuming they're legal.

How hard can that be?

Very.

You must produce the right product, in the right environment, with the right people to drive the business. You must convey the right messages, consistent messages, at the right time, via the right media, in the right way. You must deliver on your customers' expectations, keep your promises. And all the while, despite increasing costs, you must maintain margins that assure a viable business and keep your prices affordable. Meanwhile, you must match or outperform competitors who, each day, are coming up with hot new products and services.

Most business decisions are attempts to differentiate ourselves in some significant way from everyone else who is courting the same customers. And with customer choice soaring and loyalty declining, each industry has unique challenges to surmount. In *The Experience Economy,* Joseph Pine tells us that today's customers expect far more than good products and services. That's the baseline, but it's not enough. Whether they're purchasing socks, coffee, flat-screen TVs, or consulting services, customers want to enjoy the *experience* of acquiring and using those products and services, from first contact through to completion of the transaction.

So assuming your products or services are of good quality and competitively priced, one of the most powerful differentiators has to do with the conversations you have with customers. The conversation *is* the relationship. Remember? If the conversation stops (I often hang up after every attempt to get to the right person is thwarted) or is inauthentic or lacks warmth or is one-sided or canned or self-serving, then . . . well, you do the math.

A senior executive in a financial organization recently told me about a meeting that had been called to figure out why the company had suddenly arrived at a negative result with several important clients.

She told me, "As we were talking, I noticed one of our more accomplished senior managers, who is usually quite vocal, in the back of the room, deep in thought. I called on him to share his thoughts. He related that because of a series of recent events with a major client, he had been putting off a discussion with that client about fee changes.

"Up until this moment," she said, "he had felt somewhat secure in having that important 'fees' conversation at some time in the not-too-distant future. What really struck him was the sense of urgency he was now feeling to have that conversation today rather than leave it even a few more hours. He just knew that our organization was very close to 'suddenly' losing this client because of all of the missing conversations.

"By sharing his sense of urgency, he tapped into a larger awareness in the room. He brought the feeling and awareness to everyone about how our internal conversations impact what we choose to do *or not do* every day, which ultimately produces our outcomes. It was a great real-life, powerful example and a profound experience for the entire room. He actually did have that conversation shortly after the session and was able to clarify significant issues and secure our relationship with that client."

I'll never forget my first Fierce Leadership session with sixteen executives who had flown to Atlanta from around the world. I was eager to get them well launched in achieving their goals for the year.

One big problem. They learned upon arrival that they had just lost the customer that accounted for 20 percent of the company's net profit.

They were in shock. I threw out the planned agenda and helped them process this news and figure out what to do about it.

This is what came up: The client had been a difficult one, unreasonable, accusatory, combative, demanding everything yesterday for less than they originally agreed on and with extra bells and whistles thrown in for free. During the previous two years, every conversation had taken place in a war zone. No matter what good results were produced, the client never expressed appreciation or said "thank you."

It's no wonder that whenever someone thought, "I should call the client," the competing thought was, "Why ruin a perfectly good Wednesday? I'm not in the mood to be chewed up and spit out. I'll call tomorrow." And tomorrow became next week, which became next month (*gradually, gradually, you see where this is going*). Besides, even though there was no love lost on either side, this client was legally, contractually bound to the company in such a way that if it took its business elsewhere, it would have to pay a heavy penalty. It was like being stuck in the mud.

Each contentious conversation and each missing conversation took the relationship down, as emotional capital—which was never really there from the beginning—leaked out of every crack, window, and door. Have you noticed that quite often, the biggest problems and the greatest prices paid are not because of the conversations we tried to have that didn't go well, but because of the ones we didn't have? The ones we avoided. The missing conversations.

Meanwhile, who do you suppose was in there talking with this client? Right. The competition. And gradually, then suddenly, those conversations persuaded the client to come over to the other company and even managed to justify paying the penalty to break the contract.

The executives I was working with hadn't been aware of these conversations with the competition. How could they, when they had basically curtailed communication? But they were certainly aware that losing 20 percent of the company's net profit was not okay. What to do? Could *anything* be done?

First was to realize *how* the account had been lost.

Second was to ask, do we want this customer back? Are we certain?

The answer was yes, but with a greatly improved relationship. Life is short, and with some clients it feels way too long!

Third was to get the customer back the same way they lost it—one conversation at a time. So I helped them build a game plan to do just that.

The plan included humility, intimacy, accountability, apology. It included thought partnership and significant innovation, which the competition was not providing to the same degree. Mineral Rights came in handy. Eighteen months later, the client returned.

Take a moment to think about *your* customers. Who needs to hear from you? Write their names:

_____

_____

_____

_____

The House Feels Cold

Over lunch, after struggling to articulate the reason he wanted to meet with me, the head of sales effectiveness for a large organization offered this analogy: "Our people are good at designing excellent, comprehensive solutions for our clients. If you compared building a solution to building a house, they build strong houses, smart houses that can stand for all time. The trouble is, when you walk into the house, the house feels cold. We need an interior designer to warm it up."

"What words do your clients use most often to describe your people?"

"Self-serving. It's a killer. Clients use the same words over and over to describe our people: cold, no warmth, no connection, inauthentic, kept selling no matter what I said, only care about how much money you can make off of my company. It's costing us a fortune."

"What words do your clients use to describe your people?"

"Self-serving. Comes up again and again. It's a killer."

I accepted his invitation to observe three days of sales training. The theme was good old "client centricity," and it kicked off with a senior executive's presentation of the company's "burning platform," followed by a session on "inspirational leadership" (yawn), a training in negotiations, and six simulated sales meetings with salespeople who were given just one assignment: SELL.

Here's what I noticed.

The executive's opening "burning platform" focused entirely on numbers, some of which were troubling, and barely contained his pride that the company's people were always selling. At one point, he said, "Because we've been losing some talented people, we may need to raise some salaries and show appreciation for people." Something he failed to do in his ninety minutes on stage.

At the end, when asked what behaviors he would encourage, given the goals and challenges before the company, he said, without missing a beat, "Pricing! We've got to get that right."

Of course, I'm not saying that pricing and sales goals aren't important to the bottom line. But what his presentation failed to acknowledge was the humanity, the individuality, and the value of his customers *and* of his employees. No wonder the company had trouble retaining both.

There was another huge "tell" later on, when the instructor showed the following slide to four hundred people on a screen ten feet tall:

Definition of Successful Negotiation:
- satisfies the company's interests well
- satisfies clients' interests acceptably
- satisfies others' interests tolerably

I almost fell off my chair. It doesn't get more self-serving than this. After I had recovered, what I wanted to know was, when someone first floated that slide, did anyone say, "You've got to be kidding!"

By the final session on day three, stragglers were coming in late, shirts limp and wrinkled, faces damp from running. They dropped their four-inch-thick sales leadership notebooks on the table and wearily opened them to "Client Meeting Simulation #6." Time to put everything they had learned into practice and advance or close the sale.

Though I was rooting for them, I was concerned. It had become clear in earlier simulations that even when urged to demonstrate client centricity, nowhere in this training had these very smart people been taught *how* to connect with clients in a real way, much less at a deep level.

For one thing, their initial "warm-up" attempts were perfunctory and inauthentic. They simply went through the motions, and in every case, opening comments were about golf, which is about as predictable, impersonal, and insincere as you can get.

"Been spending time on the golf course?"

"A little, not much, given the big change we've got on our hands."

"Hmm, well . . . "

(awkward silence) then they would jump into active sales mode.

It might as well have been:

"How are you?"

"I'm dying."

"Glad to hear it. How much would you like to spend with us today?"

How are you?
I'm dying.
Glad to hear it. How much would you like to spend with us today?

Needless to say, no one engaged emotionally. What's more, the trainees missed the huge clues tossed out by clients (" . . . *the big change we've got on our hands . . .* ") that could have provided opportunities to learn more about the client's agenda and, in turn, could have provoked more compelling conversations, clarified appropriate "solutions," and raised clients' trust level.

When it comes to warm-ups, I'm a fan of getting to the point—no inane chitchat about golf or the weather. If it's a first meeting, why not simply say, "Thank you for your time. I've been looking forward to meeting you." *(And mean it.)* And then "What's most important to you to accomplish in our time together?" And get on with it, with stellar eye contact throughout.

If it's a second or third meeting, you can inquire about something that came up in your first meeting. This shows not only that you were listening, but that you cared enough to commit it to memory. "How was Costa Rica?" or "How did last week's meeting with your team go?"

Back at Simulation #6, the "clients" had been instructed to begin by saying, "Before you start, I should tell you the big news. We've just been acquired by ABC Corporation. So, as you can imagine, everyone here is distracted because a lot of us will undoubtedly be laid off, including me. So once the deal is inked, I might not be here."

What I wanted the trainees to say at that moment *(you would have wanted it, too)* would have been something like "That is big news. Tell me more." Or "Let's set our meeting agenda aside. How are you doing and how can I help?" And perhaps "If you leave the organization, I'd like to make some introductions. I work with several companies who might jump at the chance to bring someone of your caliber on board."

But noooooo . . . I watched three simulations, and in all three cases, the trainee's immediate response was, "Hmmm. How do you think this will affect our project?"

When I tried to tip off the last duo prior to their simulation with a note that said: "EMPATHY! Ask him how HE is?" they nodded, walked in, and said, "Thanks for the meeting. How are you?" And when the client told them about the acquisition and his possible departure, they immediately expressed concern—not about him, about the project.

"How are you" was their five seconds of "client centricity." I realized that they honestly didn't know HOW to empathize and, even more concerning, didn't seem to understand why they should.

The result? The "house" felt cold indeed. One frustrated client provided a terrific analogy: "If you came home and discovered your wife weeping in the kitchen, would the first words out of your mouth be, 'Does this mean dinner will be late?' "

At the end of the day, the head of sales training confessed to me, "This is always the point in the training where I am tempted to drink heavily." No wonder.

Happens Every Day!

No matter what your job is—whether you sell pipe fittings, design high-rise condominiums, or serve cappuccinos—the key is your *con-*

text, your beliefs about your responsibility to customers and the relationships you intend to enjoy or endure with them.

For example, if I'm in the checkout line at my local grocery store (or any checkout counter anywhere in the world), it would be easy for you to think that you're doing your job if you ring up the sale and hand me my purchases, the correct change, and a receipt. That you get points for using my name and more points if you make actual eye contact with me. That you get a bonus for pointing out reusable bags I can buy for use today and in the future. That if you have a customer loyalty program, you get more points for asking me for my membership card so you can check to see if I get a discount. And that if I don't have a membership card, you get even more points if you recommend it and I sign up.

But I'll tell you what makes the real difference. That you look into my eyes and connect with me, even if only for a few seconds. Human to human. A real smile that suggests, "I see you." This seems like such a small thing, perhaps foolish to some, yet it's what we all want, deep down where it counts. To be seen.

I'm reminded of the African greeting *sawu bona,* which means "I see you." The response is *sikhona,* which means "I am here." The order is important. It's as if until you see me, I don't exist. Raking your eyes quickly over someone's face is not seeing them. So if you want to *see* your customers, really look at them. What takes mere seconds can make people want to return again and again.

Practicing Squid Eye

What might you notice if you were practicing squid eye that would suggest you and/or your organization are not "seeing" your customers and clients as individual human beings? Check any of the following tells that apply to *your* organization.

You have an initiative called "client centricity." The fact that there is an initiative on the subject in the first place is a tell to your customers (and to everyone else) that you are *not* client centric, you are the exact opposite; otherwise, you wouldn't need an initiative in that area.

You use the term *customer facing.* This should disturb you. It implies that you have a special face that you pull out of a drawer and slap on when you're about to talk with a customer. What happened to you being *you,* consistently, no matter whom you're with? You already have a face. Yours. It's a perfectly good face. Wear it everywhere you go.

> You already have a face. Yours. It's a perfectly good face. Wear it everywhere you go.

You confuse "presentation training" with sales training. Your employees are rarely taught how to have conversations—two-way *exchanges* of ideas and sentiments—with your customers. They prefer to pitch, and even though your customers tell you that at every stage of the sale, they would greatly prefer a conversation to a presentation or a pitch, your people pale at the thought of abandoning their PowerPoint decks.

You use the term *high-performance partnering,* **though that is not your customers' experience.** "High-performance partnering" is often jargon without action, without real meaning. In actuality, there is no shared clarity in the organization about what high-performance partnering really is, how it would benefit your customers, what it actually requires, or how to sustain it once you've made the sale.

You have a relationship with your clients based primarily on very shaky ground—price. Because you are not connecting with your clients, because you have not acquired emotional capital, your price- or fee-based relationships with clients are hanging by a thread and clients are leaving because competitors are offering a similar product or service for a lower price.

You are operating on information clients shared with you six months ago. No plan survives its collision with reality, and reality changes for you and for your clients in a heartbeat, seriously complicating your favorite fantasies about how things were going to go. When was the last time you asked your customers, "What has changed since last we talked?"

Your language turns customers off. If your message or marketing materials include clichéd or insincere words and phrases like "be your own boss," "100% free," "act now," "amazing," "Dear Friend," "double your (income, satisfaction, weight loss)," "easy terms," "financial freedom," "information you requested," "instant," "limited time," "now-only offer," "satisfaction guaranteed" (and so many more), STOP IT! These words underestimate your customers' intelligence, and they'll trust you about as far as they could throw you.

You rarely challenge your customers. No matter what you're selling, you will never clink glasses with your clients to toast great results if you don't challenge a request or idea you feel is not right for them. That's true whether you're selling million-dollar solutions or prom dresses. If you enable bad habits, bad choices, bad behavior, and questionable decisions, you may struggle to look in the mirror after cashing another of your clients' checks, and it may be the last check of theirs that you cash.

You rely on software to build the "relationship." You've invested thousands, maybe millions in CRM software, which can be very valuable if it helps inform your conversations with customers, personalizing and deepening the relationship. But if CRM is primarily a data bank to be managed, sans conversations, your investment will return very little. Where in the plan do your customers, as individuals, truly reside?

You are cautioned not to use certain words that have taken on a negative connotation. The word *solutions* is an example. In the consulting field, it's considered a bad word. Apparently, customers don't like it. The question is: *Why* don't they like it? It's a tell when a perfectly good word gets a bad reputation. A further tell is that we think we've solved the problem by simply replacing the word with another. The word is not the problem. Why not focus on solving the real problem?

What Were We Thinking?

So if client centricity initiatives often fall short of expectations, why do they continue to hold such a prominent, costly place in our communications with our customers? What were we thinking?

We *were* thinking, but with only one part of our brains, the wrong part. The part that looks at relationships as only a means to an end. The part that wants to connect with customers only to the degree that it will take for them to hire us or buy our stuff so we can make money, grow the company, satisfy shareholders, pay our mortgages, and put groceries on the table and gas in the tank.

"Business," broadly speaking, has taught us to spend the minimum amount of time with customers needed to make the sale or resolve the problem, so that we can get on to the next customer. *What efficiency expert came up with that one?!*

As a result, we've made it almost impossible to make a real connection with our customers. Again, think about how hard it is for customers to reach a real person who can help them. Instead, they must listen to a lengthy list of options, none of which has anything to do with why they're calling. When they finally get to us, we come across as unengaged automatons, whose response to most queries is: "It's the company's policy." Often preceded or followed by "It's not my decision." But hey, we've been encouraged to use the customer's name! We know they like that, right?

Apparently, some companies don't want a meaningful relationship with their customers. Not really. They think, "Why should we be expected to develop genuine affection for, much less an emotional connection with, our customers? That's hard enough at home! We're pleasant enough, aren't we? We wish our customers well and hope they are happy enough with their purchases, with their decision to work with us. But we don't need to treat them like living, breathing people with families, homes, dreams, and birthdays. How about if our CRM system automatically generates birthday cards with a coupon for 20 percent off?"

If you believe this is the way business must be conducted, the way success is measured, you are destined to struggle.

What argument are *you* waging, and what are you winning if you can prove you're right?

WHAT DO YOU BELIEVE?

Take a look at the following list of beliefs and check those you currently hold.

I believe that:	I believe that:
The notion of forging a real relationship is unrealistic; I mean, really, who has time?	My most valuable currency with customers is relationship, and relationships are enriched or damaged one interaction at a time.
Customers don't want a relationship. They just want products or services.	Customers want to be seen, responded to as the individuals they are. Their "conversation" with me may be the only meaningful conversation they'll have today.
Customers can be annoying. They ask naive and stupid questions. I don't have the time or the patience to go into detail.	Customers' questions remind me how valuable my expertise is. Customers need my help.
My job in sales is to sell as much as possible for the highest amount possible, and since commission is based on that number, up-selling something a customer doesn't need is just the nature of the game.	My job in sales is to provide the best possible service to my customers. I want to sell a lot *and* I want long-term customers who come back time and time again. Sometimes that means saying, "Don't buy that."

Customers can check the status of their accounts, get answers to FAQs, place and manage purchases online. This is efficiency at its best. It's unrealistic to think we can talk with every customer. There are too many of them.

The solution to the wonderful dilemma of having too many customers to talk to is not a maddeningly pleasant voice that tells customers, "I'm sorry. That is not a valid option."

If you hold the beliefs on the left, consider the implications.

- **You will be providing poor customer service, a really lousy strategy.** This is unsustainable unless you are the only company on the planet that sells what you sell. If that isn't the case, you are already in decline. You just don't see it yet.

- **You will be underfunded.** Lacking emotional capital, you'll also have dwindling financial capital and will be forced to focus your attention on keeping the doors open or on the next round of layoffs, rather than on innovation, trends, strategy, execution.

- **Customers will leave, are leaving.** *'Nuff said.*

- **Word will get out.** Thanks to the Internet, it's easier than ever for customers to find out what others think of your company. Your company has a reputation, and it's out there. And *you* have a reputation, which will follow you throughout your career.

- **You won't enjoy your work.** Losing sales and market share or working with perpetually unhappy or departing customers is no way to live. You'll burn out, contemplate selling seashells on the seashore, which might be a good idea. Anything to relieve the stress.

Think back to the company whose salespeople held the view that their only job in client meetings was to sell. That's their context: sell, sell, sell. Growth is key—increased market share, improved margins, mega deals.

I have no argument with the overall goals of that organization. None at all. Growth *is* key! And that company's people have the intellectual chops to get it right for their clients. They know their stuff, believe in their stuff, and want to close the sale.

Trouble is, their clients have different, competing beliefs. In addition to goals achieved and problems solved, they want thought, leadership, innovation. They want to have their learning provoked, hear new ideas. They'd like to be thinking differently when the conversation is over. They want to know what other companies are doing that's smart. They want to be alerted to mistakes and pointed toward the path that is best for them. They want flexibility and innovation on the structure of the deal, as well as the solution. They see a clear line between self-serving behavior on your part and what's best for them, and they will be extremely irritated if you cross that line. And sometimes they just need someone to talk to because things aren't going so well and they've had a tough day.

In short, they don't want to be treated like customers; they want to be treated like people. That is *real* client centricity. And in addition to considerable professional expertise, it requires deep listening and the ability to connect as human beings—proven time and time again to win customer loyalty, boost profits, and make your company the kind of place where consumers like to do business and talented people like to work.

The Fierce Practice: Customer Connectivity

If you want to become a great organization, one that endures and thrives despite economic downturns, fluctuations in the global stock market, climate change, and escalating costs of doing business, then gain the capacity to connect with your customers at a deep level, or lower your aim. And this practice starts with *you;* it is the individuals in our organizations who build relationships with customers and consistently win new business one conversation at a time.

Connecting with customers is neither a naive notion nor a "soft skill." It is an essential skill, one that requires courage, because it involves a fair degree of intimacy, which is initially uncomfortable for many people.

I like the following formula from David Maister and Charles Green, coauthors of *The Trusted Advisor,* because it adds intimacy to the mix and also accounts for the significant damage done when we put our own interests (closing the sale, making our quota) before the interests of our customers.

$$\frac{C + R + I}{S - O}$$

$$\frac{\text{credibility} + \text{reliability} + \text{intimacy}}{\text{self-orientation}}$$

Most successful companies are credible and reliable, but they don't always view intimacy as an important part of the equation; in fact, many don't even have a good model for what intimacy *is,* what it would look like in action.

Remembering the names of your customers' dogs may score you some points, but it won't land you the contract. Neither will lowering the price, except perhaps in the very short term. And neither will halfhearted, meager "customer-facing" or "client centricity" initiatives. Only true intimacy—being warm, authentic, truthful, and familiar—can transform a bad relationship into a good one.

Assignment: Think about a customer relationship you value and diagnose where the strengths are and where the relationship could use some shoring up.

Jot down your insight(s):

_____

_____

_____

_____

How can you add intimacy to your conversations with customers? By having conversations with them that they can't find on any street corner. No matter what your company does or sells, whether your customer conversations are typically lengthy or brief, ideally your conversations with customers will . . .

- interrogate reality (concerning your customer's agenda and well-being)
- provoke learning (about your customer's goals and needs)
- tackle tough topics (clarify a next step to take, whether it's to produce a tall breve latte or prepare a proposal)
- enrich relationships (acquire both intellectual *and* emotional capital)

. . . leading to high-performance partnership—experienced, delivered!

In case you're thinking, "Intimacy? I sell cupcakes!" (or mutual funds or computer software or knives), let me remind you that this formula works, no matter what business you're in. If you want to sell LOTS of cupcakes (or mutual funds or computer software or knives) to happy repeat customers, there is something here for you. And what's more, while there are cultural differences across the country and around the world, the suggestions in this chapter work well no matter where you go.

Kate Carter, a barista on Orcas Island, achieves intimacy by remembering what her regular customers like and going the extra mile to provide it. The first time I met Kate, she noticed me hesitating when she asked, "One shot or two?" So she said, "How about one and a half?"

"You can do that?"

"You bet!" And now that's what she prepares for me each time I come. The perfect latte. So imagine my disappointment when I ask for one and a half shots at other coffee shops and am invariably told, "We can't do that because it's not programmed into the order system, so there's no way to charge for one and a half shots." Now I ask you, would that really be so hard? A child could do the math.

So when I'm on Orcas Island, where do you think I choose to go for my coffee? I can't begin to count the number of one-and-a-half-shot breves I've purchased from Kate. And even when she's very busy, she manages to talk somewhat intimately with each customer. It's not the coffee or the coffee shop alone that draws me, though the view is spectacular. It's the experience that draws me. It's Kate that draws me.

Connecting with customers is critical and entirely possible, in fact EASY. The customer conversation that achieves intimacy, connection, better and quicker than any other is Mineral Rights, which I introduced in Fierce Practice #2 as a way to point people toward accountability.

As you'll recall, the goal of a Mineral Rights conversation is to identify the most important issue you should be talking about, achieve greater clarity about the issue (including what part of the issue has our DNA on it), create impetus for action (accountability), and enrich the relationship. That conversation is also covered in depth in *Fierce Conversations.*

Here, we will adapt Mineral Rights for conversations with your customers. But before we do, there are several other things I encourage you to practice.

CONNECTION BEFORE CONTENT

First and foremost, stop selling! Customers don't want to be sold to. They want you to genuinely care about them, to be there. In Asian cultures, it's always connection first, business second. Many years ago, when I lived in Japan, I studied the tea ceremony, which is entirely focused on providing someone with an exquisite, total sensory experience. Not only is tea carefully prepared and served, but everything about the environment in which the ceremony is performed—sight, scent, sound, and gentle conversation—is given thought. Thus, the tea ceremony provides an experience of being cared for. Today, business meetings in Japan are often begun with a tea ceremony, not always the lengthy and formal ceremony that I studied, but at the very least an unhurried, relaxed enjoyment of tea, accompanied by equally unhurried and relaxed conversation—one that facilitates connection.

In the United States we make the mistake of business first because "that's how it's always been done." We start meetings or relationships with "all business" because it makes us look "professional." But connection trumps "professional" every time. I'm not advocating that you swing the pendulum to just "connection." I'm recommending that you balance your "content" agenda with a "connection" agenda, so that you are a "connecting professional."

Did you know that the fastest way to connect with someone is through laughter? When was the last time you and your clients had a good laugh?

Enrich the connection by checking in with your customer following the "sale": "How are things working? Are you happy? Is there anything you need?"

FOCUS ON INDIVIDUALS, NOT COMPANIES

Remember, you are selling to an organization via an individual. Or several individuals. Don't forget that ABC company didn't buy your services, ANDY did. Or Susan, Katherine, and Chad. So how do you sustain relevant relationships with individuals with the decision-making power in their organizations?

Do all that you can to ensure their success. Work to understand and embrace their agendas. Make their agendas your own. Understand what individuals are trying to do, and personalize your work with them. Be voracious about learning. Sit in on meetings. Understand their competition. Make your interest personal, authentic, and passionate. Strap on your helmet and take the field with your customers. Then stay in the game until the whistle blows.

Rally the rest of the team around the client's agenda. Make sure no one tries to sell anything that doesn't connect to the client's agenda. The right thing at the right time to the right person.

If you can influence individuals' success—whether it's by bringing them the deal that will wow their boss or by selling them the minivan that will get their kids to soccer practice on time—you will succeed. Plus, these relationships will come in handy down the line. People are mobile. A tenure of two to three years at a job is normal. That's a positive for you if you have the relationship. When you knock on someone's new door, she will let you in because she knows you and trusts you and you stayed close to her through thick and thin.

SLOW THE CONVERSATION DOWN, WAY DOWN

Consumers have become cynical. So no matter what product or service your company is selling, people's perception of your intent is far more important than any technique you might employ. When you're in a rush to close the deal, customers' trust radars will go up. Slow the conversation down so that it can find out what it really wants and needs to be about. Your goal is to earn your customers' trust by connecting with them, creating a container of safety and intimacy in which they will talk candidly about what they need so that you can help them achieve their goals—no matter how long it takes.

BE WILLING TO PLAY "LITTLE BALL"

Chris Douglas, a key executive at Fierce Inc., has season tickets to the Mariners games in Seattle and uses the concept of playing "little ball" to explain how client relationships often evolve over time. In Chris's words, "Don't go to the plate swinging for the fences. It's more important to get on base. Once you're there, you can open up the game. Often people contact us for a very specific, targeted reason. It's important to explore that and then open the conversation up to other possibilities."

This can be tough when you know there's a larger idea, product, service, or "sale" that would benefit a new client or customer significantly. When you're eager and excited to tell him about it and because it would solve multiple problems for him, it's hard to listen to him talk about this teeny-weeny solution about which he's inquiring. But if you don't really listen because you're waiting for the chance to swing for the fences, your customer will pick up on that. Think about the effect this will likely have on your opportunity to connect with this customer right here, right now.

Even though a far bigger engagement will accomplish more of what your customer needs, and your intentions are good, stop. Practice principle 3 of Fierce Conversations: *Be here, prepared to be nowhere else.* Shove all other agendas aside and pitch your tent on this conversation, this issue, this individual, this next best step. If you do, your next turn at bat might be a home run.

SELF-DISCLOSE WHEN APPROPRIATE

If you are open, vulnerable, disclosing, more likely than not it will be reciprocated and walls will come down. In contrast, if you are "steel encased in concrete," as a brilliant and lonely executive once described himself to me, your relationships will be tenuous at best, because no one will feel they know who you really are.

Do all of us and yourself a huge favor and get beyond golf, the weather, and the local sports team. Talk about your family, vacations, et cetera. Ask about theirs. Send photos of yourself and family so that they can attach a face to your voice. You don't need a professional head shot. The photo on the jacket of this book is a photo I sometimes attach to proposals, so people who are just getting to know me will get a feel for who I am. I'm wearing jeans and wellies, not a power suit, and I'm surrounded by my dogs. Beside the photo, I usually write, "I look forward to our next conversation."

My colleague Cam Tripp shares a photo of his son, Gabriel, with Fierce clients and, as a result, Cam's clients are deeply connected to Cam and even send him photos of their own families.

Go into your calls and meetings with a genuine curiosity about

the person with whom you're talking. Look at each conversation as one that may lead to or deepen a friendship. Ask a personal question, and share something personal about yourself. If you are present and stay interested, you will learn and remember personal things that can take the relationship deeper. Obviously, don't talk *too* long about yourself. One man whom I respect professionally talked ad nauseam about his daughter every time I saw him, until I found myself avoiding him. Yeah, yeah, she's a great kid, but pleeeeease spare me another long story about her achievements.

BE AUTHENTIC (ASSUMING YOU AREN'T AN A&@&?E)

Hand in hand with self-disclosure comes authenticity, which is missing in most customer conversations. Do away with the notion of "customer facing." Stop trying to project an image you imagine your customers desire, and instead, show up as YOU. Assuming you have the right products or solutions for your customers and the ability to execute, who you really are will work just fine—better than fine.

On the other hand, refrain from disclosing things about your personal life that may make customers see you in a negative light. For example, I've seen people take the unconscious strategy of trying to connect by sharing information about their messy divorce and the curse they'd like to place on their ex, or the argument they "won" last night at the bar.

Authenticity also requires that you know when to say "I don't know. Let me look into that and get back to you." This is far more productive than pretending to know the answer, and customers will respect you for admitting you might not have all the answers and for being willing to go the extra mile to get them what they need.

BECOME A RESOURCE

Most customers aren't looking for a white knight who will single-handedly vanquish all the dragons. Customers are looking for someone who will help them get it right, keep them out of trouble, and bring them resources. In a global economy where customers face increasing choices and the bar gets higher and higher, this is one of the best ways to build and enrich the relationship.

A common mistake is to underestimate what you know and overestimate what your customers know. Bring them the ideas, the innovation, that only you can bring. When there are others who can do aspects of the job far better than you can, make introductions. Because you understand the PERSON, you know the sort of people he or she will like to work with. When your clients look at the teams you have assembled to help them, you want them to have strong respect for everyone you've introduced to them and be very upset if anyone leaves.

Share articles, research. If there's a connection to be made, make it. If there is something another company is doing that might benefit your customer and you are free to disclose it, tell him or her about it. If you think a customer is about to step off a cliff, warn him or her and point him or her to the safety net, even if it isn't your net. This is about paying it forward with no agenda.

DITCH THE BUZZWORDS, THE JARGON, THE POWERPOINT DECK

Are you aware that most of your customers groan inwardly when you come to a meeting and fire up your laptop? It's true. Yet I've been told by many executives that their people would be paralyzed without their PowerPoint decks—that they don't know how to simply have a conversation, that the thought terrifies them.

I can hear you now. "But with PowerPoint, we can put up cool data on the screen that visually illustrates the case we want to make, whereas our people would have a tough time just describing it in words. Besides, some people are visual. They need something to look at."

Instead of looking at a screen, your audience should be looking at, connecting with, *you*. I love technology and am one of those visual people. And we do use PowerPoint slides in our Fierce training classes. But we use them *sparingly*. And that's the key. I can almost promise you that your next client call or sales meeting will be far more successful if you either abandon PowerPoint altogether or cut the number of slides by two-thirds. Come on, take the leap!

The same goes for jargon. It amazes me when a salesperson or consultant confuses me with impenetrable jargon—confusing, unspecific terms or phrases that mean nothing to people outside their field or organization. Are they showing off? Is their goal to be condescending and annoying?

Internally, jargon provides a useful shorthand that everyone understands, but customers are irritated when we insist on using jargon they don't understand. Compile and ban your own list of "nonwords." Above all, lose the word *centricity*. Don't be customer centric or patient centric or student centric or anything centric. Take it off your website, out of your marketing materials. It's jargon and fails to convey in any meaningful way what you intend and your customer desires.

INVITE CUSTOMERS TO PLANNING SESSIONS

Many business development and salespeople are shocked at the thought of having a client planning meeting with the actual client present. They offer lots of reasons why they shouldn't, why they couldn't, why it wouldn't work, why it would be too uncomfortable for them and for their clients. But in fact, it is a wonderful way to deepen the connection and enrich the relationship.

Think of this meeting as simply a forum for your client to tell you more. After your initial conversations with a new client, a planning session is an opportunity to ensure you heard right. Focus the meeting on further defining and agreeing on the ideal outcomes. If they are not clearly defined or are unrealistic or inappropriate, or if there is no verbal agreement or commitment to an agreed-upon "end in mind," you are setting yourself and your client up for frustration, possibly failure.

Say, "Here's what we think are your focuses and priorities. Is this right?" Clients often share new information during this meeting that is critical for your success.

During this meeting intent is far more important than what you actually say. If your intent is right, that will come across. And only after you and your client agree that you understand should you talk about some of the things you are doing with other clients and give your initial recommendations.

If you will be accompanied by a colleague, have a plan for the call. Will you "show up" as two soloists competing for airtime or as a well-coordinated team demonstrating mutual respect? If you are both skilled at Mineral Rights conversations, you might agree that both of you may probe during each step but that one of you will determine when it's time to advance to the next step.

INQUIRE ABOUT YOUR CUSTOMER'S ÜBERGOALS

At an appropriate time during an early conversation with your client— only when she trusts your intent completely—ask about her company's or department's overall goals and strategies. Tell her you'd like to understand these things because you understand that her success will be based on her ability to make better decisions on a long-term basis and that you are committed to making sure that everything you do will support her larger goals and possibly help directly with them.

Say, "Keeping your goals and strategy in mind, here are the things we'll do, the principles we'll follow to help you with these things. This is our commitment to you."

ENGAGE WITH CUSTOMERS AS EQUALS

Two frequent customer complaints are "You haven't taken the lead as strongly as needed" and "You haven't challenged us enough."

The customer conversation should be a conversation between equals, containing a feeling of mutuality, rather than talking at someone, talking down to someone, or being subservient to someone. In fact, so should all the other conversations you have in your life—with family, friends, colleagues, the CEO of your company, your favorite barista, the waiter at the Mexican restaurant, the prime minister, the butcher, the banker, the candlestick maker.

You may not agree that we're all equal, and I'm not here to convince you otherwise. But I do want you to consider that when you see yourself as less than, lower than, or subservient to someone else, he or she picks that up, and most (with the exception of a few crazy dictators) don't respond well. And it isn't healthy for you. And if you think you're superior to or better than others, well, get over yourself.

PUT SKIN IN THE GAME

Be prepared to invest. Whether negotiating a deal, making a sale, or drafting a contract, sometimes we forget that customers judge what they think *you* invested. If you try to sell an expensive piece of work that doesn't take a lot of effort or investment on your part, even if it gives your client a good return on investment, your client will not be confident in your commitment. Clients don't mind your making a healthy profit. They do mind feeling that the deal is unbalanced and you are not putting in the effort that justifies the fee. So the value is in the outcome your work produces relative to your perceived investment. All parties should have skin in the game.

WIN THE RIGHT CUSTOMERS, THE RIGHT WORK

Ah, the time, dollars, energy, and sleepless nights wasted on brightly colored Easter eggs that look pretty in the basket and are never going to hatch. I'm referring, of course, to all those sales that never closed. We were bewitched, excited, hopeful that the deal would go through. But maybe these eggs were never going to hatch from the beginning. How would we know? We can ask ourselves, "Did we spend enough time testing the client, gathering evidence that our product or service would meet his or her needs? Did we ask ourselves often enough whether we should even pursue this work? Did we do the market research to make sure we weren't chasing customers we shouldn't be chasing? Did we go after customers who insist on a first-rate result for a fourth-rate price?"

Yes, your competitive edge will be your ability to connect with customers. That said, you absolutely needn't connect with everyone. Some customers, some people, some industries, some individuals simply aren't worth the time, energy, and resources you'd have to put into them. It's kind of like fishing. You can spend as much time and energy hooking and hauling in what turns out to be an old boot as you can hauling in dinner. I bet you can think of a customer right now that was or is a giant sucking sound in your life, that has sucked up tons of your time and energy and left you parched and exhausted. Every seasoned businessperson I know has worked with very small clients who were more demanding and required more time and energy than large clients. And large clients who were, well, jerks!

One of the smartest things you can do is be more rigorous in your initial conversations with prospective customers, so that you win the right work and can focus on delivering it. When we've got a number of great clients, we tend to be more selective and don't end up fishing in so many wrong ponds and going on so many bad "dates." Some suggestions:

- Determine what your ideal win ratio should be. If you could win 50 or 60 or 70 percent of the work you go after, what effect would that have on the quality of your life, on your income, on your enjoyment of your work?

- Be realistic about how many clients or customers you can handle. No individual has the capacity to do good work for an unlimited number of customers. If you take on too much work and stretch yourself too thin, you may find yourself overworked and exhausted, and your results for ALL your customers and clients will suffer.

- Upgrade your prospective client list so that they contain only viable prospects. Consider declining blind requests for proposals where you have no relationship.

- Look at the potential yield from a prospective customer over the course of a year. Does it make sense for you to spend the same amount of time on unprofitable work that will suck the life out of you as you would on profitable work that is enjoyable?

ACKNOWLEDGE MISTAKES

Ideally, you'll deliver what you agreed to deliver on time, within budget. Otherwise, you're just noise. Charming, perhaps, but just noise. But given that you're not perfect, sometimes you'll make mistakes. How you handle this, stepping up to the issues when things are challenging, is beyond important; it's critical. Ducking the issue or trying to dodge responsibility is the quickest way to the exit. Remember, you should be modeling accountability at all times! Be forthright and transparent about any missteps you've made, as soon as you know you've made them.

A tip on how to apologize: Don't say, "I'm really sorry you feel that way." That's the response of someone who won't acknowledge his or her contribution to the problem. Don't be sorry someone *feels* that way. Be sorry that you did whatever you did (or didn't do) that *caused* the person to feel that way. Say, "I'm sorry that I [fill in the blank]. I messed up, and I want to correct this, make this right." Stop there. Don't go into WHY you messed up, all the reasons and excuses for messing up. Just say you're sorry and move into "fix-it" mode.

MEET WITH CUSTOMERS IN PERSON

Nothing replaces or beats connections made face to face. When two people are in close physical proximity, the heart reads and understands the other heart (i.e., intention, spirit, et cetera). Stop advocating for larger budgets for technology that "manages" an online customer conversation. Advocate for larger travel budgets so that you can visit clients face to face. Individuals on the Fierce team have traveled, at our expense, to Brussels, Sydney, London, Dubai, and other points on the compass to meet with key contacts face to face, even if only for a few hours. This has invariably resulted in deeper connection and intimacy and is a very real demonstration of our investment in the relationship. Is air travel costly? Yes, it is. But the cost of lost customers is higher.

LIST OF "DONT'S"

Don't try to go around protocol or bypass a customer who is ambivalent or seems hostile toward you by going over his or her head. This will alienate the person you tried to avoid and make an enemy for life. Don't criticize him or her to others and don't violate his or her values unless not doing so would violate a core value of yours.

Don't give clients a position on difficult issues, then back off it when challenged. This will not only confuse your clients, but damage your credibility.

Don't convey the attitude that you disrespect your primary competitor or anyone else in the business.

Don't make presentations. Don't "present," period. It shuts people down. Have a conversation instead.

Don't be so sensitive to internal politics that you are scared to tell customers what they need to know because you're trying to protect your relationships within the company. If you are unable to dissuade someone from doing something you feel would damage his or her company, you need to take action.

Don't train new people on the backs of client relationships. In other words, don't bring in new people then quickly move them, so that just when a customer feels someone is getting to know him or her, that person is gone. It's not about whether your people are good or bad. It's about their ability to gain a client's trust and confidence.

Don't mistake customer apathy for customer loyalty. Don't assume that because a client is still with you, he or she is loyal to you. He or she may just not have gotten around to making the switch. Customer loyalty lasts only as long as the transaction. If you do a bad job, you're replaceable. You win and retain work in a competitive context. Always.

Let's look at Mineral Rights, the best customer connectivity conversation I've ever experienced.

Mineral Rights with Customers

There are essentially two gears in customer conversations—active and receptive. In active gear, your goal is to sell—whether it's a product, a service, a plan, or an idea. You do most of the talking; the customer listens. You are often smiling, talking fast, enthusiastic about your subject. You might not always recognize that your customer is tuning out, turning off.

In receptive gear, the goal is to understand the customer's agenda through a balance of questioning and listening. The challenge is to lower your internal dialogue so you can focus on the other person. Your customer does most of the talking. This is not a passive gear. It takes energy to concentrate, to pay attention to what is really going on. If you don't listen to exactly what your customer is telling you, you won't be able to ask good questions. And if you don't ask good questions, you won't find out what you need to know. Many people miss opportunities because they fail to draw out the key information that will help them get the best results. Plus, when you're good at the receptive gear, asking questions and listening intently, it raises customers' energy level and increases their engagement in the conversation. Many customers, if they're not being asked good questions, disengage.

Most people, especially salespeople, are skilled in the active mode. But Mineral Rights requires that you be strong in both gears and be able to fluidly shift between them. It is the combination of active and receptive gears that allows a breakthrough to honest ground and expanded possibilities with your customer.

Whether your goal is a one-time transaction or a long-term relationship, the Mineral Rights conversation will help you gain a deep understanding of your customers' needs, rather than make quick assumptions *("Oh, I know just what this customer needs")*. It will help you stop talking and listen to learn rather than to pitch. The conversation should be a mutual exploration during which you resist suggesting products or solutions. Remember, products and solutions have no inherent value—relationships have the value. Mineral Rights builds these relationships not only by clarifying needs but also by uncovering emotions. I think of it as a Swiss Army knife we should carry with us at all times!

The secret sauce, the element that differentiates the Mineral Rights conversation from all others you may have had with customers, is that it allows you to surface your customer's emotions by inquiring about what is at stake to win or lose if his or her goals are not met. If you can feel yourself putting the brakes on as you read this (maybe you think that asking about emotions seems awkward or unprofessional or not "you") remember that people—customers—make decisions first for emotional reasons, second for rational ones. We talked about that in Fierce Practice #2. If your house is cold, you could lose the business or the sale because there is no real "heat" (emotion), nothing for a lit match to ignite.

Note: I always ask "What do you feel?" rather than "How does that make you feel?" Nothing makes us feel anything. Our emotions are an inside job, a choice we make, often unconscious.

The Mineral Rights conversation will also help you determine if this is a viable opportunity for you or your organization. After all, do you want to make a run for everything that crosses your path, or might it be wise to scrub your pipeline, so you can focus on key opportunities?

The model helps you sense when to change drill bits and probe deeper. Part of your job is to slow this conversation down so it can discover what it really wants and needs to be about, to help your customer identify the core issue, so that you can partner with your customer in identifying the best product or solution. To recap, the steps in a Mineral Rights conversation are as follows.

STEP 1: IDENTIFY THE ISSUE.

You are essentially asking: "Why are we talking? What is the *most* important thing we should be talking about?" The biggest error salespeople make is to suggest products or solutions at this stage or immediately jump to a story about how they solved this exact problem for ABC Company and what a spectacular result they got. DON'T DO IT! Even if your customer asks about solutions, don't dive into your sales pitch. Instead, realize that your mission is first to understand what matters most to your customers, where it hurts, what they're trying to achieve or resolve. Until you do, you won't know which of your products or services, if any, will be the best fit.

Don't be so quick to assume you know what's important to your customers. You could be in for a big surprise. Hold off and return to the problem they're trying to solve and the result they're trying to achieve. There's much you could talk about. You want to choose exactly the right product or solution to focus on, and it's way too early in the conversation to do this. Additionally, I'm sure you've noticed that what a customer asks for isn't always what a customer needs.

STEP 2: CLARIFY THE ISSUE.

This is where you'll work to identify the real issue and begin to determine how (and if) your company can address it. There may be multiple issues. You may not be dealing with the real or most important issue. Is the issue your customer is presenting a symptom or a root cause? Might your organization be able to solve the entire problem or just part of it? Or none of it?

Check your assumptions as well as theirs, particularly those that could cause both of you to miss the mark. Assumptions such as

- There actually *is* a problem and a solution.
- There is only one problem and only one solution.
- I understand what the problem is.
- I have the solution.
- I've got a solution, and I'm pretty sure you've got a problem, and even if you don't, the solution is so cool, you should want it.

STEP 3: DETERMINE CURRENT IMPACT.

This is where you begin to qualify the "opportunity." Is this a viable opportunity for your organization, or should you decline? Draw out the customer. What evidence is there that the problem exists? What results is this producing? Is the evidence hard or soft (anecdotal, opinion-based, not measured effectively)? How do you measure this? How is it impacting the organization? Who else is this affecting? How is this affecting *you?* When you consider everything you just described, what do you feel?

STEP 4: DETERMINE FUTURE IMPACT.

Clarify the importance of this issue. Is this truly a priority relative to other problems or initiatives? Will there be sufficient ROI when this is resolved? What systemic implications must be considered? Will solving/achieving this cause even bigger problems elsewhere? Who is committed to solving this problem? Take away the solution and see if the customer cares.

If they fight for it, great. If they don't you just learned there's no opportunity here.

STEP 5: EXAMINE INDIVIDUAL CONTRIBUTION TO THE ISSUE.

This topic is rarely explored in conversations with prospective customers. Asking it will certainly differentiate you from your competition, and though this level of inquiry may seem risky, it will likely send your credibility skyrocketing. It indicates that you're courageous in your search for all of the relevant "truths" that are key to resolving the customer's problem or achieving his or her goals. And occasionally, the biggest obstacle to success is the individual sitting in front of you.

Problems can be caused by systems, by individuals, by both. Ask your customer or client, "How might you have contributed to this problem/issue? In other words, what piece of this issue has your DNA on it? Might you and/or others find it difficult to make the changes required for resolution? If yes, what would it take to create impetus for change?"

STEP 6: DESCRIBE THE IDEAL OUTCOME.

So far, the conversation has been focused on the problem, what the problem is costing the organization, and your customer's emotions around the problem. Now it's time to lighten up and clarify ideal outcomes, specific goals, what "winning" would look like, how it would be measured, and what your customer's positive emotions would be if outcomes were achieved.

STEP 7: COMMIT TO ACTION.

If there is interest and willingness, on both sides, to pursue this opportunity, and it's clear that partnering with you will provide more value to your customer than going it alone, it's time to determine mutuality of effort and next steps. Find out what could get in the way. Ask, "How will the decision to stop or move forward be made? Who will be involved in that decision? What do you see as the next most important steps? What might get in the way, and how will we get past that? What's the time frame? When would you like to meet again? Who else should be there?"

Sometimes when I demonstrate a Mineral Rights conversation at a training session, I ask the audience to note what questions they would have liked to ask during each step. I am always impressed and humbled by the terrifically insightful questions they come up with and wish I had thought to ask them myself. So don't be bound to the words I've suggested. Ask the questions that make sense given the topic. Just don't stray out of a step onto a rabbit trail that derails or confuses the conversation.

STEP 8: OFFER SUGGESTIONS.

By now, your customer will be sincerely interested in hearing your ideas because something invisible and critical has developed—a real connection. You've gained credibility because you've kept the focus on his or her problem and goals, not on your products or services. Once you've earned your customer's trust and given the in-depth exploration you've facilitated, whatever you suggest toward the close of the conversation or meeting will be far superior to anything you might have suggested earlier in the conversation.

At this point, you'll also want to ask your customer if he or she has all the information he or she needs about you and your organization to make a decision about going forward. And you should ask about your competition. With whom has the customer talked? Is he or she pleased with the ideas he or she has heard so far? If not, what would have to be different?

You've earned the right to ask this last question because you've achieved intimacy—the key, often-missing ingredient in conversations, the ingredient that tips the scale on how much information a potential customer shares with you, as well as the final decision.

$$\frac{\text{credibility (20)} + \text{reliability (20)} + \text{intimacy (60)} = 100}{\text{self-orientation} = 0}$$

Your score = 100. You win. And so does your customer.

I've never—and I mean NEVER—had a customer pull back or resist this conversation. Many customers even find it so useful that they begin to practice this model with their customers. They lean in—we both do—because even though it may be a formula, it is the right formula, there for the right reasons: not to manipulate, but to connect, to understand, to enrich the relationship and get it right for the customer. Of course, in any business, the goal is still to sell, but to sell the right things to the right people or organizations, at the right time, in the right way. Big bonus: genuine affection for and emotional connection with your customers, which translates to returning customers who trust you.

During a Fierce Conversations training at Starbucks, after practicing Mineral Rights, the managers recognized that one of their top executives has used this conversational model for several years and consequently has differentiated himself from others in leadership roles, excelling at creating value for the people he leads, even during challenging economic times.

WHEN MINERAL RIGHTS ISN'T PRACTICAL.

Of course, there are always going to be situations where it is neither practical nor appropriate for you to take your customers through Mineral Rights. For example, if you worked at a coffee shop and someone ordered a nonfat latte, they'd think you were nuts if you tried to launch a Mineral Rights conversation, and your manager would point out the long line of customers waiting! *How do you feel about skim milk versus one percent? Can you identify your emotions surrounding this issue?* So when your typical transactions are quick and fairly basic, what can you do to connect with customers?

- For starters, LOOK AT THEM. I acknowledge that there are cultures where making eye contact is considered disrespectful, but those are exceptions. Since a basic need of most human beings is to be seen, not looking at your customer is a missed opportunity. I've shared the African greeting *sawu bona* (I see you), and the response, *sikhona* (I am here). If you aren't looking at your customers, the message you're sending is that they don't exist. Not a good strategy to encourage return business.

- Smile. I'm sorry if you're having a bad day or if you don't feel so hot, but don't transmit your sour mood to your customers. When things are seriously "off" for you, either stay home or learn how to fake it! This is about them, not you.

Taking It to the Organization

Think back to the story I told you about the cold house. Your company could have the most solid foundation and the most sturdy structure, but if it is freezing inside, no one will want to come over for dinner. The point is, "sell" isn't a wrong message. But *how* you sell will make all the difference, so in addition to training your sales force in Mineral Rights, here are some broad ideas that can help your organization connect with customers in a warm, meaningful way.

ENCOURAGE CUSTOMER RELATIONSHIPS AT ALL LEVELS OF THE ORGANIZATION

Too often, leaders and executives write white papers, craft case studies, and build PowerPoint decks while avoiding conversations with the living, breathing people upon whom the success of the company truly depends.

I know an executive whose people go the extra mile for the company and its customers in part because this executive talks with customers one on one, inviting candid input and listening intently to whatever customers say. She's a busy woman who runs a large company, and everyone would understand if she only left her office to attend meetings, but she understands the importance of acquiring both intellectual *and* emotional capital. One of her employees told me, "When she's with you, she's really WITH you."

Some executives might think that building relationships with customers is a job for the sales team or for the customer service department. And it is, but everyone in the company—no matter what their rank or position—should have a personal connection with customers, at least on some level.

MEASURE AND REWARD CONNECTIVITY THROUGHOUT THE COMPANY

What gets tracked and rewarded tends to improve. So if connectivity is important to you, track and reward it. This is one of the things they do at Starbucks, where connecting with customers has always been and continues to be a key to the unique Starbucks experience. An idea—Blended Beverage BINGO—conceived in 2001 by John Moore and Paul Williams is still talked about today as an example of a great program that encouraged Starbucks employees to connect meaningfully with customers.

When John was asked to develop ideas for a store-level incentive contest to drive sales of Frappuccinos, he turned to Paul for help in coming up with a creative approach to product sampling, which had been a major driver of the company's success.

When it comes to sampling, there are two approaches. Passive sampling is when customers help themselves to a sample of a product sitting on a table or near a register. Active sampling is when a store partner (employee) physically hands a customer a sample and engages him or her in a conversation. It's probably no surprise to you that active sampling is by far the best way to connect with customers and drive product sales. The challenge for John and Paul, then, was to create an incentive for employees to walk around the store inviting customers to actively sample products.

On FastCompany.com, John Moore posted John and Paul's story in "The Anatomy of a Starbucks Customer Experience Program."

> PW: As we were brainstorming, we started talking about how much fun we had playing timeless childhood board games like Candyland, LIFE, Connect Four, and Mousetrap. The kitschier the game, the better. We thought it would be great to connect with store partners by turning the incentive contest into a board game—like the ones we used to play as kids. I mentioned that I had recently played BINGO with some friends and that is where we had our EUREKA moment.
>
> JM: Paul suggested we model the incentive contest around BINGO. We wouldn't use numbers. Instead, we would replace the numbers with a fun activity that would ask a store partner to interact with a customer all the while sampling them a beverage.
>
> PW: For example, we created activities like: Sample a Mocha Frappuccino to a customer working on a laptop; sample Tazoberry to a customer wearing a red article of clothing; teach a customer to order their favorite blended beverage using the "Starbucks drink language." For the center squares, we got really wacky with one that asked store partners to get five customers and two partners to form a "conga" line in-store.
>
> JM: Not only was this program fun for store partners, it was fun for customers. I remember one store sent us their completed BINGO card and a laminated poster that featured photos of their store partners and customers doing all twenty-five activities on the BINGO card.
>
> PW: The end result was sales of blended beverages increased and the morale of store partners increased as well. Just last week, I was at a meeting where someone mentioned this tactic from 2 years ago! Time and time again, Blended Beverage BINGO has been mentioned as one of the most successful ways we helped partners deliver great customer experiences.

Moore added that not only was this an innovative way to enhance sales and drive profit by making sampling fun and top-of-mind, but it enhanced the Starbucks culture by encouraging meaningful interaction between store partners and their customers. "It created dialogue, offered our customers a special treat and delight, and provided store partners the chance to step out from behind the bar and interact with their customers."

What could your company's version of Blended Beverage BINGO look like? How would it be played? Where would it be played? By whom? With whom? What would you call it? What would be the ultimate goals? How could you capture activities? In addition to having fun, connecting with customers, and increasing sales, what incentive would excite your employees or team members?

Of course, people want to be stars, want to get credit for their ideas, want to "own" the customer relationship. This ambition is natural, given that many people are evaluated or compensated based on performance—and this is often linked to the business they bring in or the sales they make. But remember, the deal or the sale should be secondary to the relationship. So I'd advise you to reward or incentivize your people for making the connections, not just closing the deal.

KEEP EVERYONE ON MESSAGE

It goes without saying that everyone in your company should get the message about the importance of building deep, authentic customer connections and that you should practice what you preach and back this up with actions.

If your "burning platform" focuses entirely on financial scorecards but fails to address, capture, and enrich your customers' experience, you're in no danger of bringing customer connectivity to life. Worse, you're out of integrity.

For example, a goal of an organization I've worked with is to target and win "heavenly clients." Based on my experience of it, the organization needs to *become* a heavenly client for its own vendors. They cannot attract what they themselves are not demonstrating. Case in point was

Fierce's extended arm wrestling in the circus tent with someone in the organization's legal department (let's call him Fred), whose demands were so inappropriate, uncalled-for, and arduous, the only way we could get through it was to laugh. And the contractual nightmare we had to go through to get a reasonable agreement in place, just so I could pay the organization the visit it had requested, gave us serious pause.

Another huge tell that something was seriously wrong in this organization was that Fred resisted a conversation. He did not supply any phone number we could call and ignored requests for a phone call, which meant a lot of unhelpful e-mails back and forth. Even though an eventual conversation helped us arrive at clarity and agreement, Fred continued to nitpick with a lot of legal garbage around stupid details—all via e-mail—which required more unnecessarily time-consuming work on our side. We determined that if we continued working with the organization, we'd have to raise our fees to cover the legal costs incurred by our dealings with Fred. Some people are jumpy around spiders. Apparently, Fred is spooked by the "threat" of a conversation. Wonder what he's like at home!

The point is, just one bad apple in an organization can sour the entire relationship. So build a compelling message or "stump speech" for your organization and make sure everyone—and I mean everyone—gets it. Ask yourself:

- **Where are we going?** *This is an opportunity to paint an inspiring future vision that includes your ideal relationship with your customers. Write it from your customers' point of view. What is it you do for them that matters to them?*

- **Why are we going there?** *There must be something beyond the stock price. Obviously, it makes good business sense, but what's in it that is deeply meaningful for the company, for you, for your customers beyond making money?*

- **Who is going with us?** *This is an opportunity to flag key attitudes and behaviors you desire in the people who work in your company, such as the ability to connect with customers and build long-term relationships with them.*

- **How are we going to get there?** *This is an opportunity to emphasize and reinforce key elements of the strategy.*

If you'd like a copy of the stump speech with which I launched Fierce Inc., e-mail me (contact information is at the back of this book) and request it. We revisit it annually, and it continues to serve us well, even as we've adapted our business model and strategy to meet the needs of global customers, including our Fierce in the Schools division.

FORM A CUSTOMER ADVISORY BOARD

How would your customers, your clients, describe the conversations your organization is having with them? Throw yourself into the deep end and get feedback from demanding clients with high standards who push you to raise the bar. Get them together at least once a year to give you the good, the bad, and the ugly. Clarify what would make an "opportunity" a *yes* or a *no* for you and your organization. Make *no* be okay.

Personal Action Plan

1. Make a list of customers who need to hear from you, expanding the list you made earlier in this chapter. Include clients who bring very little revenue to the table. Write down these customers' names—the people's names, not just the company names. Write down the core issue (roadblocks) or other issues that need resolving. Don't be too confident that there are no issues, that all is well. Consider that "pricing" is often a mask for other issues. Write down your deadline for having these conversations. There should be urgency here.

Company/Contact	Issue(s)	By When
_____	_____	_____
_____	_____	_____
_____	_____	_____
_____	_____	_____

Before you have these conversations . . .

2. Bring together the best connectors within your organization. Share your thoughts about what your customers want and need that you and/or your company are not providing. Get their thoughts on how you can:

   a. Make it easier for your customers to tell you what they really want and need, even if your customers don't think you can help with those issues.

   b. Expand your work with customers. Perhaps you've been merely playing in the yard when there is a large field of possibilities nearby. Your goal is to maximize the possibilities such that your customers leave with more than they expected, and you leave with the maximum they are willing to give.

   c. Say, do, or offer something that will demonstrate that you have your customers' best interests in mind—versus your company's needs or your personal sales quota.

3. If you would like to do something "crazy" for your customers—something above and beyond the normal precedent or protocol—make a compelling case to your boss and ask for permission.

4. Be prepared to go off script. Nothing turns customers off more than a scripted presentation loaded with jargon, like "solutions." Don't "present" and don't flatter. Go into Mineral Rights mode. Ask, "What is the most important thing you and I should be talking about?" Also ask questions such as, "What has changed since the last time we talked?" and listen! Be yourself, natural. Let the conversations go where your customers want them to go, understanding that each conversation may be quite different because every customer is unique. If a customer becomes emotional, even angry, thank your lucky stars! You're close to something real, something important for you to understand and to which you can respond.

5. Whatever you promise to do for a customer, do it by the time agreed or earlier.

6. Take personal accountability for any missteps you or your organization may have made. No buck passing.

7. Loosen your death grip on pricing, and focus on imbedding. You're

in this relationship for the long haul. What little step can you take now?

8. Respectfully challenge a customer's thinking if you are convinced it is wrongheaded or shortsighted. On the other hand, clarify your walk-away point, even with a large customer. Some customers' demands are unworkable, and at times, saying good-bye is the most productive thing you can do.

9. Have conversations with your customers in person, if possible, even if it means getting on a plane. When budgets are tight, this is a big ask but one that's well worth it. The greatest opportunity to enrich a relationship with a customer is when you are face to face. You know this. Fight for it.

10. Finally, remember that you are always building or destroying your reputation and your relationships with your customers. The direction is up to you. People will buy an inferior product from someone they like over a superior product from someone they don't like. *How do you suppose Microsoft would be doing if more people liked them?* If someone likes you and what you do, they'll tell twenty-five people; if they don't, they'll tell one hundred twenty-five. And though many would argue this point, a relationship with a customer is not a means to an end. The relationship itself, is the end, the goal. When you connect with a customer at a deep level, the rest will come.

Conclusion

Remember that what gets talked about and *how* it gets talked about determines what will happen. Or won't happen. And that we succeed or fail, gradually then suddenly, one conversation at a time.

Remember that every conversation with someone, whether a co-worker, a customer, or a family member, either enriches that relationship, flatlines it (so what's the point), or takes it down, so if we lose emotional capital with the people who are important to our success and happiness, gradually, then suddenly, we may find ourselves out on the street corner, alone, in the rain.

Remember that when you and I see a newspaper headline about a bankruptcy or the leave taking of a key executive, or when we learn that someone is estranged from a family member or getting a divorce, we're seeing the "suddenly" part. The result was influenced gradually, gradually, gradually, until the outcome became inevitable and we arrived at suddenly.

While in London last year, I was invited by Mark (not his real name), the newly appointed UK rainmaker, to view his organization's brand-new client "war room," which had been designed to impress clients and win consulting work. Mark wanted to know what I thought of it.

The room was high-tech nirvana. An oblong, beautifully crafted, low conference table with six cushy leather chairs around it. Embedded in the tabletop were two computer monitors, so that looking into what at first you might think was a glass top, you could see graphs, charts, PowerPoints, video.

There was a podium for the senior consultant (the rainmaker) from which he or she could push buttons, like the Wizard of Oz, sans curtain. There were two small monitors to the right and left of a larger monitor at one end of the table. There were seven-foot-tall wraparound screens enveloping the conference table and chairs, on which softly colored graphics and provocative phrases drifted, fading in and out.

Floating above the conference table was a screen onto which clouds were projected. Inspiring music and mood lighting completed the scene. I sank into one of the leather chairs and was taken through a simulated client presentation.

Graphs on one screen. Faces of consultants and clients on another. Filmed case studies of impressive work on the big screen at the end of the table. And videos of happy clients touting successes backed up by numbers. The wraparound screens showed the results of electronic input provided by the prospective client—in this case, *me*. I pushed buttons to vote, prioritize issues, introduce additional concerns or goals, et cetera. It was damned impressive.

At the end of the "show," a floor-to-ceiling curtain opened, revealing a view of a stunningly beautiful harbor and the beginnings of a spectacular sunset. I was offered a drink and chose a Shiraz. Music set a relaxed, convivial tone. We toasted technology. We toasted the budget for the room. Two million, I seem to recall.

Mark, his assistant, and the man who had taken me through the simulation leaned back in their chairs, smiling.

Me: Spectacular.

We sat for a moment, sipped the wine.

Me: Okay, here's my question.
Mark: *(Raised eyebrows)*
Me: Where was the conversation?
Mark: *(Eyebrows inch higher)*
Me: I love technology, so this place knocks my socks off, and you had me when I walked in to great music and was seated in a stylish, comfortable chair. I loved the intimate setting, felt cocooned surrounded by screens. You impressed me with tales of successful engagements. And the sunset over the harbor, well, here's to major ambiance. This Shiraz is excellent, by the way. But when did you connect with *me*, rather than with the computer monitors?
Mark: *(Silence)*
Me: I was here for an hour, was exposed to an onslaught of technology, resulting in a sensuous derangement of intimacy. I get that you've gone beyond PowerPoint decks, that you can do some amazingly creative things with technology, but I actually temporarily lost touch with who I am, and I have no idea who you are. There was little eye contact. No one talked to *me, with* me. You talked *at* me.
Mark: *(Silence, a bit uncomfortable now, and I am feeling pretty low myself. Two million is a lot of money.)*
Me: So, for example, what if in this amazing room, you periodically put a gorgeous, nondistracting background on the screens, turned the music off, looked at your clients, asked questions, and listened.
Mark: *(Eagerly)* We do all that on the front end. From the first call and subsequent meetings, leading ultimately to this session, we

do our due diligence before we come up with a solution and build a presentation like this.

Me: It's clear you've done due diligence, which has its place in this meeting. I just don't think you should lead with it, because for global clients like yours, reality is a moving target. Something significant may have changed since last you spoke with them. So for example, even if you checked in with them last week, you might want to begin by asking them if there's any late-breaking news you should be aware of. And though this presentation demonstrates your capabilities, your competition has similar capabilities (yes, I know you don't agree) and may pitch similar solutions. When they've seen everyone's pitch, assuming expertise and reasonable fees, your clients will most likely hire the people they think they'll enjoy hanging out with the most over the long haul.

(The discomfort was obvious.)

Me: I'm not saying don't use what you've got here. I'm suggesting that you layer in eye contact, time to respond, to question, to listen. So the client will feel seen, heard, understood. In fact, it has to be more than a feeling. Your client *will* be seen, heard, and understood, which meets a basic human need and is good business practice. Otherwise, you won't get to the heart of what your client on their best day would look like. And don't have someone standing at a podium. Everyone should be seated, so this feels like a conversation, not a pitch, and your people must be willing and prepared to go off script. They must be willing to go wherever the client wants to go during the conversation.

(Silence!)

Me: What are you thinking, but not saying?

Mark: Well, to be completely candid, most of our people, those who would be using this room, would be uncomfortable without a prepared, scripted presentation. Free-flowing conversations, as you call them, would be very difficult for them.

Me: You've got to be kidding me!

Mark: *(Shakes head)*

Me: Well, then here's where I suggest you begin. Train your people to have conversations, especially ones that enrich relationships.
(Silence.)

Me: Here's another idea you'll likely choke on. Since you can make anything happen on these screens, when it's time to just talk with the client, why don't you change the monitors embedded in the tabletop to a crackling campfire, possibly even with sound effects—very low, of course. Most people have good memories about campfires. The smell of wood smoke. Easy conversations, scary ghost stories. We connect with families and friends around campfires. It would be a fun touch, a human touch, unexpected.

Mark took my suggestions to heart, including the campfire idea. His current win ratio is so impressive, he currently heads up the firm's "mega deal" team.

Here's the thing. The first organization in any industry to really connect with clients will win the field. It might not be the biggest competitor out there. It could be a quietly emerging company you don't even see coming. It might not have the fanciest product or the cheapest prices or the cleverest ad campaign—but if it has the relationships, emotional capital with its customers, it will take the hill.

And as a leader, you may be highly competent, convinced that your product or service is superior to those of your competitors. But at the end of the day, your competitive edge is *you,* specifically your ability to connect with your customers at a deep level. Once you achieve intimacy and connection, I predict that innovation, partnership, execution, and success won't be far behind.

Fierce Practice #6

From Legislated Optimism to Radical Transparency

There are few diseases for which the cure is more dangerous than the affliction. Alethophobia—an intense, abnormal or illogical fear of the truth—is one of them.

It sounds like a rare and serious psychiatric disorder, but I'm betting that two out of three people suffer from alethophobia. And the approved cure, administered by companies all over the world, is far worse than the disease.

How many times have you told someone—your boss, a colleague, a customer, your spouse—what you thought he or she wanted to hear, rather than what you were really thinking? Painted a false, rosy version of reality, glossing over problems or pretending they simply didn't exist? Tossed out the ceremonial first lie?

Telling it like it is, speaking the ground truth as opposed to the official party line (which we know to be bogus) is no one's notion of exalting. It's so upsetting, alarming, and risky that we're willing to place a FOR SALE sign on our integrity to avoid it. After all, we've all witnessed a kind of violence—a lost promotion, raise, or place at the table—visited on those who've spoken their hearts and minds, and it is raw.

Weak leaders want agreement. But fierce leaders want to know the truth. As leaders, we need to encourage those we lead to tell us the whole truth, paint the whole picture, even if it's ugly, unpleasant, not what we wish it to be. Because only then can we put our best efforts forward to fix what needs fixing.

Several years ago, following a training in Fierce Conversations at Washington Mutual, the participants were wildly enthusiastic about the bank's need for these practices. They were sobered by the idea that their careers, their organization, their relationships, and their lives were succeeding or failing—gradually, then suddenly—one conversation at a time. There was unease in the room and during the debriefing after a Beach Ball conversation, they were eager to bring Beach Ball conversations to all levels of the organization. Executives didn't see it that way. Gradually, committed to a failed strategy, WaMu spiraled downward, arriving at "suddenly" on September 25, 2008, when JP Morgan Chase acquired the deposits, assets, and liabilities of what was left of Washington Mutual's banking operations. Good for JP Morgan Chase. Sad for WaMu. Now, whenever I look at the WaMu tower, the most beautiful office building in Seattle, in my opinion, I wonder if things might have turned out differently if Kerry Killinger, the CEO, had frequently gathered people around him who could have alerted him to trouble and advised him what was needed to turn things around.

The first frontier is finding our own courage. You know how it goes. Someone speaks the truth out loud, in the presence of leaders, and soon it is difficult to breathe. Tension fills the room. The leader stiffens, gives us the *look,* sweeps the room with it. Then there's more silence, lots of fidgeting and darting eyes, until finally, the leader speaks solemnly, as if to a carrier of dengue fever. "I'm aware of these concerns, John (Jane, Larry, Linda). We've got it covered." Translated: "What part of 'team player' did you not understand!"

And this is a shame because our first thoughts, unfiltered, uncensored, are usually on to something. We may not even know how or why we know what we know, but we *do* know, and these thoughts are usually the most true, most honest, yet all too often we are scared to capture and voice them. (Later in this chapter, I'll invite you to capture your own first thoughts.)

Admittedly, sometimes what we "know" is off because we don't have the whole picture. I've often wondered what the first day would be like for a newly elected president of the United States. A briefing by all the agency heads: "Mr. President, we feel we should begin this briefing by informing you that aliens do exist. . . . "

But while you and I may not be privy to everything there is to know, our BS detectors sound the alarm when something doesn't look, sound, or smell right. And it's the courage to admit it to ourselves and point it out to others that signals the presence or absence of fierce leadership in our companies: "Thank you for telling me about this. Let's work to correct it." NOT "Don't mention this to anyone else. There's nothing to worry about."

What Is Legislated Optimism?

So what happens when honesty is discouraged, when leaders distort reality and insist that everyone perpetuate their rosy version of the current disaster? I call this legislated optimism, and I've saved this practice for last because it may hit a nerve, possibly *your* nerve, as this practice is largely about ego, about our insistence on building a public story of our lives into one we can live with, even if it's a fantasy. It's a protection mechanism. By God, we *will* be viewed as heroes, not jesters or villains.

Don't get me wrong. I am a card-carrying, verging-on-lunatic optimist who tends to see a burning bush where others see a brush fire. I'm all for upbeat, and I suspect that optimism is one of America's most valuable contributions to the world, a powerful asset that helps individuals and organizations reach and surpass lofty goals. Optimism isn't the problem. It's the "legislated" part that should concern us.

Legislated optimism is the purview of the one-way leader. When optimism is legislated, meetings produce more nothing than something. Ideas die without a funeral or proper burial. Communication is primarily from the leader to everyone else. The reverse is not valued, not welcomed, because the leader and his inner circle of advisers know best. Always have, always will. And the message is always upbeat. Accurate information is presented with a coat of whitewash and abracadabra laid over it, as if leaders would have us believe they've sent all the Death Eaters flying. *Naysayers will be sent to Azkaban.*

In a culture of legislated optimism, leaders know only the sound of one hand clapping. They ask questions not because they want answers, but because they want to hear how they *sound* asking them. In this environment, conclusions are reached at the point when everyone stops thinking, which is often short of brilliant. The leaders have already done the thinking for us and have called it good. No point in telling them what we're actually dealing with every day, since to do so would not be a career-enhancing move.

Reminds me of Jon Stewart's imperson-ation of former president George W. Bush: "You either agree with my position or you're looking to have a thermonuclear reaction bake your shadow instantly into the sidewalk."

> Conclusions are the point at which everyone stops thinking, which is often short of brilliant.

In short, legislated optimism is the tactic of those who attempt to camouflage rotten news with pretty words, confusing words, empty words. It's the tactic of those who replace the bold headlines with the small print—the kind of false advertising that allows credit card compa-nies, mortgage brokers, and wireless carriers to raise rates unexpectedly, for no apparent reason, or the kind of euphemisms that result in the misleading labels on things we buy every day. Organic (read *overpriced*). Low-fat (read *low flavor*). Healthy (read *not really*). New and improved (read *new and improved price*). Free (read *sucker. nothing is free*).

The *Today* Show recently ran a segment about how food manufac-turers are shortchanging the consumer by "downsizing" the products. One example was Skippy peanut butter. The standard jar looked the same as it always had, but in fact, Skippy had reduced the jar size from 18 ounces to 16.3 ounces by creating a large hemispherical "dimple" in the bottom of the jar while retaining the same jar height and diam-eter. Even though the price of Skippy had gone up slightly, consumers felt the manufacturer was basically holding the line in tight economic times. In truth, consumers were paying more for less. If it sounds like deception, it probably is deception.

Which reminds me of a poem by Tony Hoagland called "The Big Grab."

Big Grab

The corn chip engineer gets a bright idea,
and talks to the corn chip executive
and six months later at the factory they begin subtracting
a few chips from every bag,

but they still call it on the outside wrapper,
The Big Grab,
so the concept of *Big* is quietly modified
to mean *More or Less Large,* or *Only Slightly Less Big than Before.*

Confucius said this would happen:
that language would be hijacked and twisted
by a couple of tricksters from the Business Department

and from then on words would get crookeder and crookeder
until no one would know how to build a staircase,
or to look at the teeth of a horse,
or when it is best to shut up.

We live in that time that he predicted.
Nothing means what it says,
and it says it all the time.
Out on route 28, the lights blaze all night
on a billboard of a beautiful girl
covered with melted cheese—

See how she beckons to the river of late night cars;
See how the tipsy drivers swerve, under the breathalyzer moon!

We're in the wilderness now,
confused by the signs,
with a shortness of breath,
and that postmodern feeling of falling behind.

In a story whose beginning I must have missed,
without a name for the thing
I can barely comprehend I desire,
I speak these words that do not know
where they're going.

No wonder I want something more-or-less large,
and salty for lunch.
No wonder I stare into space while eating it.

Of greater concern than misleading advertising, though, is that the practice of legislated optimism—withholding ground truth, assuring us that all is well, that the grab is big, urging us to sing the official hymn, *In Leadership We Trust,* insisting that you're "either for us or against us"—is dangerous and extends to those who lead countries, as well as those who lead companies. The price paid by people all over the world is heartbreaking. I'd like us to rail against this practice, to insist that *all* leaders, whether leading companies or countries, tell us the truth, surface *mokitas* (more about that later), and find out what we're made of.

Human beings are hardwired to solve problems and are usually successful when they address the *real* problems, the root causes of whatever miseries they're experiencing. But often those who recognize the *real* problems hesitate to name them because (a) they are afraid they will be seen as party to creating the problems; (b) they don't know how to solve them, which would be embarrassing; (c) somebody else might figure out how to solve them, which would be more embarrassing; (d) what kind of leaders would they be if they didn't "lead," as in devise the plan and issue directives?; and (e) as Sinclair Lewis said, "It is difficult to get a man to understand something if his salary depends on his not understanding it."

I was once working with the key executives of a company when it was acquired by another company. One of the first pronouncements from the visiting executive was, "Our culture is one of compliance. This means if you're told to do something, don't ask questions. Just do as you're told." Most of the men and women I had known for a year, accustomed to regularly interrogating reality and a steady diet of candor, declined to remain.

At Fierce Inc., thanks to Cam Tripp, who pushed back repeatedly on my determined plan to build a stable of world-class facilitators, we instead began developing world-class materials and empowering clients to become certified and teach our courses themselves. I admit that when Cam first floated this suggestion, my exact words were "Over my dead body," but luckily, I was able to open myself up to his suggestions—and in the end was extremely happy I did.

"Dead body" is now a joke in the company and the code for a possibly crazy and brilliant idea that is about to be suggested. As in, "This could be one of those dead body ideas that could take us to the next level."

When someone says, "This is how it's going to be. This is the truth, the right way to go. ALL IS WELL!" in spite of rumors or what you're feeling in your gut, in spite of the dead and dying, and having failed to interrogate reality and solicit competing views, well, that person doesn't just burn her bridges to brilliance, to innovation, to employee engagement, to high levels of collaboration and cooperation, to a healthy top and bottom line, she blows them up.

For the Rhythm of Your Home

Of course, there are some things leaders keep under wraps—such as impending mergers or acquisitions or the newest top secret gizmo in development—for security or legal reasons or to avoid wild swings in the stock price. But when leaders keep secrets or cover up or sanitize risky material in order to avoid or postpone the recognition of failure, they put the company and everyone in it at risk. This practice is not fierce. It's insulting, deceitful, and foolish.

Consider NASA's refusal to divulge its disturbing survey data on airline safety because knowing the truth would upset air travelers and hurt airline profits (*Is it just me, or does anyone else suspect concerns over profits trumped concerns about you and me possibly being upset?*); the CIA's destruction of videotapes of harsh interrogations (read *"waterboarding"*), of suspected al-Qaida operatives, despite repeated, detailed requests by members of the September 11 Commission for documents and other information related to interrogations; and Merck and Schering-Plough's admission that they had known for two years and failed to disclose that their widely used cholesterol drugs, Zetia and Vytorin, not only failed to slow the accumulation of fatty plaque in arteries but actually seemed to contribute to plaque formation (*Why tell the truth when it will trigger an immediate net worth–ectomy, even though millions of people are taking a drug that doesn't benefit them and in fact may raise their risk of heart attack? After all, the overriding purpose of all business is to make a profit!).*

We all recall the breathtaking collapse of investment bank Bear Stearns, one of the most alarming indicators to flash on the U.S. economy's dashboard. Yet days earlier, the CEO of Bear Stearns had assured investors, employees, and the press that there was no cause for alarm.

In the fall of 2008, it took nothing less than the failure of Lehman Brothers, Fannie Mae, Freddie Mac, Merrill Lynch, AIG, Washington Mutual, and the top U.S. automakers and the subsequent devastation on Wall Street for many executives and political leaders to admit the gravity of the situation. Brian Williams interviewed CNBC experts who, with refreshing candor, didn't try to sooth and smooth. They were worried and said so.

How long had these fires been smoldering? How did these companies go bankrupt? "Gradually, and then suddenly."

If the leaders of these organizations had caught their downward trajectories early in the game, and owned up to them, rather than painting a rosy picture to assure shareholders, and the world at large, that everything was A-OK, would their stories have had a happier ending? Optimism is not warranted when "management" withholds or manipulates the truth as the organization slides toward illness. When a company's pronouncements don't match reality, the company's immune system is weakened, making it vulnerable to getting sick when faced with tough developments—a downturn in the economy, a competitor's fabulous new offering, the rising price of oil. These and other challenges can kill a company whose immune system is already compromised.

Reminds me of a television commercial for a scented air freshener that could be programmed to spritz an odor-masking fragrance every five minutes, fifteen minutes, or sixty minutes. The tagline was "For the rhythm of your home."

If your house stinks to high heaven, don't go looking for whatever expired under the sink; just mask that odor with a different one. If the smell is really bad, set the air freshener on "high."

Doesn't that sound lovely? *The rhythm of your home.* But of course, air freshener doesn't get out the nasty smell, it just hides it. If your house stinks to high heaven, don't go looking for whatever expired under the sink, just mask that odor with a different one. If the smell is really bad, set the air freshener on "high."

In the news recently, I learned that room deodorizing sprays and drier sheets can cause physical harm to those who use them. This perfects the metaphor. Cover-ups are unhealthy, which begs the question, what is the rhythm of *your* home, your team, your organization? Is there an odiferous issue that you or others have been attempting to mask?

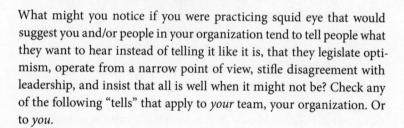

Practicing Squid Eye

What might you notice if you were practicing squid eye that would suggest you and/or people in your organization tend to tell people what they want to hear instead of telling it like it is, that they legislate optimism, operate from a narrow point of view, stifle disagreement with leadership, and insist that all is well when it might not be? Check any of the following "tells" that apply to *your* team, your organization. Or to *you*.

Only the usual suspects are invited to the table. It's always the same people, the same flow, the same distractions, the same argument for the same strategy, which nets the same outcomes. We're committed to implementing option A, while the guys in the warehouse are suggesting option Q (which could save us). But they weren't invited to the meeting.

You hear words like *burning platform* and *playbook*. This grandiose verbiage is a special language spoken from the bully pulpit. It's an attempt to add weight to the task at hand, to add importance to what we're doing, like the Wizard of Oz behind the curtain, operating his thunder machine. No one really buys it.

The "corporate nod" is prevalent. When people are asked what they think of a leader's ideas or plans, heads lower around the table, eyes are averted. If the leader calls on someone to speak, he or she adopts a thoughtful expression and nods his or her head, which is mistaken for agreement. In actuality, there is little or no agreement, but since those who point out problems are considered troublemakers, no one pushes back.

Mokitas abound. *Mokita* is a term from Papua New Guinea. It means "that which everyone knows and no one speaks of." The health of any community is judged by the number of *mokitas* that exist within it. *Mokita* is apparently also the name of an umbrella drink. I assume that is because when enough goes in, the truth comes out.

There is a gap between "official truths" and "ground truths." When a company nears disaster, people who work there admit they knew it was coming, based on the reality with which they were confronted daily. In spite of the CEOs' exhortations to the contrary (the official truth), all was not well at Enron, Bear Stearns, Fannie Mae, Freddie Mac, Washington Mutual, AIG, GM, Ford, Chrysler. . . . By the time this book is in your hands, the list will have grown.

There is a dearth of innovation. When optimism is legislated—the forecast is always sunny skies, no chance of rain—forget about innovation. Since all is well, we can relax, keep doing what we've been doing. We're good, we're great, we're successful; we've got it figured out. Nothing can touch us. Tra, la, la, la, la. Take the rest of the day off.

We experience implementation agony. If we've been assured that all is well, why struggle to implement new initiatives that require us to change? If a new initiative is difficult to implement, we assume it's because it is unnecessary, the wrong thing to do. So we move slowly, drag our feet, point at obstacles.

There is an absence of accountability. We're not fond of taking accountability for the success or failure of someone's decision if our input was not solicited and valued in the first place, especially when leaders peddle rosy predictions and deny corporate dysfunction. Our leaders can hold us accountable all day long, and nothing will change. This is *their* plan, *their* bright idea, not ours.

We declare war on the wrong things. The problem isn't HERE with me, with us. It's over THERE. It's YOU. It's THEM. It's THAT. It's THIS. Production engineering, not manufacturing. Offshore, not on shore. Sales, not merchandising. You, not me. Our competition's brilliant products. Not *our* lack of innovation. Not *our* unworkable plan.

If our organization were a car, many of the warning lights would be flashing red. While the CEO or the press secretary smiles broadly into the camera and denies that there is reason for concern, those privy to the real numbers are talking with headhunters, hoping to bail out before the whole thing comes crashing down. What are the rest of us pretending not to know?

We may not cook the books, but sometimes we cook the truth. We tell ourselves that technically, withholding, obfuscating, avoiding, reframing the truth isn't lying, it's just being optimistic. The last frame of a *Dilbert* cartoon captures my thought about this: "If you hear a whistling noise, that would be your soul escaping through your nose." That sound would be your immune system deflating. That would be your team exiting, your world crashing.

If any of this is occurring in your organization, what part has *your* name on it? Could be a lot or a little, depending on your beliefs.

What Were We Thinking?

Take a look at the following list of beliefs and check those you currently hold.

Leaders *do* know best. That's why I am a leader. Let me lead.	Leadership doesn't imply omniscience. No one has all the answers. I certainly don't.

As a leader, I'm privy to more information than others, so others aren't equipped to advise me.	The best decisions are made with input from multiple sources. If anyone's point on the compass indicates danger, I want that person to speak up.
I get paid the big bucks, so I do the heavy lifting. Others get paid to implement my decisions and strategy.	A strong leadership bench requires that people think and behave as if they are at least one level beyond their current role. I want everyone to *think*, as well as do.
Most people can't handle the truth. Why upset them unnecessarily?	People *can* handle the truth and need to know it so they can help us figure out what to do.
I speak in order to present myself, my ideas.	I speak in order to *become* myself. I hope to be different when the conversation is over.
I rarely ask a question unless I already know the answer. Makes me look good.	I *never* ask a question to which I already know the answer. I want ideas and actions to move in one direction only— forward.
If I openly share all my ideas, people might steal them and pass them off as their own.	I freely share my ideas with colleagues so we can engage with one another, counsel one another, maintain energy and momentum.

WHAT ARE YOU WINNING?

To the extent you hold the beliefs on the left, be prepared for the consequences. When we lie or distort the truth, we do so at a horrific cost to ourselves and others. When people are fed a story they know to be at odds with real-

> When people are fed a story they know to be at odds with reality or downright untrue, there is psychological breath holding. Souls asphyxiate.

ity or downright untrue, there is psychological breath holding. Souls asphyxiate, which creates a chronic wound, so great in some that they eventually blow our cover. People whose beliefs lie on the left may call them whistle-blowers, try to find out who they are, then make their lives hell on earth. A prime example of declaring war on the wrong thing.

Whistle-blowers aren't the problem. The problem is that we aren't asking ourselves why anyone who works for us would feel he or she had to go behind our back or over our head to express serious concerns about our practices. *Unless, of course, our practices are dead wrong, illegal, and/or putting others in danger. Let's not let that out!*

Another consequence of a culture that subscribes to the beliefs in the left column is that when people are told not to question reality, just DO, they are unlikely to look for and point out threats and opportunities or share information on a day-to-day basis that could be relevant to things like new product innovation. What's more, are these yes-men really the type of people you want working at your organization? What person with a healthy self-image, high emotional intelligence, and an appetite for personal development and career growth will be attracted to or remain in a culture of compliance?

An additional cost of legislated optimism, or hiding or shying away from the truth, is employee misunderstanding—and this is expensive. The CEO of an airline told me that if he could capture the cost of misunderstanding to his airline, it would probably be one of the largest numbers on his P&L statement. In June 2008, a white paper commissioned by Cognisco determined that employees in the United States and the United Kingdom were costing businesses $37 billion every year by not fully understanding their jobs. The study defined "employee misunderstanding" as actions taken by employees who have misunderstood or misinterpreted (or were misinformed about or lacked confidence in their understanding of) company policies, business processes, job function, or a combination of the three.

The research suggests that by ignoring problems or issues, firms erode employee confidence, compliance, and productivity, risk public safety and legal problems, and damage both brand reputation and customer satisfaction. In fact, all four hundred companies surveyed reported that employee misunderstanding had placed them at risk of injuries to employees or the public, and 99 percent cited risk of lost sales and reduced customer satisfaction. And much of this is because, despite very real evidence to the contrary, their employees are assured that all is well: "We're doing great!"

Carl Jung pointed to the inevitable consequence of legislated optimism: "What we do not make conscious emerges later as fate." In other words, in the end, we will win precisely what we have been attempting to avoid, pretending not to know. Our fate is already sealed, and by trying to hide it, we make it inevitable.

> "What we do not make conscious emerges later as fate."
> —Carl Jung

Letting the Fresh Air into the Room

So, given the deadening effect legislated optimism has on an organization, why is it still so prevalent?

Well, there truly are people who believe that while *they* can handle the "truth," the rest of us can't. Perhaps they view us as the human version of fainting goats or suspect that when we understand what a dreadful hash they've made of things, we'll throw them out. They could be right on the second point. We are not fond of those who've made one wrong move after another, while lying to us along the way. And as far as fainting goats, we really, really don't enjoy being patronized, as if we needed protection from the tough world out there. We're bigger than that, thank you very much. So go ahead, lay it on us.

There's also the popular myth that it's lonely at the top. That leaders must privately bear their cross—that decision making falls to them and them alone, which requires them to hole up in their private brainpans, pull the shades, and ruminate until they've arrived at a conclusion.

What a crock! It is most definitely NOT lonely at the top. Leaders are smack dab in the middle of a vast community of good, talented, often underutilized people who would love to be invited to the table to lend their expertise to any challenge you could name. And this may surprise you, but nobody cares that you, the

> It is most definitely NOT lonely at the top.

leader, scorched a gazillion of your brain cells staying awake all night thinking this through and have now arrived at a brilliant decision. We get no sense of fulfillment that you are apparently a genius. You were alone when you made your brilliant decision. You're alone with it now. For the sake of the company, we hope it was a good one, but please stop waving it in our faces. We're busy trying to attract attention to ourselves.

Another false belief some leaders hang on to is that if they tell people how dicey things are and that the immediate future doesn't look good, their best people will leave, customers will desert them, the stock will plummet, the board of directors will hand the CEO his head on a plate, and . . .

These things only happen when we disclose seriously bad news *that no one has seen coming.* For example, it was hardly a surprise when the U.S. government initially refused a $30 billion bailout for the auto industry. What had the people who ran those companies been pretending not to know? And why, when the CEOs of GM, Ford, and Chrysler first pleaded for money, could not one of them produce a credible plan to quickly turn things around? Remember, problems arise gradually, and it's only when we're taken by surprise, having ignored or suppressed all the signals, all the signs, do we arrive at a negative "suddenly" and the now-inevitable, drastic consequences. Whereas when we're honest with ourselves and others from the start, we can spot trouble coming and form a sound plan, allowing us to turn things around.

In the spring of 2008, Starbucks reported a significant decline in sales, laid off people at every level, and closed a number of stores nationwide, yet most who left hoped to return when the situation improved. Meanwhile, everyone wondered how bad things were and how long it would take for Starbucks to turn around. Howard Schultz announced, openly and honestly, at the company's annual meeting, that there was no "silver bullet" for fixing Starbucks, whose stock had dropped 40 percent over the previous twelve months. Given everything that was going on in the U.S. economy, he admitted, a $4 cup of coffee was no longer affordable for many people, and Starbucks's U.S. expansion plans had been too aggressive.

What happened? Goldman Sachs immediately dropped the stock

from "growth" to "neutral," and no one wanted to touch it. But because Starbucks's management fully disclosed its problems, talked down expectations, crafted and implemented a sound plan, and kept revenue moving up at the rate of 20 percent a year, the company and the stock began to benefit from the law of modest expectations and from the turnaround plan.

As this example shows, even if a stock has been abandoned by Wall Street, if there has been full disclosure about the extent of the bad news and there is a sound strategy that the company can implement, hitting modest targets with relative ease, the stock may begin to move up again.

Still, at our own organizations, many of us lose sleep over the stock price and keeping shareholders and the board of directors happy, when we should be disclosing organizational shortcomings, even if it means we'll take a short-term hit. But instead of coming to terms with our problems and looking for new and innovative ways to solve them, we hide our heads in the sand, avoiding the conflict we fear will be our daily lot if we fully disclose our sad state of affairs. Why tell it like it is if we can manage to keep things relatively peaceful?

Yet a strong leader—a fierce leader—knows things will improve only by coming to grips with how bad things are and how they got that way, building a good plan, and staying the course. Steve Hankins, the former CFO of Tyson Foods, once told me, "Sometimes we really *can't* get there from *here*. So we have to go someplace else to start."

> "Sometimes we really *can't* get there from *here*. So we have to go someplace else to start."
> —Steve Hankins

An obstacle for most of us—I include myself—is that we are in love with our beliefs and practices, so convinced that they are true and right, irrefutable, that we do not entertain the possibility that our truths may have only an *element* of truth in them. Or that they were true once upon a time but are no longer true today. Or that they may be true in theory, but in reality, they aren't working.

When our false version of the truth is cast in bronze, when we suppress all evidence to the contrary by silencing those we lead, we continue to practice old habits and are ultimately left contemplating the ashes of our downsized opportunity. We wonder when the next turning point is going to come along, failing to recognize that we'll incinerate that one, too. Someday history may judge us badly, or worse, accurately.

The point I'd like you to consider is that being "strong" and "right" can be turnoffs, not turn-ons. Modesty is called for here. Humility. You may be great, you may know stuff, but you're not *that* great, and you don't know everything.

What is needed now is for leaders to become more open, more flexible, less egoistic, and less hypocritical. We must loosen our death grip on whatever we believe to be the truth simply because it is how we *want* the truth to look. We must be honest with ourselves and invite honesty from others.

We can do this. We can let the much-needed fresh air—fresh voices—into the room. As Martin Luther King said, "We will have to repent in this generation not merely for the vitriolic words and actions of the bad people, but for the appalling silence of the good people."

The Fierce Practice: Radical Transparency

WHAT IS RADICAL TRANSPARENCY?

A post on Wikipedia describes radical transparency as

> a management method where nearly all decision making is carried out publicly. All draft documents, all arguments for and against a proposal, the decisions about the decision making process itself, and all final decisions, are made publicly and remain publicly archived.
>
> The only exceptions to full transparency include data related to personal security or passwords or keys necessary for physical access required to carry out publicly negotiated decisions. Any technical actions which are perceived to be controversial or political are considered to lack legitimacy until a clear, radically transparent decision has been made concerning them.

Okay, but it's more than that. Throughout this book, I've attempted to persuade you that human connectivity is the key to exponential growth for companies and for individuals, a sustainable, competitive edge. Radical transparency is at the very *center* of our increasingly hyperconnected world. In fact, it is already a trend. And I recommend it as a way of life. If you're not moving toward open-source thinking and full disclosure, please note that this particular train has left the station. But if you run, you can still jump on.

In the nineties, many organizations adopted Jack Stack's "open-book management" approach. This practice involves giving employees all relevant financial information about the company so they can make better decisions as workers. This information includes, but is not limited to, revenue, profit, cost of goods, cash flow, and expenses.

The basic rules for open-book management are

- Give employees all relevant financial information;
- Give employees training to understand the financial information;
- Give employees responsibility for the numbers under their control; and
- Give employees a financial stake in how the company performs.

We do this at Fierce. Everyone understands our financials and has ongoing access to the data, a liberal amount of decision-making power, and a discretionary budget to do what's needed to achieve our goals. Our president meets with the team once a month to review our goals, our "critical numbers," and our performance against those numbers. Based on results, everyone in the company (EVERYONE) receives a quarterly profit-sharing check. The number may be big or small, but what's important is that everyone understand how each of us influences that number by what we do every day—by the quality of the decisions we make and the strategies we design and how well and how quickly we execute them.

You can adopt this fierce practice of full disclosure, too—in your job, at your company, even at home with your family. Want to start a college fund for the new baby? Remodel your home? Buy the newest hybrid car? Save up for a dream vacation? If your partner and your kids are aware of what goes into these decisions and what sacrifices they might entail, they may come up with new and interesting ways to go about it. *Here are my ideas. What are yours?*

This is lightning in a bottle.

But why stop with the financials? Why not fully disclose everything and fling open the doors for suggestions and ideas? We've done this at Fierce from day one, and I swear by it. The best ideas have come as a result of ongoing, fully transparent free-for-alls to which everyone, including our clients, is invited.

This is what radical transparency means to me and to my company, but before I describe how you can put radical transparency to work in your organization, let's talk a bit more about what it is and clarify what it requires of you and others and what results you can expect.

THE "SEE-THROUGH CEO"

Clive Thompson wrote a terrific article titled "The See-Through CEO" for *Wired* magazine. It's a long article worth reading, in which Thompson cites CEOs and companies who have revealed flaws in their strategies, confessed missteps, solicited input from employees and customers—in other words, practiced radical transparency—and seen their business grow as a result.

For example, when the real estate firm Redfin posted internal debates about the underbelly of the real estate business on its website, it did not discourage customers. Instead, it radicalized the conversation about problems and got customers pulling for Redfin. Sun Microsystems' CEO, Jonathan Schwartz, is respected because he dishes company dirt and apologizes for start-ups he's accidentally screwed. And after JetBlue trapped passengers for hours in its storm-grounded planes and canceled 1,100 flights, CEO David Neeleman won back consumer loyalty and confidence by airing a blunt mea culpa on YouTube. Even Microsoft, once a paragon of buttoned-down control, now posts uncensored internal videos—and encourages its engineers to blog freely about their projects. A company-wide wiki at Zappos.com, the rapidly growing online shoe retailer, lets staff members complain about problems and suggest solutions.

Thompson makes a strong case for voluntarily and promptly broadcasting a company's news—both good and bad—and actively soliciting an ongoing, robust dialogue with all those who are interested. And why not? With just one click on Google, people will find out what's really going on anyway!

Speaking of Google, that's another company that practices radical transparency. There are many internal e-mail lists at Google dedicated to the discussion of particular ideas, issues, and complaints. For example, on the "Google Ideas" website, Googlers regularly submit their thoughts on product improvements or suggestions about how to make things better around Google. Their colleagues can then weigh in by rating the suggestions from 0 (dangerous or harmful if implemented) to 5 (Great idea! Make it so). The management team pays very close attention and is responsive to issues that Googlers deem important enough to discuss on one of their internal e-mail lists. Sometimes, the conversations started on one of these e-mail threads actually become topics of larger discussions. Plus, the highlight of Google's quarterly "Kick-Off" meetings for its North American Sales Organization is the very candid, no-holds-barred Q&A session with Google's entire senior management team.

If you're still hesitant to do business in the buff, Thompson's article may change your mind:

> Fire the publicist. Go off message. Let all your employees blab and blog. In the new world of radical transparency, the path to business success is clear. . . . Radical forms of transparency are now the norm at startups—and even some Fortune 500 companies. It is a strange and abrupt reversal of corporate values. Not long ago, the only public statements a company ever made were professionally written press releases and the rare, stage-managed speech by the CEO. Now firms spill information in torrents, posting internal memos and strategy goals, letting everyone from the top dog to shop-floor workers blog publicly about what their firm is doing right—and wrong.

> **"Fire the publicist. Go off message. Let all your employees blab and blog."**
> **—Clive Thompson**

"You can't hide anything anymore," Don Tapscott, coauthor of *The Naked Corporation,* says. . . . If you engage in corporate flimflam, people will find out. He ticks off example after example of corporations that have recently been humiliated after being caught trying to conceal stupid blunders. . . .

Secrecy is dying. It's probably already dead. In a world where Eli Lilly's internal drug-development memos, Paris Hilton's phonecam images, Enron's e-mails, and even the governor of California's private conversations can be instantly forwarded across the planet, trying to hide something illicit—trying to hide anything, really—is an unwise gamble. . . . Radical transparency has even reached the ultrasecretive world of Washington politics: The nonprofit Sunlight Foundation has begun putting zillions of public documents in elegantly searchable online databases, leaving it to interested citizens to connect the dots. . . . All of which explains why the cult of transparency has so many high tech converts these days. Transparency is a judo move. Your customers are going to poke around in your business anyway, and your workers are going to blab about internal info—so why not make it work for you by turning everyone into a partner in the process and inviting them to do so?

Some of this isn't even about business; it's a cultural shift, a redrawing of the lines between what's private and what's public. A generation has grown up blogging, posting a daily phonecam picture on Flickr and listing its geographic position in real time on Dodgeball and Google Maps. For them, authenticity comes from online exposure. It's hard to trust anyone who doesn't list their dreams and fears on Facebook. . . .

Google is not a search engine. Google is a reputation-management system. And that's one of the most powerful reasons so many CEOs have become more transparent: Online, your rep is quantifiable, findable, and totally unavoidable. In other words, radical transparency is a double-edged sword, but once you know the new rules, you can use it to control your image in ways you never could before. . . .

But here's the interesting paradox: The reputation economy creates an incentive to be more open, not less. Being transparent, opening up, posting interesting material frequently and often is the only way to amass positive links to yourself and thus to directly influence your Googleable reputation.

The notion of a "reputation economy" makes sense. In our world of blogs, YouTube, and social networking, if you let down one person, you run the risk of being publicly exposed to hundreds or even thousands of that person's closest friends!

Want to know something fantastic about radical transparency? It deepens accountability. When decisions, strategies, the debates behind them, and bumps and successes along the way are openly shared with an organization's community, our arguments, our deeds of derring-do and what-was-I-thinking are there for all to see. Corrections and improvements are encouraged along the way, often stopping poor decisions in their tracks, before they're implemented.

So if you want to model accountability and hold others able, as I talked about in "Fierce Practice #3," radical transparency is your ticket to the land of "I did it. I own it."

SURFACE *MOKITAS* AND GET TO GROUND TRUTHS

The fierce practice of radical transparency requires that our conversations reveal *mokitas* (that Papua New Guinea word for "that which everyone knows and no one speaks of") and get to ground truths—what's *really* going on—rather than the "official truth." Such conversations compel us to change when change is called for and help to ensure that any changes we commit to come from our best thinking, our A game, rather than the same idea mold as our predecessors and perhaps some of our current leaders.

I suspect we all want this, so it's puzzling that, even though radical transparency is destined to win out in the end, it remains a fairly rare experience. Unfortunately, many of us have gotten so used to saying what we think others want to hear, that we forget that some people actually want the truth.

In *The Summer Book,* Tove Jansson captures questions I wish more of us asked:

"Why do you use so many euphemisms and metaphors," the grandmother replies. "Are you afraid?"

—Tove Jansson,
The Summer Book

"Why do you use such harsh words?" the grandmother's old friend Verner asks her, when he comes for his yearly visit to the island. "I was only telling you the news." "Why do you use so many euphemisms and metaphors," the grandmother replies. "Are you afraid?"

Perhaps *you* are afraid, at times, to disclose the truth, your truth. My hope is that you will do it anyway. So to encourage you, let's talk about *what* truths need disclosing and how to go about it.

Interrogating Reality Through Beach Ball Meetings

A goal of our work at Fierce Inc. is to enhance the collaboration, alignment, and accountability of teams and to track and celebrate the healthy cultures and financial results that go hand in hand with this. And what we've found is that when a team or company can't come up with the right answers, it may be because it is asking the wrong questions. So much of our work with leaders has involved helping them master the courage and the skill to interrogate reality, to ask the right questions.

reality
    1: the quality or state of being real.
   2a: a real event, entity, or state of affairs; the totality of real things and events **b:** something that is neither derivative nor dependent but exists necessarily—in reality: in actual fact.

reality check
    1: something that clarifies or serves as a reminder of reality, often by correcting a misconception.

When realities outside our organization—and often outside our control—change, it can affect our plans. Think about advancing technology, scientific breakthroughs, global warming, hurricanes, earthquakes, and other challenges nature hurls at us (some of which we bring on ourselves). Think about a rocky economy, bankruptcies, an erratic stock market. Think about changing demographics and how this affects *who* our customers are and what they want and need from us today. Think about the changing landscape of competitors and what this requires of us. Think about internal organizational changes, new leadership, dwindling resources, which affect our decisions and our ability to execute.

Not to mention the changes in our personal lives—partners, children, parents, pets, health issues, geographic moves, balancing goals, balancing budgets, trying to keep everyone happy and whole.

Mastering the courage and the skill to interrogate reality is where Beach Ball meetings come in. We talked about them in "Fierce Practice #4." As a reminder, picture your organization as a beach ball. Each person in your organization—as well as each of your customers, vendors, and advisers—stands on a different colored stripe on the corporate beach ball and experiences reality from that perspective.

Who owns the truth about what color your organization is? That's not a trick question. The answer is that every person connected to your organization owns a *piece* of the truth. No one owns the whole truth. Those who think they *do* make it doubly difficult for the rest of us. You and I may know a lot about a particular topic, but we don't know all there is to know on that topic, and, while we may have a lot of great ideas, we don't have all of them, so when there's an important decision to make or a problem to solve, it's essential that we examine the multiple, often competing realities existing simultaneously on every topic under the sun.

Interrogating reality is complicated. Things get even more interesting when you expand the notion of "reality."

So far, we've referred to lowercase *r* realities. Before we talk about how to utilize Beach Ball meetings to tap into radical transparency, let's examine reality with a capital *R*—the reality of our own intellectual, physical, or emotional capacity and contribution. This is where the *courage* in "master the courage to interrogate reality" comes in, because *R* reality has to do with a *self*-examination, being transparent about our own role in creating or sustaining any current reality—positive or negative.

As you know, each practice begins with yourself, so let's go there.

STEP 1. PREPARE YOURSELF.

R reality may arrive unexpectedly as input from our boss, our peers, our direct reports, our customers, our spouse. What if we learn that we often leave a negative emotional wake or that people don't feel we've been clear with them, that our leadership style is ineffective, or worse, offensive? What if we learn that a customer feels ignored, undervalued, made wrong. We are advised, "Don't take this personally." But we do, because there's no other honest way to take it. Our careers and our lives *are* deeply personal, or what's the point?

The bravest among us actively seek a glimpse of *R* reality by asking, "What am I pretending not to know about my contribution to this situation or problem?" While interrogating realities about business performance, the question good leaders invariably ask is, "Where am I in all of this? What did I bring to the party? How have I behaved in ways guaranteed to produce the results on my plate, on our plate?"

Where am I in all of this? What did I bring to the party?

For example, in the middle of a recent conversation with a prospective client, I sensed that the client was distracted. I was disappointed and a bit annoyed that she had asked for time with me and yet was so unengaged. And then the recognition hit me that I was distracted, too. My mind was drifting to the article I needed to write by the end of the day. The instant I realized what my Reality was in the situation and brought all of my attention back to the prospective client and the problems with which she was dealing, she became animated and energized, and we had a terrifically enjoyable and productive conversation.

Let's return to the dictionary.

virtual reality

an artificial environment that is experienced through sensory stimuli (as sights and sounds) provided by a computer and in which one's actions partially determine what happens in the environment.

Sans the computer, given this definition, virtual reality is the reality in which each of us lives every day, all day. Our own actions *do* determine what happens in the environment. Our companies, our teams, our marriages are an accurate mirror reflecting us back to ourselves. There is simply no other place to look.

To truly understand our own leadership potential is to truly understand ourselves—capital *R* reality. It's about taking ownership for our results and making choices with clear intentions. We can learn the skills and the tools, but true leadership is about learning to maintain a state of being that is both authentic and powerful.

> To truly understand our own leadership potential is to truly understand ourselves— capital *R* reality.

Leaders are ineffectual if they fail to move quickly and honestly to their own inward essential character. It is like the water that flows underneath the earth's surface. If you dig a hole down deep, you'll realize that water is down there under everything. It's been there for a long time. Your character—your gifts and your flaws—influences everything and everyone around you. But first you have to go deep to find it, tap the water table.

Self-examination is not ethics, nor judgment, nor a quest for perfection. It is recognition, awakening. Thomas Merton said, "If you want to identify me, ask me what I am living for, in detail, and ask me what is keeping me from living fully for what I live for."

Where are *you* going? *Why* are you going there? What are you living for? Are you on the right path, headed in the right direction? The right direction not from someone else's perspective, from *yours*.

Only when we better understand ourselves and our own direction can we change the beliefs and practices that are keeping us from happiness and success. And once we change, the people around us can change, our careers can change, our companies can change. The world can change.

I'll let you in on a personal story. Nine years ago, many people were urging me to turn my fierce conversations workshops into a book, but I had no desire to write nonfiction, plus I knew writing a book would take time I couldn't spare and was probably a guaranteed way to go broke. I had just left a long-term marriage and had money on my mind. I could pay my monthly bills but didn't earn enough to save for retirement. Besides, I had been thinking about an idea for an Internet start-up that I was convinced was a good idea.

I hired someone to help me in the incubation stage of the business plan and assembled a board of advisers. I spent five months and most of my savings to flesh out the plan. With growing excitement about the success I was certain to enjoy, I pitched the idea to venture capitalists, all of whom turned me down.

Surprised and a little discouraged, I remembered a man who had deep pockets and was well connected to others equally well heeled. He had told me several times that he was my biggest fan, so I bought an airline ticket, met with him, and pitched the plan. He turned me down.

I told him, "If you don't see the value and potential of this business plan, it's not because the plan isn't good; it's because I'm lousy at pitching it. I'd like to leave it with you. If you get bored, take another look at it." He agreed to keep it, though I suspected he was just being polite.

I returned to Seattle. It was December, the time of year when I take stock, reviewing my answers to the "stump speech" questions: Where am I going? Why am I going there? Who is going with me? How am I going to get there? And as I imagined what my life would be like if, by some miracle, I got enough money to launch the new company, I remembered something Annie Dillard wrote: "How we spend our days is how we spend our lives."

I was fairly certain that if I did not spend the majority of my days in the high art of serving others, even if I accumulated money, possessions, titles, and all the trappings, I could expect the following:

- deep regret
- the slow death of my soul
- empty rooms

- a weakened immune system
- no joy

My stomach clenched when I imagined spending my days doing what it would take to launch and run the Internet company I had conceived and the inevitable, ongoing, capital-raising treadmill that is the fate of most start-up CEOs. I know you're thinking, "Well, duh! Didn't you think about that earlier?"

No, I didn't. I should have, but I was thinking about doing something others would think was really cool, about stepping into that high-tech world filled with possibility and potential. Mostly, though, I was thinking about how much money I would make and how I would spend it. I wasn't thinking about my life and how I would spend *that*. This was personally legislated optimism at its finest. I had convinced myself that the plan was a good one and, in spite of rejection by venture capitalists, I believed I would ultimately succeed. And be happy. And wealthy.

But once I was finally honest with myself, once I finally interrogated my Reality, I realized that if I was "successful," depression would probably be my lot. Which prompted the question: "What is the *one* thing that if I got to the end of my life and looked back, I would regret not doing?" The answer was immediate and clear. Write the book.

I argued with myself. I went back and forth. *I'll spare you the details.* And finally, fairly exhausted emotionally, I gave in. *Okay, I'll write the book and go broke! Satisfied?!*

Well, actually, yes, I *was* satisfied. The decision felt so good, so right, it was almost embarrassing. I felt ridiculous. What had I been pretending not to know about where my life really wanted and needed to go?

The next day, my wealthy acquaintance called and said, "I get it. I'll give you ten million of my own funds and go to others for the rest on the condition that you run the company."

When your heart is in your mouth, it's difficult to speak. So I barely managed a whisper. "Can I call you back?" And then I sat and stared, paced and debated. Ranted and raved. "Accept ten million dollars or paper my bathroom walls with rejection slips from publishers? Take the money or go broke?"

I landed on "go broke." I called him back and said, "You're going to think I'm nuts, but I've decided not to do this." He did. And I began a year of writing, which, to my amazement, resulted in a book deal, a generous advance, and the launch of Fierce Inc. Meanwhile, the high-tech world took a dive. There is no doubt my start-up would have tanked. And I would have been not only miserable and broke, but guilty of having mishandled other people's money.

To say that I have no regrets is an understatement. I am in the right place, doing the right work, with the right people, at the right time, in the right way—for *me*.

Please don't take this story to suggest that I imagine *you* are in the wrong place. I don't. But if your heart has been lobbying for a reality check, then I urge you to give it one, even if confronting reality leads to a change that initially complicates your life. Fierce leadership meets nobody halfway. Without a clear sense of what's important, without principles and values to be "true" to, it will be difficult to do the hard things that happen to be the right things.

Fierce leadership meets nobody halfway.

If you want to take an honest look at your capital *R* reality, please take a moment now to answer the "stump speech" questions below. Twice.

Where am I going?
Why am I going there?
Who is going with me?
How am I going to get there?

First write down where you are actually going right *now* and why, whether you like your answers or not. Then write down where you would like to go, if you could go anywhere, do anything, with no one to please but yourself. Be specific. For example, many people say they want to make a difference, want to have a positive impact, want to give back, want to influence others. Sorry, these vague statements won't cut it. In writing your stump speech, you want to clarify a powerful, specific direction that wakes you up and gives you goose bumps. What, *specifically*, is the difference you want to make? What, *specifically*, is the positive impact you want to have? How, *specifically*, do you wish to influence others?

I'll give you an example. My friend, Michelle, has loved animals all her life. Over the years, she's talked about wanting to learn sign language to work with chimps, wanting to volunteer at the zoo, all kinds of things. But, apart from caring for Bosco, her Labrador, she never did anything about it. About two years ago, she began mentioning this horse she often passed on the side of the road on her way home, and how it looked unhappy and malnourished and dirty. After the fifth time she mentioned how bad she felt every time she saw this poor horse, I said, "Well, why don't you see if they'll sell it to you?" What followed was a very long list of excuses about how she couldn't afford a horse, had nowhere to keep it, et cetera.

But her husband and I kept encouraging her to take action, and after much soul-searching, Michelle finally bought the horse, which she named Dodger, and found a wonderful place to board him and a creative way to pay for it—by offering the owner her website design services in exchange for the horse's board. By confronting her Reality, by asking herself what she really wanted, what was really important, she shifted from wanting to make a difference to actually *making* a difference, a profound difference in the life of one horse. She changed Dodger's life forever, and hers in the process.

Happy ending.

The poet Mary Oliver asks, "Tell me, what is it you plan to do with your one wild and precious life?" One's career direction, much less one's life direction, can be tough to wrestle to the ground, so don't be hard on yourself if the answer doesn't immediately spring to mind, but that's the question on your plate, and the answer will be worth the work. I encourage you to write down whatever comes up for you, first thoughts, no editing. Right down what your *real* goals are, not what you imagine *other people* think your goals should be, or even what *you* think your goals *should* be. Take the *should* out of it and name your heart's desire.

> "Tell me, what is it you plan to do with your one wild and precious life?"
> —Mary Oliver

Where you are going doesn't need to sound lofty or inspiring to anyone else. This is *your* life. Be straight with yourself. Tell it like it is. Radical transparency starts with you.

Where am I going?

_____

_____

_____

_____

_____

_____

_____

Why am I going there?

_____

_____

_____

_____

_____

_____

Who is going with me?

_____

_____

_____

_____

_____

_____

How am I going to get there?

_____

_____

_____

_____

_____

_____

Given your answers, what are the most potent next steps you need to take?

1. _____

2. _____

3. _____

STEP 2. PREPARE OTHERS.

Now that you've clarified your own capital R reality, let's talk about how to make radical transparency part of the woodwork in your organization. And what this requires of *you, as a leader.*

Is it possible that, as William Stafford suggests, a pattern others made still prevails and, following the wrong god home, you are missing your star? Is there something you and others are pretending not to know?

In *Good to Great,* Jim Collins quoted Fred Purdue, an executive at Pitney Bowes, who said, "When you turn over rocks and look at all the squiggly things underneath, you can either put the rock down, or you can say, 'My job is to turn over rocks and look at the squiggly things,' even if what you see can scare the hell out of you." So Pitney Bowes created a long-standing tradition of forums where people could stand up and tell senior executives what the company was doing wrong, shoving rocks with squiggly things in their faces and saying, "Look! You'd better pay attention to this."

Fierce leaders create a culture where people turn over the rocks and look at all the squiggly things underneath, not one where people put the rocks down and keep quiet for fear of what the leader would say. When people are more concerned about pleasing the leader than about interrogating reality, it is a tell that there are bad times ahead. If you suspect that essential bits and pieces of reality are being edited out of your conversations with people essential to your organization's success, *you* may be the problem. The question is, "How can I become the kind of person to whom people will speak the truth?"

This requires fierce resolve, passion for your work, passion for your customers' success, depth of understanding of both context and content, the ability to engage both head and heart, lots of practice, and authenticity. And all of this requires radical transparency. We cannot

The question is, "How can I become the kind of person to whom people will speak the truth?" be "authentic" when we legislate optimism, shielding ourselves from challenging, unpalatable truths.

A word about authenticity. You simply cannot fake "fierce," fake "real." I remember attending a wake for a man, Jac, who had been very important to me and many others, who had died suddenly at fifty of a brain aneurysm.

At the wake, one of his supposed best friends put on a dramatic display of mourning that was so over the top and inauthentic that it left many of us sickened. There's a difference between uncontrollable grief and a *show* of uncontrollable grief. I thought back to other times I'd been in the same room with this man. He was always "onstage," posing as if for the best camera angle. I wondered what it would be like when *he* died and, bereft of any pretense, God might greet him with puzzlement, saying, "I've never seen this man before in my life." *But I digress.*

The point is, because no one can be everywhere and see everything that's going on in a company and be aware firsthand of every broken or limping segment of an organization, as a fierce leader, you need to ask yourself, *What don't I know?* And who *does* know?

A good way to answer these questions is to gather together the people whose realities deserve interrogating and ask them to share their perspectives. Don't just *ask* for the truth, *really* ask for the truth. Our radar informs us when someone is not really asking, doesn't really want to know. And when that happens, we don't really answer.

If you want people to tell you the truth, you'll need to be on your best behavior. Your accomplishments are due as much to how you facilitate people, ideas, and situations as to your education and skill set. You must become a highly skilled facilitator, one who is able to engineer epiphanies for each individual in the room, one to whom people listen closely and who listens closely yourself, one who knows how to advocate a position, while inviting others to push back on your thinking and that of others and, in doing so, to expand the possibilities.

As I said earlier, a Beach Ball meeting is radical transparency at its best, because everyone comes out from behind themselves, into the conversation, and interrogates multiple, competing realities and perspectives.

So, if the goal of the Beach Ball meeting is to interrogate reality and achieve radical transparency, whom should you invite? I have found that it is important to look for the people with the best vantage point on the topic at hand. Who is standing right at the juncture where things are happening? Who has the fifty-yard-line seat on the action? That person isn't always the designated leader. Be creative in your thinking about whom to invite. Err on the side of *including* people, rather than leaving them out.

Once everyone is assembled, how this meeting will go is really up to you. Your primary responsibilities are as follows:

- Act in a way that is consistent with your objective of honesty. In other words, model it yourself. Say things, confess things that scare you.
- Set a tone and an atmosphere in which competing ideas, opinions, and styles are not just encouraged, but expected.
- Engage people intellectually *and* emotionally.
- Ask people for specifics regarding context (meaning), as well as content.
- Involve attendees in two-way discussions—rather than coming across as a "presenter" who is merely a talking head.
- Moderate interactions to avoid inappropriate comments, nonconstructive criticism, and grandstanding. Blunt honesty is useful; offensive comments are not.
- Make needed adjustments in pacing and participation to ensure that you involve and hear from everyone present.
- As always, start and end the meeting on time.

These kinds of meetings help organizations surface and resolve *mokitas,* so let everyone know that you expect everyone to step up to the plate in terms of the degree of intelligence, creativity, energy, and candor they bring to the table.

Acknowledge that you don't have all the answers. Tell those assembled that you are willing to be wrong, that you hope to be different when the conversation is over. Tell people that you want them to . . .

- **Surface mokitas.** Explain what a *mokita* is and provide some common workplace examples, such as these, courtesy of Howard Rheingold:

1. A sizable percentage of our marketing doesn't work.
2. Most departments have people who have retired on the job and at least one or two who are crazy.
3. The boost from last year's motivational speaker evaporated by the time he reached the parking lot.
4. The CEO tells everyone how important training is and then quietly slips out the door.
5. People who are unreliable are rewarded with less work.
6. The first-line supervisors know more about employment law than the folks in the executive suites.
7. The HR department is frequently regarded as more of an adversary than an ally.
8. Middle managers are afraid to fire people.
9. Frequent reorganizations are used to disguise poor management.
10. Our strategic plan is not working.

Resist the desire to print out a list of *mokitas* and staple it to a colleague's forehead. Instead, declare a *mokita* amnesty day and then extend it indefinitely. Let people know you want to bring to the surface anything that isn't being talked about that needs to be talked about relative to whatever topic is on the table (and also topics that *aren't* on the table because they're *mokitas!*), so that you can work on resolving them!

Remember, a careful conversation is a failed conversation, because

> **A careful conversation is a failed conversation, because it merely postpones the conversation that wants and needs to take place.**

it merely postpones the conversation that wants and needs to take place. Tell people that you don't value *careful*. You value *honest*. Tell them that you define *honesty* as full disclosure, to oneself and others, with good intent. Name-calling and blaming doesn't have a place here. Naming the issues and focusing on solutions does.

- *Think further.* To see truth as it really is, to see all the options and arrive at the best choices, we must think further. Thinking further is a practice. To do this, first we must truly want to. Then we must ask another **Thinking further is a practice.** question, and another, and another, until we lead ourselves out of our normal, limited range of thoughts and ideas. We will see new things; consequently, we will have more to choose from.

- *Be contrarians.* Dave Daly, the CEO of Evergreen-Washelli, the largest cemetery in the state of Washington, was my favorite contrarian. During nice weather, we would talk while walking the winding paths of the cemetery. While everything looked meticulous and beautiful to me, Dave always spotted *something* that needed to be fixed or done and made notes to talk with people when we got back to his office.

  During his thirteen years as a member of one of the CEO groups I chaired, Dave could always be depended on to throw a wrench into our conversations, just as we were about to concur on a recommendation. We were initially irritated when Dave, after listening quietly for a long time, would say things like "What if instead of rearranging the furniture, you moved it to a different floor?" or "What if it's not the *cat* that needs skinning?" But eventually we had to acknowledge one thing—the man was brilliant.

  Though Dave's ideas usually involved rethinking and reworking existing plans—and often starting from square one—they were always worth exploring. Had he not been there, we would rarely have discovered ourselves capable of original thought. (Several years ago, he died of the heart attack even *he* expected and is buried on the grounds we walked so many times.)

  So if the debate in your company is between those who believe the company should turn right or left, be a contrarian like Dave and suggest a route off the beaten path.

- *Understand the place of consensus.* Consensus has a place, but in my view, it's a small one. I've seen teams committed to consensus, consense (is that a word?) themselves into a coma. Or confusion. Think about the stock market. If past experience is any guide, the consensus opinion is not even right about the *direction* of the market, let alone the scale of change.

  In a truly fierce company, people know they won't get their way all of the time. They know that sometimes they'll be asked to implement plans and strategies with which they're not in complete agreement. But they'll do it anyway and put their backs into it if they feel they've been heard.

STEP 3. DO IT.

Now it's time to turn your team into an internal think tank. Like all things fierce, radically transparent Beach Ball meetings are straight-forward. You don't have to pick up a burning cauldron with your forearms and sear the image of a dragon into your flesh. You just have to get your own head on straight and put a few guidelines in place, such as:

The answers are in the room. We have them.

1. We need contradiction to get to the truth. Let's surface and use it rather than push it out and pretend it doesn't exist.
2. The answers are in the room. We have them.
3. Surface *mokitas;* no more battling what we're not saying.
4. Think further.
5. Ask questions! Ask more questions!
6. Don't ask a question to which you already know the answer.
7. Replace *but* with *and.*

Call a meeting and have a fierce conversation with your team about a truth you've been avoiding or a *mokita* that needs surfacing. Make it clear that you yourself are on a quest for genuinely new conclusions rather than persuading people of foregone ones.

You could ask people to come to the meeting having thought about their answers to open-ended questions such as the following:

What's the most important thing we should be talking about today?

What do we believe is impossible for us to do that if it *were* possible, would change everything?

Are there integrity outages that need correcting?

If you could give me just one piece of advice, what would you advise me?

What do you need from this team that you're not getting?

What could you contribute to this team that you're not contributing?

Or put a specific topic on the table and ask:

Given our current reality, if nothing changes, what are the implications?

Given this current situation with X, what would you advise?

Life at Fierce Inc. feels like an extended Beach Ball meeting, since we schedule them whenever there are decisions to make, goals to set, or strategies to design. Sometimes the question we aren't eager to hear answered yields the most value.

STEP 4. DEBRIEF.

At the end of the meeting, ask everyone at the table to briefly comment first on "What could we do better the next time we meet?" And then go back around and learn "What did we do well?"

End on what you did well, anchoring the value of how people interacted and contributed. Comments are often emotional, heartfelt, and directed at specific individuals, which reinforces those individuals' desire to behave similarly in future meetings. Everyone leaves hoping for more of the same and with a clearer picture of reality than when he or she walked in.

STEP 5. DO IT AGAIN.

Your meeting may suggest the need for additional meetings on a topic that surfaced but had to be "parked" for lack of time. Don't despair. You won't get caught in meeting hell. Beach Ball meetings can be impromptu and brief—just grab those who can spare you a few minutes and several of their brain cells.

Taking It to the Organization

Remember that the most powerful way to introduce any practice to your organization is not to talk about it, but to live it, so as always, I recommend that you quietly model the fierce practice of radical transparency at all times. Remember, no matter your rank or role in the organization, you can see to it that several of the following suggestions are taken.

1. Hire for raw ideas. Don't always hire in the company's image or you'll struggle to get to new "truths" and innovation.
2. Allow for experimentation, mistakes, dead ends. If every idea adopted, every decision made, every step you and others take is right on, start to worry. You're not stretching, not reaching enough. And people will get lulled into thinking that they can't make a mistake or that if they do, heads will roll.
3. Get at least one blog up and running that actively solicits and acts on complaints, compliments, and suggestions from employees, customers, and management. The top dog should weigh in from time to time.
4. Tell the ground truth, especially during tough times. When people are given official truths, they know it and lose trust.
5. Declare a *"mokita* amnesty" day and thank everyone who named a *mokita*. Consider publicly honoring the person who named the mother of all *mokitas*. Serve him or her a mokita cocktail, which I discovered online actually exists.

Looks a bit sweet for my taste, and the alcohol content is seriously low, but what the heck! Why not create your own recipe!

MOKITA

GLASSWARE   Double cocktail glass

INGREDIENTS   2 centiliters amaretto
1 centiliter strawberry syrup
1 centiliter gomme (sugar) syrup
4 centiliters coffee
2 centiliters cream

PREPARATION Shake together amaretto, strawberry syrup, gomme syrup, and coffee. Pour into chilled cocktail glass. Float the cream on top.

Personal Action Plan

Radical transparency is not only a fierce leadership practice. For me, it's a way of life. Even for personal decisions that require no one else's input, I find that if I let even one person in on my private thinking, I end up thinking further, deeper. Remember that if there *is* a problem, it exists whether you cop to it or not. And only once you accept a problem can you be open to the fix. As my friend Paul Lindbergh says, "A car will run with one flat tire, but you won't enjoy the slow, bumpy ride, and at some point, with even a slightly broken part, your vehicle will stop. I can live life with a flat tire, or I can fix it. You see people metaphorically running on their rims and thinking it's totally cool. And it may be, for them. Not for me."

So here are a few tips to help you practice radical transparency in all situations, at all times:

1. Find the courage to speak truth to power, to get in trouble with the king or queen if you have a genuine concern. In *The Horse Whisperer,* Robert Redford's character says, "Knowing something's easy. Saying it out loud is the hard part."

2. If what you say publicly is different from what you say privately or different from what you tell yourself, vow to tell the truth from this moment on—at work and at home. *This one will change your life.*

3. Press for the truth from others. When you hear something that just doesn't sit well, doesn't seem entirely truthful, ask about it. Respect requires candor—both ways. Be bold.

4. Capture first thoughts. In writing courses, instructors often use timed stream-of-consciousness exercises to get at first thoughts, unfiltered, unedited, where the good stuff resides in us, stuff we can't get at by sitting and pondering. Write down whatever comes up—no crossing out, no pauses, no worry about punctuation or spelling.

First thoughts are far more interesting than second and third thoughts, unobstructed as they are by our internal censor or by political correctness or by cultural norms about who can say what to whom. First thoughts neither edit nor cover up what we are really thinking and feeling; therefore, they contain tremendous intelligence and often result in that elusive thing most companies seek: real innovation—the kind of innovation that moves us into blue ocean territory, where there is little, if any, competition.

> First thoughts are far more interesting than second and third thoughts, unobstructed as they are by our internal censor or by political correctness or by cultural norms about who can say what to whom.

Typical brainstorming doesn't always get at the truly brilliant idea, because we're still simply water-skiing on the surface of the same pond in which our competitors are swimming. We cannot jump from the pond into the ocean until we have accurately named the problem we wish to solve or the opportunity we wish to evaluate, including underlying issues that aren't always readily apparent. Fierce leaders are scuba divers, not water-skiers.

Here's an exercise for you. Write down whatever pops up for you in response to the following question:

If you could give your boss (or spouse or sister or best friend or son) one piece of advice, what would you advise him or her?

Pick a person and write for two minutes without stopping. If you run out of space, write in the margins. If you want to write longer than two minutes, go for it. Don't lift your pen from the page. Don't think. Don't get logical. GO!

_____
_____
_____
_____
_____
_____
_____
_____
_____
_____
_____
_____
_____
_____
_____
_____

What do you feel right now? Are you startled by the truthfulness and wisdom (stop being modest) of what you wrote? Do you want to write more, knowing that there is more to surface? If so, put this book down, find some paper, and keep writing.

What has prevented you from surfacing and disclosing these thoughts before? If you chose your boss, what would prevent you from going to him or her as soon as is humanly possible and sharing these thoughts? I know that not every boss (or spouse or sister or best friend or son) has indicated that input like this would be valued, but I also know that fierce leaders speak first thoughts and encourage others to do so, as well. In fact, they won't stand for anything less.

Conclusion

Many would say that it's the day-to-day grinding it out that moves the dial. The ruthless execution. Rallying people around results like stock prices, quarterly revenues, profits and losses. Yeah, yeah, yeah . . .

A leader—let's call him Charles—told me he thought his division had achieved "RUP"—rational, unified process. *More jargon!* But there was a discrepancy between official truth and ground truth. Behind the green on the corporate dashboard was lots of red. People were burned out, unaligned on objectives, having implementation and control issues because of reporting structures. Trust was a scarce commodity. In other words, there was nothing unified about their progress at all. As one "kingdom" within the company grew, others shrank. The word *productivity* caused eyes to roll. The vision of becoming the "vendor of choice" was not inspiring anyone. They were ethical but incompetent. Why? There was a bad leader in the group: *Charles.*

Charles's fatal flaw was that after years and years of rubbing shoulders with those who practiced the dark arts—those who said, "GROWTH IS THE MANDATE, NO MATTER WHAT IT TAKES"— he wasn't looking for conversations or answers. He was looking for facts to support his case for growth; consequently, new revelations by his staff were ignored, and because his modus operandi was to lob ideas over the transom for others to implement while he came up with more ideas, people were desperate to get *anything* done and felt like failures because so many of Charles's ideas were only partially implemented.

Charles couldn't conceive of questioning his ideas, much less starting from scratch. Though he had traveled the globe, he didn't seem to have gone very far. He may have tasted exotic meals in different countries, but his soul remained the same flavor. His mission was to change everyone around him, but he saw himself as in no need of change. Therefore, he was unable to journey with his employees and colleagues, even though I believe he sincerely wanted to. In fact, he told me that his goal was to become the chief executive within two years, which required a cheering section from his direct reports. They were not cheering.

The board of directors let him go one costly, painful year later, when no one could deny that his only utility to the culture was as a caricature. The moment he left, employees donned T-shirts that read, "Chaos, panic, disorder. My work is done here."

Don't be this man.

Become bored with puffery and posturing, ducks and dodges. Recognize legislated optimism when you hear it, and decline to play that game. Lobby for getting to ground truths early in the game, so that your challenge becomes how to respond to opportunities, not how to fix problems.

Think about the day *you* move on—and you will someday. What would you like the T-shirts to say? Behave accordingly.

Conclusion

Crossing the Bold Line

One of the greatest challenges we all face is understanding and embracing our own leadership potential. Even the most highly paid executives struggle with internal questions about their personal effectiveness as leaders. This is normal. Our results, attitudes, beliefs, prejudices, fears, hopes, glories, and broken places have led us all to practices that others celebrate or question, that *we ourselves* celebrate or question.

At the same time, we are all leaders in some capacity or another. It doesn't matter if we have the title or not. But there is a profound difference between having the title and being the kind of leader to whom people are drawn and to whom people commit at a deep level. The former are just leaders, while the latter are fierce leaders. These are the leaders others look to for advice and opinion and gratefully follow wherever they go. These are the leaders who engage others whenever they are present. Call them natural leaders, if you will. I would call them natural, period.

Fierce leaders aren't born that way; crossing the bold line between leadership and "fierce" leadership takes courage and work. It requires that you hone your faith in others *and* in yourself. Not blind faith, but rather the faith that comes from paying attention, being present. Crossing the line requires that you screw your courage to the sticking place and summon all your skill, reach, in fact, for skills you don't yet have.

Replacing worst "best" practices with fierce practices is challenging, and that's the point. *And, so what?* You cannot differentiate yourself or your company by taking the well-worn, familiar path.

Joseph Campbell explained that the "hero" is heroic because at some point he steps off the path that everyone else is on and heads into the woods where there is *no* path and no indication of help. But he does it anyway. It's that first step into the woods that is the heroic moment. And then everything changes. Help appears that is exactly what he needs, when he needs it. It is there for him alone.

What is the path *you* have to step off of?

In February of 2006, I was in Kenya for twelve days—three working in Mombasa, then nine on photographic safari with my granddaughter, Maizy, who had just turned nine. We knew we were in strange and wonderful territory when we spotted two giraffes as we landed at the Mombasa airport.

Mombasa was hot and humid. I was there to train fifty-five executives and country heads with CARE International—courageous, brilliant people accomplishing impossible tasks in difficult, sometimes dangerous environments—in the art of fierce conversations. Two weeks before we arrived from all points on the compass, the head of CARE in East Africa and his wife had been driving home from church when a car pulled in front of them. He gave the robbers his money and the keys to his car. The money wasn't as much as they wanted, so they made him kneel and in front of his wife, as he pleaded for his life, they shot him. So that day, there was a palpable sense of grief and sorrow. And incredible courage. Most people I know don't have to worry about things like this.

At the training session, there were many languages spoken, interpreters, headphones. Maizy asked to sit in, since she'd never seen me "in action" before. At lunch someone told her it would be okay if she drew on the flip chart in the back of the room. During the next break we noticed a green giraffe named Bob . . .

. . . who loves to have conversations, thinks that a conversation is a relationship, and has had many fierce ones (see the picture of Bob on the next page).

Everyone loved Bob, because Bob got it. Someone said, "From now on, let's prompt each other by asking, "What would Bob do?"

With a simple drawing, my granddaughter had inspired these brave, smart, powerful, and successful leaders from around the world to practice the art of fierce conversations. No doubt she'll be a fierce leader herself someday.

The next day, Maizy and I headed to Nairobi. A gentle, professional young man named Zacharia Njau ("Zack"), was our knowledgeable

Bob the giraff.

loves to have conversations! :)

He thinks that a conversation is a relationship.

And he has had many fierce conversations.

guide and hilarious companion as we flew over grasslands and mountains in twelve-seater airplanes, navigated muddy ravines on game drives, and shared exotic foods for breakfast, lunch, and dinner. (That's Zack and Maizy in the photo on the next page.)

Picture gentle people speaking English with the soft accent of those for whom Swahili is the mother tongue. Imagine a cozy cottage with a view of elephants. An "international airport" consisting of tarmac and a gazebo. A luxurious tent above a river filled with hippos. The soft skin behind the ears of the only tame black rhino in Kenya. Standing on tiptoe to offer bits of banana to colobus monkeys on the roof of a tea plantation. Drifting in a hot air balloon through the early-morning smoke above a Maasai village, then breakfasting in the company of giraffes.

Maizy and I now know what an embarrassed ostrich looks like. One

day a female sprinted down the road, then tripped and sprawled right in front of our vehicle. Once we knew she was okay, we couldn't stop giggling, as she collected herself, shook her feathers, and—we were certain—pretended she'd done it on purpose, just for our benefit.

We know the location of a stork nest—at the Mount Kenya Safari Club—that boasts a golf club. We saw it happen and applauded the stork's theft, strength, and chutzpah. We'd be willing to bet there are sunglasses, cameras, and an iPhone or two in that nest. Shiny objects are apparently seductive even to storks.

We straddled the equator, one foot in the Northern Hemisphere, the other in the Southern. We forded rivers, mud up to the rims, in the Land Cruiser, went off road to get a closer look at a cheetah, hung out with a pride of lions preparing for the evening's hunt, and drove slowly into the middle of the real "peaceable kingdom" in a valley in Amboseli National Park. We turned off the motor and sat quietly, surrounded by thousands of zebras, gazelles, wildebeests, eland, crown cranes, and warthogs, serenely being themselves. They didn't mind or fear us. Many walked past us a few feet away.

I know I'm in the conversation business, but while on safari, I didn't really want to talk with anyone except Maizy, Zack, and our driver. So I spent twelve days in Maizy's sweet company, mostly with my own thoughts and only the edge of others', luxuriating in silence broken only by birdsong or the grumble of hippos returning to the river after feeding in midnight fields. Some words lose their meaning in the Maasai Mara. Like *tax return*. Others take on new ones: *Beauty*.

Best of all, we spent time in a Maasai village, talking with the chief, visiting with families, communing with cows. In these villages, the huts are brown (made of cow dung and mud), the ground is brown (the cows trample it at night), the people are brown. There is no electricity, no running water. No toys, no shelves or closets filled with clothes, dishes, stuff. There is no art on their walls; there are no walls! The *people* are the art, each of them uniquely adorned, living serenely in the official middle of nowhere.

So what does any of this have to do with fierce leadership?

It inspired a few epiphanies.

While it was tempting to romanticize the Maasai, I did not fantasize about living in a hut of dung and mud. I did fantasize about acquiring their demeanor, their serenity. All that time to think, to really be awake, alive, to focus on relationships, human connections, rather than arbitrary, empty notions of fulfillment and success. The freedom in that.

But just a few days later, back in my familiar world, with its own kind of beauty and its own brand of crazy, I found myself turning on the TV again, getting caught up in the latest celebrity news. What occurred to me was how big a difference there is between a celebrity and a hero, between the people our culture follows and emulates and the leaders in cultures like the Maasai. So I began thinking about how to somehow hold the Kenya experience, how to let it inform whatever came next, how to share some of my learning with others who work in a typical corporate culture.

Maizy and I spent a lot of time simply *looking* while we were in Kenya, and this taught me a valuable lesson. All leaders should spend more time looking and listening than they do talking and selling. More time laughing than frowning. More time delighting one another than irritating one another. More time embracing change than clinging to old ways, under the delusion that motion and direction are the same thing. And to do this, we must become fierce.

For me, there is a pull between the two definitions of *fierce: fierce* as in *real*, honest (and often sweet), and *fierce* as in *fiery*. You might be surprised to learn that the fiery side of me is a fan of the "haka," the ritualistic, fierce "dance" of New Zealand rugby players, which involves slapping the palms of their hands on their thighs, rhythmically drumming their feet on the ground while locking eye contact with an opponent, and ending by drawing a finger across their throats. The message is clear. But I love the haka and look for the player who, though he makes the same movements as the other players, is focusing on gathering strength, presence, and intensity within *himself*. His strength doesn't come from trying to intimidate the other side or from sending violent signals. Like a tai chi master, with each movement, he gathers strength from within, where it remains. He is centered. He gives his strength to the team.

Yesterday, I asked a prospective client a question about his leadership that required some potentially catastrophic introspection. He said, "Honesty isn't really a problem with you, is it?"

"No," I admitted. "And I've yet to meet a client who initially considers this an asset."

We laughed and fell silent, and then he answered the question. During the conversation, we began to connect and agreed to work together. This was a conversation that embodied both definitions of *fierce*.

Last night, I was talking with Maizy about my friendship with people who hold very different beliefs from mine. Their thoughts are not my thoughts. Nor mine theirs. What is right for one person may not be right for another. When I told Maizy that I was trying to be open-minded, she giggled and said, "Your brains might fall out."

I suspect my brains *have* fallen out, and I suppose I should put them back in, but the fact is, my head isn't on business as usual, it's on business as it *could* be.

It is not enough to be a leader. This world is full of leaders who cause us to wonder how in the world they achieved that position. I want a world full of great leaders. I want *you* to be a great leader, a fierce leader. I want us all to stop thinking only in terms of accomplishments, of task and completion, of beating the competition, of gathering income and merchandise, of winning praise, and instead, live our lives forging the deepest relationships we can with ourselves and with one another. I want us to respond to adversity by deepening our engagement in our lives. It isn't complicated.

We've got to make connections—at a deep level. Create them. Every day. On purpose. Make more and more of them. Connect the people in our homes and businesses and cities and countries, so that we and our children and our colleagues and customers breathe connection in and out like oxygen. Souls rising. Resulting ultimately in that elusive concept we call peace on earth.

I won't settle for less. I am trying to do my part. I really am.

Someone recently asked me, "If Fierce were a car, what kind of car would it be?" My answer was immediate, with a big grin: "A Toyota Safari Land Cruiser. That sucker can go anywhere!"

And so can you.

For you, for me, in our particular companies, on our particular fields, whether small or large, domestic or global, the progress of the world truly does depend on our progress as individuals now. And if we are to cross the bold line into the territory of fierce leadership, we must do our own version of the haka, gathering strength, honing it, sharing it.

I'll leave you with a comic strip, *Mutts*.

Two birds sit on a wire.

"I wrote a NEW song!" one says.

"A NEW song!?! But we've been imprinted in our hearts to sing the SAME song for thousands of generations."

"Yes, but mine ROCKS!"

The practices of fierce leadership can be scary—but they rock. They sing to the soul and want to change us.

We could talk about them all day, but where they live is out there in the marketplace, in the hallways, offices, meeting rooms, living rooms. This is a good time to remember that like attracts like. When we embrace higher practices, we are soon surrounded by higher practices. When we indulge in inferior practices, we can expect to produce inferior results. My hope for *you* is that you will keep an open heart with others and serve as a conduit for deep connection. Don't talk about it—

do it, be it. *Your* song will rock because the grand sum of your fierce "practices" will create an incredible workplace, enduring relationships, a unique, satisfying life you would not gladly change for another. State of the art; state of the heart. Laminated in bliss.

Love is a practice, too. Give it a try. When outside influences are challenging, allow your quiet heart to lead you. Let me know how it's going. You can reach me at susan@fierceinc.com. Standing by.

Conversations I Need to Have

Name   Topic

_____   _____

_____   _____

_____   _____

_____   _____

_____   _____

_____   _____

_____   _____

_____   _____

_____   _____

_____   _____

_____   _____

_____   _____

_____   _____

_____   _____

_____   _____

_____   _____

_____   _____

_____   _____

_____   _____

_____   _____

_____   _____

_____   _____

_____   _____

_____   _____

_____   _____

_____   _____

_____   _____

_____   _____

_____   _____

_____   _____

_____   _____

ACKNOWLEDGMENTS

I am grateful to the many individuals and organizations who contributed to this book—some unwittingly and some on purpose. For the former, I know it's not customary for paparazzi to send a thank-you note after publishing photos of subjects cavorting naked in their backyards, so let me just say that I did my best to disguise you. If you recognize yourself, I'm sorry, but your antics were just too crazy to pass up.

For help of the intentional, voluntary variety, I would like to thank my agent and friend, Janet Goldstein, and the team at Crown—Roger Scholl, Michael Palgon, and Talia Krohn—for your unfailingly enthusiastic support and the benefit of your reading and astute observations. Thanks to Paul Lindbergh, whose introduction to squid eye gave me the thread I'd been looking for, to Louis Pollack for "A Ritual . . . ," and to Jim Sorensen, whose personal stories, insights, and brilliant facilitation inspire me.

Thanks to my friends, Michelle Twohig, Jan Harding, and Jan Dressler, for checking in from time to time and coaxing me out to play when they noticed leaves and twigs in my hair. Great food and wine was a serious plus.

I'm forever indebted to the core Fierce team—Halley, Deli, Chris, Cam, Aimee, Traci, Myra, Pam—for cutting me the slack needed to write this book and providing candid feedback, from "You've got to be kidding!" to "Huh?" to "I absolutely love this part!" Now that the book is done, can I have my office back?

Blessings on Chris Doherty, who crafted my Orcas Island tree house and worked around me when I insisted on moving in two months before it was finished. The last chapter of this book and considerable polishing of the manuscript took place in the tree house.

RECOMMENDED READING

Prescription for defending against the dark arts . . . Hafiz, Rūmī, any poetry that speaks to you. To borrow Robert Bly's wonderful language, Hafiz poems are "as nourishing as an old apple that a goat has found in the orchard." Take one poem, twice a day, till end of course.

Ardagh, Arjuna. *The Translucent Revolution: How People Just Like You Are Waking Up and Changing the World.* New World Library, 2005.

Barasch, Marc Ian. *Field Notes on the Compassionate Life: A Search for the Soul of Kindness.* Rodale Books, 2005.

Barbery, Muriel, and Alison Anderson. *The Elegance of the Hedgehog.* Europa Editions, 2008.

Blanchard, Kenneth H., and Spencer Johnson. *The One Minute Manager.* William Morrow and Company, 1982.

Bly, Robert, ed. *The Rag and Bone Shop of the Heart.* HarperPerennial, 1993.

Bortoft, Henri. *The Wholeness of Nature.* Floris Books, 1996.

Coetzee, J. M. *Elizabeth Costello.* Penguin Books, 2004.

Collins, Jim. *Good to Great.* Collins Business, 2001.

Gladwell, Malcolm, "Most Likely to Succeed," *The New Yorker,* December 15, 2008.

Goldberg, Rube, "Artwork Gallery: Simplified Pencil Sharpener." http://www.rubegoldberg.com/.

Green, Michael. *One Song: A New Illuminated Rumi.* Broadway Books, 1997.

Jansson, Tove. *The Summer Book.* NYRB Classics, 2008.

Kelly, Kevin, "What Is Your Dangerous Idea: More Anonymity Is Good." *The Edge, 2006*. http://www.edge.org/q2006/q06_4.html?kelly.

Ladinsky, Daniel. *The Gift, Poems of Hafiz*. Penguin Books, 1999.

Lindbergh, Paul. *Running as Designed: A Nuts and Bolts Approach to Re-assembling Your Life and Using It to Get What You Really Want.* This is self published. 2008.

Maister, David H., Charles Green, and Robert M. Galford. *The Trusted Advisor.*

Markle, Garold L. *Catalytic Coaching: The End of the Performance Review.* Quorum Books, 2008.

MBA Jargon Watch 2.0, http://www.johnsmurf.com/jargon.htm.

McEldowney, Brooke, "*9 Chickweed Lane*," Seattle Post-Intelligencer, March 23, 2008.

McEwen, William J. and John H. Fleming, "Customer Satisfaction Doesn't Count," *Gallup Management Journal,* March 13, 2003.

Neilan, Paul. *Apathy and Other Small Victories.* St. Martin's Press, 2006.

Piercy, Marge. "The Seven of Pentacles" in *Circles on the Water.* Alfred A. Knopf

Pink, Daniel. *A Whole New Mind: Why Right-Brainers Will Rule the Future.* Riverhead Books, 2005.

Rutledge, Tim. *Getting Engaged: The New Workplace Loyalty.* Self-published in 2008.

Shaffer, Mary Ann, and Annie Barrows. *The Guernsey Literary and Potato Peel Society.* Dial Press, New York, NY, 2009.

Sullivan, Robert. *Rats: Observations on the History and Habitat of the City's Most Unwanted Inhabitants.* Bloomsbury, 2004.

Tapscott, Don, and David Ticoll. *The Naked Corporation: How the Age of Transparency Will Revolutionize Business.* Free Press, 2003.

Thompson, Clive. "The See-Through CEO," *Wired,* March 2007.

Toltz, Steve. *A Fraction of the Whole.* Spiegel & Gray, 2008.

Twiname, Dr. Linda. "In Search of Well-Being in the Workplace," Waikato Management School, 2008.

And if you still haven't read *Fierce Conversations,* get on it!

About the Author

SUSAN SCOTT is the founder of Fierce, Inc., a global training company whose clients include Yahoo!, Starbucks, Cisco, BP, General Dynamics, New York Life, Nestlé, Four Seasons Hotels and Resorts, LEGO, CARE, Best Buy, Coca-Cola, and Ernst & Young. Scott is the author of *Fierce Conversations: Achieving Success at Work & in Life, One Conversation at a Time*. She lives in Seattle, Washington.

free resources for fierce leaders

Visit www.fierceleadership.com/resources
to download these free resources

"Spot the Tell" Audio

Developing "squid eye" will help you
spot the "tells" that predict an
organization's future more accurately
than the stock price.

When you spot a "tell," you see what
others haven't noticed. You see more,
see differently, and given what you see,
are compelled to act.

In this audio interview you'll learn
about squid eye and try it on one of the
most popular worst "best" practices of
leaders today.

Susan talks *Fierce Leadership*

The term "best practices" is used to
describe the "best" techniques used in a
company or industry. Unfortunately,
companies often confuse latest with
best, with the practices of one era
quickly replaced by those of the next.

For example, there is the adage that
a leader should ensure growth at all costs.
Ironically, there is a dawning recognition
that human connectivity is the primary
"means" to drive that growth.

In this video clip, Susan Scott discusses
how, if you want to be a great leader, you
must gain the capacity to connect with
others at a deep level—or lower your aim.

Take the Fierce Assessment

This assessment will give you an overview of your ability to have direct, courageous, clear, successful, and enriching conversations.

Make your selections fast, go with your gut and remember, this is not about who you want to be but who you are now.

6 Practices Poster

"You're always practicing something. The question is, what are you practicing?" —Martial arts sensei.

Fierce leadership is a state of mind. A fierce leader doesn't simply do the practices in this book like items on a To-Do list.

Fierce leadership itself is a practice, one that becomes woven throughout all that you do, wherever you are, in the same way that an Aikido sensei or a Buddhist monk behaves according to core principles of his or her discipline at all times.

Post this 6 Practices printout where it will help you integrate the core disciplines into your daily leadership routine.

any conversation **can**.
www.fierceinc.com

a special offering

Keynote Opportunity
with Susan Scott

In her refreshingly candid, no-nonsense style, Scott busts six of the worst "best" business practices and reveals a technique she calls "squid eye"—the ability to see the obvious, once we know what to look for and to spot the "tells" that we're falling prey to disastrous behaviors before they cripple us and our organizations.

Informed by over a decade of conversations with executives at Fortune 500 companies, Scott offers surprising alternatives that leaders and managers at every level can put into place. With new approaches to everything from employee feedback, to corporate diversity, to customer relations, Fierce Leadership provides audiences with an honest look at what might be holding them back—and what to do about it.

Scott is the founder of Fierce, Inc., whose diverse, global client list underscores a basic truth: Business is fundamentally an extended conversation—with colleagues, customers and the unknown future emerging around us.

Whether you focus on implementing key initiatives, managing top talent, improving customer acquisition and retention, developing leaders, or simply igniting productive dialogue that generates clarity and impetus for change—success occurs one conversation at a time. To inquire about a keynote for your organization, call 1-888-FIERCE4 or go to www.fierceinc.com

"conversations" newsletter

Sign up for our newsletter and stay connected to ideas, events and articles that will stimulate your thinking and ignite conversations that can change your life for the better.

our foundational workshop

What gets talked about in an organization and how it gets talked about determines what will happen.
Or won't.

Based on the principles of Susan Scott's best-seller, "*Fierce Conversations: Achieving Success at Work & in Life, One Conversation at a Time*" this foundational, hands-on workshop will introduce you to transformational ideas and principles that will shift your basic understanding of conversations and the power they hold in leadership, relationships and results.

You'll learn to master team conversations, coaching conversations, delegation conversations and confrontation conversations—all essential to your individual and collective success.

To learn more about Fierce Conversations® and our other programs, go to www.fierceinc.com